A Camera in the Garden of Eden

A Camera in

the Garden of Eden

THE SELF-FORGING OF A BANANA REPUBLIC

Kevin Coleman

UNIVERSITY OF TEXAS PRESS   AUSTIN

Requests for permission to reproduce material
from this work should be sent to:
    Permissions
    University of Texas Press
    P.O. Box 7819
    Austin, TX 78713-7819
    www.utexas.edu/utpress/about/bpermission.html

The paper used in this book meets the minimum requirements
of ANSI/NISO Z39.48-1992 (R1997) (Permanence of Paper). ∞

LIBRARY OF CONGRESS CATALOGING-IN-PUBLICATION DATA

Coleman, Kevin P., author.
    A camera in the garden of Eden : the self-forging of a
banana republic / by Kevin Coleman. — First edition.
        pages cm
    Includes bibliographical references and index.
    ISBN 978-1-4773-0854-7 (cloth : alk. paper)
    ISBN 978-1-4773-0855-4 (pbk. : alk. paper)
    ISBN 978-1-4773-0857-8 (library e-book)
    ISBN 978-1-4773-0856-1 (non-library e-book)
1. Photography—Social aspects. 2. Plantation workers—
Honduras—Social conditions. 3. Banana trade—Honduras—
History. 4. Visual communication—Social aspects. 5. Honduras—
History. 6. Photography—Honduras. I. Title.
    TR183.C66 2016
    770.97283—dc23   2015024075

doi:10.7560/308547

For my mom and dad,

and

Hema and Saagari

Taken and retaken by sea rovers, by adverse powers and by sudden uprising of rebellious factions, the historic 300 miles of adventurous coast has scarcely known for hundreds of years whom rightly to call its master. . . . The guns of the rovers are silenced; but the tintype man, the enlarged photograph brigand, the kodaking tourist and the scouts of the gentle brigade of fakirs have found it out, and carry on the work.

O. Henry, *Cabbages and Kings*

CONTENTS

Fig. 0.1. *Courtesy of the Rafael Platero Paz Archive.*

Foto Arte and Corporate Seeing

In the early 1930s on the Caribbean coast of Central America in a town called El Progreso, a domestic servant posed for a studio photographer named Rafael Platero Paz (figure 0.1).

As she leaned against the front porch rail, her demeanor was serious. With her gaze slightly askance, she watched the photographer, who was also her employer. Her clothes were neat and clean. Her earrings were modest, her sandals, practical. She was employed by Platero Paz to help his family with the cooking and cleaning. She was probably around seventeen years old when he took this picture. So many years later, no one in the family is able to remember her name. For whom was the photo made? For the worker herself? Or was the photographer simply testing out a new camera on the closest available subject?

In the background, we see the house of Platero Paz's neighbors, Pedro Amaya and his wife, Gertrudis (everyone called her Tulita). The laundry drying on the line was probably hand-washed by Tulita, or by a young woman whose social status was similar to that of the one depicted here. Platero Paz

Fig. 0.2. Rafael Platero Paz created this advertising still and projected it onto the big screen at the local movie theater, Teatro Moderno. *Courtesy of the Rafael Platero Paz Archive.*

Fig. 0.3. Self-portrait by Rafael Platero Paz. *Courtesy of the Rafael Platero Paz Archive.*

took this picture on the veranda of a house that he rented from Manuel María García, a wealthy Mexican lumberman and local benefactor. This was the place that Platero Paz called home. Above the door facing the street, he tacked up a shingle that announced the name of his business: Foto Arte— Naturalidad, Arte y Belleza.[1]

Inside, he had a studio and darkroom where I lived for several months while I was looking into the histories of images and politics in El Progreso. Throughout the twentieth century, El Progreso thrived as a town that serviced the vast banana plantations of the fertile Aguán Valley of northern Honduras. Situated near the industrial city of San Pedro Sula and connected by railroad to the port of Tela, El Progreso has two excellent access points to the world economy and to the cultural worlds pulsating beyond the shores of Honduras.

For a relatively small city, El Progreso has had a disproportionate impact on the life and culture of the nation. Smallholders and mahogany traders founded the town in 1893. By the 1920s, the United Fruit Company had acquired much of the fertile land across the Caribbean coast of Central America. In 1954, workers for the United Fruit Company, now known as Chiquita Brands International, went on strike for sixty-nine days. The town

Map 0.1. Map of Honduras. *Reprinted with permission from Microsoft Corporation, copyright 2010 Navteq, 2011 Microsoft.*

of El Progreso served as a primary base of support for the striking workers. In the 1960s and 1970s, thousands of subsistence farmers, or campesinos, organized a massive and relatively successful movement for land reform. From 1926 to 1983, Rafael Platero Paz was there to photographically document each of these social transformations.

He was also there to make more mundane images, like the one of this domestic worker leaning on a rail of his front porch. But she is not the only person who is pictured here. The young fellow wearing the ball cap is Ricardo Platero, one of the photographer's sons. The boy "shouldn't be" in the photo. And if he does appear, he "should not" accentuate the theatricality of this photographic event. As he watches his father take a picture, young Ricardo Platero's presence in the frame denaturalizes the resulting image, underscoring that the photographer did not simply "capture" and "record" everyday life. With his camera, he intervened in it.

The simple fact that this image exists points to the way that photography can be used by otherwise marginalized people to make modest claims to dignity and to thereby create new ways of thinking, speaking, and acting. In this particular picture, a young woman who was largely excluded from social and political power negotiates with the photographer, who stands for an unreturnable gaze that she confronts. She participated in making this image. And even if she was just pretending for the sake of the camera, in doing so, she was elaborating an intelligible, readable sense of herself. Through photographs such as this one, people who had been abandoned by state and corporate power were able to create structures of meaning in which their experiences and social positions were revalued. Thus photography enabled the excluded, like this domestic worker, to see themselves in a new light and to make themselves visible to others. It allowed people with little power or influence to rearrange the signs of their exclusion and purported inferiority such that they could then see themselves, and others could see them, as worthy of respect.

THE GAZE OF A CORPORATION

If the picture that Rafael Platero Paz took of the young woman in her go-to-church clothes is about self-forging in the midst of multiple male gazes, a United Fruit Company photograph of banana workers lined up outside their barracks is about microscopic aspects of imperialism (figure 0.4).

A condensation of the intimacies of commercial empire can be found in this image from the Medical Department's annual report of 1929, which

Fig. 0.4. "Typical Scene During Malaria Field-Surveys. All inhabitants of a camp submit to blood tests, and those found positive for malaria parasites receive quinine and plasmochin treatment. This is one of the two most important measures in malaria-control work." *United Fruit Company Medical Department, "Annual Report, 1929," 114.*

renders what it deems a "Typical Scene During Malaria Field-Surveys." The photograph is "typical" in that the company implemented the same malaria-control measures throughout its divisions in Latin America and the Caribbean. As a technician for one of United Fruit's divisions in Honduras notes in the report, "In our efforts to effect a control that would materially reduce sickness, and increase labor efficiency and earning power, we have adopted the plan of making routine blood examinations of all inhabitants in camps and treating all those found positive for malaria." This wide shot portrays a certain instrumental mode of seeing, one whose first premise is that healthier workers are a means to increased profits. As the caption suggests, the photo merely reproduces and makes visible from afar a "scene" that is already a spectacle in the company's camps. Near the center of the compositional space, a man in a bow tie sits behind a table as workers gather around him.[2]

The company sought to reduce the incidence of illnesses specific to the tropics and to disentangle climate and race, reading the symptoms and signs of disease from the bodies, fluids, and corpses of its employees. Studying how abnormal conditions affect the human organism did not require that banana production be halted, and could even make it more efficient. As the company's technician explains, "We have found that the surveys and the treatment of the individuals found positive can be carried out on a large scale in conjunction with the daily routine work—systematic effort, efficient cooperation, and hard work being the essentials for success. A rapid worker can collect 500 to 800 thick films in one day; and the only assistance necessary is to have someone record the names of the subjects as the bloods are taken and to give the films a corresponding serial number."[3] For the company, its plantations were not simply a place for growing bananas, but a giant clinic in which the workers were specimens, not subjects; they were examples, transitory bodies that carried diseases, physical and ideational.

Beyond any individual case of illness, the company's gaze moved across its plantations, from Cuba and Jamaica to Guatemala, Honduras, Costa Rica, Panama, Colombia, and Ecuador. The United Fruit Company explicitly compared its medical achievements with those of the British colonial army in India, the US Army and Navy, the Panama Canal Zone, the Sumatra plantations, and the Rand Mines of South Africa.[4]

Through medical interventions, United Fruit insinuated itself into the banana workers' everyday lives. In the company's view, malaria was "a serious and constant menace to the health and progress of communities located in areas where the infection is endemic." As an "epidemic," malaria was a collective phenomenon afflicting large swaths of its labor force. Controlling malaria required a multiple gaze, capable of cross-checking viewpoints, revisiting the camps after determined intervals, and compelling workers to submit to additional blood tests to finally isolate and treat its object of sight.[5] The medicine used by the United Fruit Company to treat the epidemics that afflicted its employees had to be supplemented by a coercive apparatus of farm overseers and foremen who were themselves backed up by regional police and military forces. The company took the malaria survey depicted in the photograph above to be crucial to its control over the disease, systematically surveying its ports and all of its labor camps four times a year. "The overseer of a farm is notified one day ahead, so that he can have his people ready. He knows the working population of his district, including the members of the families of laborers; and we prepare sufficient slides for blood smears, according to his estimations." Through such measures, the company reported that 86 percent of the total population of its Panama division submitted to quarterly blood tests, enabling it to reduce the incidence of malaria from 58.8 percent in 1928 to 8.6 percent in 1931.[6] Capital's surplus-oriented gaze transformed the worker into an object of observation and a site for improving upon existing medical treatments and the year-to-year balance sheet.

From health policies to disciplining its workers, the company used the same structures of oversight to create a labor force that could efficiently produce bananas. Education and the restructuring of workers' lives were crucial to this endeavor: "We learned to realize that, without active coop-eration on the part of the people, the work is only partially successful; and it is a matter of time, effort and patience before the masses can be made to understand the benefits of such a campaign."[7] Thus United Fruit sought to enlist knowledge producers—from universities such as Harvard, Johns Hopkins, and McGill to the Rockefeller Institute and the US Public Health Service—against the pathogens and the ignorance of the inhabitants of its plantations. From this scene of a malaria field survey, the thick smears of the workers' blood would be subjected to another kind of seeing, under a microscope operated by a company agent empowered to name the disease and to thereby initiate a course of treatment that would place designated workers under more intensified scrutiny. Hence the authority of company physicians and medical researchers derived not only from the social and material apparatus that supported their looking but also from the system-atic methods they employed as part of an enterprise that builds knowledge through the accretion of microscopic observations. This way of seeing and the truths that it produced were harnessed to maximize productivity on the company's banana plantations.

Yet not only did these malaria field surveys harness science for corporate ends, they also reflected a slow and steady thinking about techniques of observation and how an enterprise could practice a better, more systematic way of seeing. As United Fruit scientists attempted to reshape nature, they were refining their own abilities, and the capacity of the company, to more efficiently extract bananas out of tropical soils by improving their meth-ods of observing, identifying, and influencing what went on at a level that remained inaccessible to the unassisted human eye. In other words, like the photograph that Rafael Platero Paz took of the young woman on his front porch, this picture of a malaria field survey is also about self-sculpting. Making this photograph de-automatized a certain way of seeing and pro-duced a representation of the company's systematic methods for detecting malarial larvae.

These two photographs are allegories for the story that follows. The photo that Rafael Platero Paz took of a smartly dressed domestic servant posing on his front porch highlights how ordinary people used photography as a means of self-forging, reworking the relationship between their social ascriptions of identity and their chosen appearance before a camera. This was about people presenting their best selves to the world. In contrast, the photo of a United Fruit Company malaria field survey emblematizes a technical use of photography that was central to the company's profit-oriented vision of land and labor on its plantations. The company used photography to refine production processes, to demonstrate its scientific methods, and to coordinate between its headquarters in Boston and its various divisions throughout the tropics of Latin America and the Caribbean. These two uses of photography collided with each other in El Progreso and, more broadly, in the history of modern capitalism. Indeed, any account of the production of a commodity in our era will also entail a parallel, but often hidden, story of the workers producing that commodity. What is true for bananas grown in Central America is no less true for iPhones manufactured in China. The "unconscious optics" of the camera, to borrow Walter Benjamin's metaphor, reveal the rationalization of landscapes and the orchestration of the movements of workers.[8] Yet that same mechanical recording device also enables the recovery of the acts of laborers producing themselves as citizens and self-emancipating subjects.

ONE

Photography as a Practice of Self-Forging

In *Conquest of the Tropics*, his 1914 "Story of the Creative Enterprises Conducted by the United Fruit Company," Frederick Upham Adams wrote, "We of the United States spend tens of millions of dollars to bring our deserts to cultivation, but our statesmanship declines to glance south of the Rio Grande, where uninhabited empires of rich soil are already provided with water and with the climate which must have existed in the Garden of Eden."[1] Blinded by his imperial fervor, Adams tried to simply wish away the people of the "American Tropics," arguing that the United Fruit Company should work closely with the US government in the conquest of new frontiers, from Cuba and Honduras to Guatemala and Colombia. In the early twentieth century, the Boston-based company saw itself as a vertically integrated corporate empire, controlling the production, distribution, and marketing of what was becoming the most widely consumed fresh fruit in North America. The economic, political, and cultural power of the company challenged the sovereignty of the countries in which it operated, giving rise to the notion of "banana republics."

The banana republic, as we will see, was an imperial constellation of images and practices that was locally checked and contested by the people of the Honduran town of El Progreso, where the United Fruit Company had one of its main divisional offices. As banana plantation workers, women, and peasants posed for pictures and, more indicatively, as they staged the general strike of 1954, they forged new ways of being while also visually asserting their rights as citizens. Photography and visuality were thus put to use in reshaping landscapes and livelihoods, even as countervailing claims to sovereignty, belonging, and the right to make public demands of one's employer and national state were also forcefully made through photographs and public performances that were staged for a camera and the implied spectator that it promised.[2]

The town of El Progreso offers a microcosm for understanding the broader historical experiences in Latin America's early twentieth-century agro-export economies. The imperial visuality that Adams called for in *Conquest of the Tropics*, and which the United Fruit Company enacted and materialized in its banana plantations and company towns, was refracted through the ways that working people in Latin America and the Caribbean looked both inward and outward as they participated locally in what were often cast as national projects of agrocapitalist modernization. For ordinary people in company towns in Central America and the Caribbean, these structural processes were enmeshed in their everyday encounters with each other and the company.

El Progreso was Macondo, but without the 1928 massacre. Yet whereas in Gabriel García Márquez's fictional banana-company enclave, a gypsy named Melquíades brought the daguerreotype laboratory to the town in which no one had ever died, it was the Salvadoran Rafael Platero Paz who brought the first fully fledged photography studio to El Progreso. Rather than a group of "gypsies," it was Palestinian immigrants who imported all manner of wares into El Progreso from the United States, Europe, and the Middle East. And whereas José Arcadio Buendía traded his mule and two goats for two magnetized ingots, the first *progreseños* traded their land and the sweat of their brows for promises of railroads, Stetson hats, and the stability of wage labor. So while nearly all of the people whose pictures are included in this book have long since passed away, the fact that Platero Paz was there, as José Arcadio Buendía saw daguerreotypy, to "fasten them onto a sheet of iridescent metal for eternity" allows us to get a glimpse of who they were and who they wanted others to believe they were.[3]

In this local history of subaltern photography, I attempt to rethink how a US-based capitalist venture harvested bananas and profits from tropical soils and peoples, changing how we see Latin America and how Latin Americans came to visualize US power. What *progreseños* experienced in the early twentieth century—a great banana boom and a degree of shared prosperity followed by the loss of land to a multinational corporation and the proletarianization of independent producers and peasants—is typical of what happened in other banana-company towns throughout Latin America. While local and national dynamics varied greatly, the fundamental values and approach adopted by United Fruit remained quite consistent. Company policies were, after all, centrally directed from Boston.

A Camera in the Garden of Eden moves back and forth between looking from and looking at El Progreso, throwing into relief distinct ways of seeing oneself, one's community, and one's racial, cultural, and national others in a site of hierarchical encounter. As visual culture theorist Esther Gabara has shown, several scholars of Latin American cultural studies have drawn a basic distinction between "looking at" and "looking from" Latin America. Ricardo Salvatore, for instance, developed the notion of "sites of knowledge" ("lugares del saber") to describe the way in which research enterprises are moved by apparently antagonistic impulses toward localism and transnationalism, rendering ways of seeing and thinking that seem to be from nowhere in particular. In contrast, Latin Americanists have worked to develop an analytics in and from a particular place ("en y desde un lugar particular").[4] The town of El Progreso is an ideal site for studying how a diverse group of local actors interfaced with the rhetoric and policies of Honduran liberals and the imperial ideologies and practices of the US fruit companies.

El Progreso was an imperial contact zone, a disputed space of encounter where peoples and cultures asymmetrically grappled with one another. As a company town, El Progreso was a meeting ground in which claims to sovereignty were made and contested. Hence examining the politics of this town not only enriches our understanding of the circum-Caribbean, it also enables us to refine our thinking about the role of the United States in the region. Historian Paul A. Kramer has called for "a U.S. historiography of spatial exceptions: extraordinary power exercised at and through the interstices of sovereignty, often underwritten by essentialisms of race, gender, and civilization."[5] El Progreso was just such a spatial exception. The banana zone decoupled a section of Honduran territory from its national laws, carving out a juridical space in which the company effectively ruled. In the 1954 strike, the workers challenged the continued existence of an exceptional space that was designed to extract their labor while also imposing modern, scientific agricultural techniques. The enclave and its archetypal "American Zone" had long been represented as models of progress that kept tropical disease at bay to establish outposts of modernity in an Edenic and primal space. Yet through the strike, the workers challenged not only the legality of the United Fruit Company's labor practices and the fabrication of an extrajudicial imperial hamlet, but also the moral and aesthetic codes that preserved this spatial exception. Hence the enclave was itself a visual form that could be reworked by local subjects: it was a point of view, a site from which its occupants looked out at Honduras and out further to the United States. If the enclave was a camera obscura, then the strike was the workers forcing images out of the darkened chamber so that spectators in the wider world could see what was going on in the banana zone.

A VISUAL DENUNCIATION

In his studio, photographer Rafael Platero Paz took a picture of an injured man in a white undershirt and stained pants (figure 1.1). The man had been assaulted and his body disfigured. His pant legs were deliberately and unevenly rolled up to reveal the injuries to his left knee and right shin. His left cheek was bruised, and his forehead was bandaged. The man had been physically attacked. By whom? Why? I do not know. The photograph comes without an accompanying text. From oral history interviews I know only that this man was a local Chinese merchant.

Fig. 1.1. *Courtesy of the Rafael Paz Archive.*

This image presents us with the subject displaying his wounds for the camera. In the moment of the photographic event, these injuries were a part of what was. They were neither rumors nor figments of the imagination. They were, rather, marks inscribed on a body at a specific time and in a specific place. They were marks of abuse, of hatred or instrumentality. These bodily and photographic inscriptions affect me, the viewer. The people, or person, who injured this man may have simply cared more about robbing him than they did about his bodily integrity. Thus, they could have been found and punished.

This photo of the injured Chinese merchant made the claim that these injuries were wrong and unnecessary and socially produced. Further wounds of this kind, the photograph declared, could be prevented. The inscriptions on photographic paper enable any viewer to think back to the moment in which this photo was taken and to wonder about what happened to the man that landed him in this bruised state. The burden of preventing these kinds of injuries now falls on the spectator, who is responsible for what she sees and how she responds.

Was this photograph taken to the police to serve as an indisputable record of a particular injury? Was it taken to the mayor's office so that the local authorities might do something to protect vulnerable residents? I do not know the answers to these questions. But I do know that the photograph was taken in Platero Paz's studio in El Progreso, that the image itself exists, and that the injuries the man suffered were real.

These two pictures that Rafael Platero Paz took—of the domestic worker posing for the camera and of the Chinese merchant who had been physically beaten—survive as records of two vulnerabilities. The young woman was not considered to be a full citizen; unable to vote and subject to patriarchal rule, she was present in a body whose sexuality was coveted by some men and protected by others. The Chinese immigrant was, meanwhile, a noncitizen, subject to the whims of power without the protections afforded by citizenship. One was denied the benefits of citizenship based on her sex, and the other on the basis of his race and national origins. Most likely, these two individuals never brought their unique struggles together as part of a single cause. They probably did not see themselves as connected in any meaningful way. In all likelihood, they are linked only by their images in the Platero Paz archive and in my analytical narrative.

But neither of these links is arbitrary.

The same photographer, in the same town, and in roughly the same place, photographed both people. Each sought to be represented, and in doing so, each one of them overcame a social position of vulnerability to make a picture. Like tens of thousands of other people scattered across the early twentieth-century globe, these two subjects individually addressed themselves to others through images. And just as the photos of the domestic servant and the malaria field survey revealed new ways of representing oneself before others, in the image of the Chinese merchant who had been physically assaulted, photography was put to use for the purpose of improvement. But this time the organism that the photographic subject was consciously and microscopically attempting to modify was not the self or the corporation, but the society in which he lived.

ARCHIVES AS COLLECTIVE BIOGRAPHIES

Early in my research for this book, I went looking for photographs of the 1954 banana workers' strike. I had seen pictures of the strike reprinted in magazines, newspapers, and books, but I had not been able to figure out who had taken those shots. Because El Progreso was the epicenter of both the Honduran labor movement of the 1950s and the campesino movement of the 1960s and 1970s, I began working through the internal records of the local municipal government and of the Jesuit priests who had been based in El Progreso since 1946. I also conducted a series of oral history interviews, attempting to understand the confluence between popular Catholicism and the iconography of the subsistence farmers who had created one of the most successful movements for agrarian reform in Central America, helping Honduras to head off, at least according to the traditional historiography, the crisis that convulsed the rest of the region in the 1980s.[6] As I went along, I would ask people where I might find photographs of the 1954 strike. Several of my interviewees pointed me to Juan Bendeck, the son of immigrants from Palestine and the owner of TeleProgreso, a local television station: "Don Juán has lots of old pictures!"

So one day, I took a taxi out to the offices of TeleProgreso to see if I could meet Don Juan. As I walked into the studio, I immediately saw the kinds of pictures that I had been yearning to see. On the walls, some two dozen framed black-and-white photographs hung with brief captions that narrated the history of El Progreso, including, at long last, photographs of the workers on strike in 1954. After looking at a couple of pictures, I walked up to the receptionist, introduced myself, and asked if it might be possible to get an appointment with Juan Bendeck. She hesitated and asked me some questions. As I described my interests, a middle-aged man interrupted me from behind the receptionist. "Those pictures aren't Don Juan's," he said. "They were taken by my grandfather. Everybody thinks that these photos are Don Juan's."[7] It had been only a few minutes since I had asked about the pictures, and already the key issues—of who owned the images, who had produced them, and who cared for them—forcefully presented themselves. From behind the large desk, the confident man in an apricot-colored shirt and black trousers introduced himself as Oswaldo Castillo, the manager of the TV station.

Together Oswaldo and I looked at the photographs on the wall. He explained that his mother had curated an exhibit in El Progreso's Casa de la Cultura to display these photographs. She had selected which images would be presented and had written the captions. Image production seems to run in the family: his grandfather was the town's first studio photographer, his mother displayed the images that her father had taken, and Oswaldo was now the manager of the local television station and the host of his own TV show. Oswaldo then took me back into the studio so that we could talk some more. As we sat on the set of TeleProgreso, with a backdrop that simulated a window looking out at the clock tower in the Plaza Ramón Rosa, he began to tell me about the station—whose corporate slogan is "The Channel of Our Identity"—and about his grandfather, Rafael Platero Paz. After a while, he suggested that we drive over to his mother's house so that she could tell me about her father, the photographer.

Oswaldo's mother, Profesora Aída López de Castillo, is a retired school-teacher, a dedicated local amateur historian, and the guardian of the photographs that her father took over the course of more than fifty years of working in El Progreso. She greeted us at the front door and brought us out onto her patio to chat. After we got to know each other a little, she took me into a part of the house that she had converted into a small dressmaking shop that opened onto the main street. On the walls, she had displayed her father's pictures, with a short description carefully affixed to the bottom of each one. I was taken by the breadth of subject matter depicted, from the photographs of political events that I had just seen displayed on the walls of TeleProgreso to the pictures of local beauties that I was now being shown. We continued talking, and she brought out some family albums with pictures of her father. An hour or so later, she led me through the house and into a nonoperational bathroom that the family had converted into a vault. In the dry shower stall, Profesora Aída showed me ten cardboard boxes, each 10 × 12 × 24 inches. She opened a couple to reveal that each was chock-full of thin negatives and occasional paper prints. I would estimate that each box contained at least five hundred negatives. The next day, I was to board a plane to return to the United States. My three months of exploratory research had come to an end.

As an artisan and an entrepreneur, Rafael Platero Paz dedicated fifty-seven years to documenting everything from children receiving their First Communion to the 1954 banana workers' strike. With his photos, he enabled a racially and ethnically diverse labor force, as well as women, subsistence farmers, and children, to inscribe themselves as honorable, respectable participants in the construction of a new national imaginary. When Platero Paz died, he left everything—including the ten boxes of prints and negatives as well as three of his old cameras, some lenses, receipts, and other equipment—to his daughter, Aída Dolores López de Castillo. As an amateur historian, Profesora Aída has published several pamphlets on the local history of El Progreso. She took a keen interest in my project and would subsequently help me as I struggled to understand the links between visuality, the local and transnational agents of capitalist development, and the ways that working-class people have sought to gain a measure of autonomy over their own lives. Within a year, I was back in El Progreso, digitizing nearly two thousand negatives on Profesora Aída's back porch and interviewing her about the contents of the images.

But before returning to El Progreso, I headed to Cambridge, Massachusetts, to spend a few weeks working in the United Fruit Company Photograph Collection at Harvard University. This collection of more than 10,400 photos records the company's operations in Latin America and the Caribbean from 1891 to 1962. This archive of one of the first and most powerful multinational corporations contains 1,426 photographs from the company's Honduran divisions. The United Fruit Company Photograph Collection invites a broader meditation on visuality, labor history, and inter-American politics, as well as an inquiry into the status of photographs as primary source material. But whereas the Platero Paz archive appears to be the result of the photographer's decision to keep a copy of almost every negative that he produced, the United Fruit Company collection is the result of an aggressive attempt to shape what researchers can find out about the company. Thus it has been purged of photographs that we know the company took but which would have provided evidence of the way it used photography to surveil its workforce.[8]

It might be helpful to think about these two archives within a broader framework that visual culture theorist Nicholas Mirzoeff has developed. Adapting historian Dipesh Chakrabarty's discussion of "two modes of history," Mirzoeff argues that Visuality 1 is "that narrative that concentrates on the formation of a coherent and intelligible picture of modernity that allowed for practical, even heroic, action."[9] The United Fruit Company used photography to transform landscapes, to scientifically monitor its field experiments, and to train the gaze of North American consumers who were led to prefer one particular kind of blemish-free, ripe yellow fruit. Insofar as the United Fruit Company Photograph Collection was a tool of industry and applied science, it exemplifies Visuality 1.

In contrast, Visuality 2, Mirzoeff suggests, is "that picturing of the self or collective that exceeds or precedes that incorporation into the commodification of vision by capital and empire."[10] Rafael Platero Paz's photo of the young woman on his front porch fits within this second species of visuality. This ambiguous photo also reveals that Visuality 2 is not the polar opposite of Visuality 1. If Visuality 1 is capital's way of picturing the world, Visuality 2 is not necessarily anticapitalist or antimodernist. Although it sometimes can, Visuality 2 does not necessarily encode a radical politics. Indeed, the vast majority of the images in the Platero Paz archive are rather traditional and conservative: First Communions, happy nuclear families, great men, and picturesque landscapes. Such images rarely interrupt, and often reinforce, capital's narrative of progress, order, and modernity. Nevertheless, the Rafael Platero Paz archive, with its thousands of unordered black-and-white negatives, exemplifies Mirzoeff's notion of Visuality 2.

In the Platero Paz collection, I had an archive of labor and much more; in the United Fruit Company Photograph Collection, I had an archive of capital. Between these two enormous collections of images—one providing the foundation for understanding an important episode in the history of Central American plantation labor and the other a history of transnational capitalism—I then inserted the collections of family photos of the local bourgeoisie, Palestinian immigrants to Honduras whose influence was greater than that of the workers and peasants but far less than that of the banana company.

Descended from a prominent family, Guillermo Mahchi maintains a large collection of photographs that his paternal grandmother bequeathed to him. Sammie Gabrie, another merchant of Palestinian descent, also cherishes his family photo albums, some of which include prints that bear the stamps of the Armenian photographers who took the pictures that his relatives sent, nearly one hundred years ago, from Jerusalem to El Progreso. Consisting of hundreds of images, these family photograph collections reveal how this ethnic group navigated the social and cultural journey between their homeland in the Levant and their host land in the Americas.

Narrating the history of El Progreso and his family's role in transforming a small village into an important medium-sized city, Guillermo Mahchi distilled his own memories into a rich photo-essay that he called *Archivo fotográfico del ayer: El Progreso, 1900-1965*.[11] Mahchi is the grandson of Salomón (Selim) Mahchi Lorenz, who was born in Palestine in 1892 and immigrated to El Progreso in 1913. The meanings of Mahchi's imagetexts are of course personal—he took many of the photos from the family albums of his parents and grandparents—and social, as he situates his family's experiences within the broader context of Palestinian immigration, the founding of El Progreso, and the familial networks of local elites.[12] Guillermo Mahchi also has boxes of loose photographs, many of them taken by Rafael Platero Paz.

Families like the Mahchis played a role in creating new international routes of circulation from various outposts in Latin America to major port cities in the United States, then across the Atlantic to Europe, only to then move southeast through the Mediterranean to Palestine and, finally, back again. A postcard that Salomón Mahchi received from his brother provides a glimpse of these early twentieth-century itineraries:

> Paris, 6th October, 1924
> My dear brother,
> I am writing to you on this card and who knows whether it will arrive before me or me before it. I am now in Paris, and on the 11th of this month I will head to New York and once I arrive there I will send you a telegraph. From New York, I will head to New Orleans and directly from there to Honduras. Tomorrow I will send you a letter explaining to you my travel in detail so you can gain insight about this and be aware of it. Keep well for your loving brother.
> [Signature][13]

In a common self-referential gesture, the postcard also bore an image of him on the front, posed as if he were piloting an airplane, evoking the mobility that he was enacting en route to Honduras (figure 1.2). Like the ethnic Chinese in postcolonial Java whom Karen Strassler has described,

Figs. 1. 2 and 1.3. Front and back of a picture postcard to Salomón Mahchi from his brother. *From the private collection of Guillermo Mahchi.*

Palestinian immigrants in Honduras attracted the suspicion of the state precisely because they tapped into transnational networks and their movement went largely unregulated.[14]

The other large visual archive that I probe is the dispersed world of images that circulated in periodicals. By 1930, Honduran newspapers and magazines regularly used photographs in their publications. These photojournalistic images did different kinds of social and cultural work. Circulating in the major cities and towns, such images became vehicles for negotiating civic identity. They usually articulated the viewer to the nation, through glorifying governing elites or by providing what Robert Hariman and John Louis Lucaites have called "performative models for citizenship." Photographs of schoolchildren, for example, with their hands raised waiting for the teacher to call on them do more than simply report; they provide imitable syllabi for civic life. Newspapers regularly published photos to emphatically denounce injustices, especially crime, poverty, and squalor. Even more straightforward are the advertising images that stoked the desires of consumers for whiter teeth, higher-quality cigarettes, or gentler relief of constipation. While advertising images always functioned as a means of persuasion, photojournalistic images often did too. The right image provided the affective resources for motivating people to buy a particular product or to identify with a certain official or church leader. Insofar as they offered assurances about the nature and legitimacy of the public world and specific validations of public action, such images, to again borrow a term from Hariman and Lucaites, "underwrote" the political community.[15] Thus, images from the archives of newspapers and magazines reflect, and in some cases constitute, shifts in public culture. By the mid-twentieth century, pictures of great men like General Tiburcio Carías Andino gave way to those of a protesting populace.

Throughout the book, I anchor my analysis of the photographic record to sources found in traditional archives. The contextual bedrock for this story is formed from the municipal records of El Progreso, a cache of internal memoranda from the United Fruit Company, the Honduran state's registries of immigrants, land tenure transactions, and the records of adjudicated criminal cases. Declassified US government documents, newspapers, neoimperialist company-boosting tracts, and pop-cultural phenomena make up the loose soil in which images competed for nutrients.

I consider these archives, and the collective biographies that they amount to, to be characters in a story of self-forging in an exceptional space. Placing these archives in relation to one another enables me to read each against the other, such that absences in one become presences in another. Each of these storehouses of meaning was the result, even before my intervention, of the selection, placement, and assembly of image objects that were themselves products of distinct ambitions, whether social, economic, or familial. Each archive was produced for an anticipated future. Each was the result of an accretion of choices to photograph one thing rather than another, to keep one picture rather than another, to send one postcard rather than another. Before I began to look in these archives, each one had already visually emplotted stories of belonging, love, accomplishment, and community.

In the discrete acts of taking pictures and posing for them, as well as in the aggregative acts of creating an archive, the subjects creating these images and storehouses of images extract themselves from the dull time of ordinary being to put themselves into the existential time of their projects and goals.[16] The temporal modes of photographic time and archival creation anticipate a spectator-historian. In attempting to reconstruct the conditions and dispositions under which any given photograph was produced, that anticipated spectator-historian might, through the archived image, catch a glimpse of a past under construction. In any given photograph and in the archive itself, the historian finds material remains of individuals shaping themselves toward their goals. In some rare instances, the photochemically encoded acts of self-poiesis are those of a collective agent.

Every photograph is, on its own, an archive of a certain moment from a certain point of view, a trace of a particular present that has passed.[17] Once each of these microarchives, these photographs that are themselves zipped files of events that took place outside the frame, is deposited in a box for some implied future spectator, it begins to acquire additional meaning. It comes to refer not only to a specific site and slice of time but to other images in the same archive. As depositories of state or capitalist value, institutional archives tend to narrate stories of linear progress—dominating wild nature and turning backward subjects into modern citizen-workers—performing their achievements in an overconfident language that prompts one to look for what is not shown. The privately held Rafael Platero Paz and Palestinian family archives are, in contrast, repositories that have been built up through the individual, familial, and collective creation of cultural value. As secular archives in which the language of Christianity is imbricated, both collections trace the incorporation of the spiritual into the personal, as well as the ways that individuals secularize—through the very act of posing for photographs—their own self-sculpting and their efforts at moral improvement, quietly working within and subtly challenging nationalist, capitalist, and religious promises of progress, wealth, and salvation.

Taken together, the photographs that make up each of these archives offer a sort of visual biography of a collective agent. The workers, new mothers, brides and grooms, campesinos, teachers, merchants, and politicians make up the graphic life story of El Progreso. The scientists, agronomists, and managers who worked with land, labor, and machinery to produce bananas together form the corporate person that called itself the United Fruit Company. The immigrants from Palestine who posed next to their general store or their new green 1930 Buick and who filled their albums with postcards received from loved ones back in Bethlehem and Jerusalem display an ethnic community making itself in a new land. Within each of these conglomerated biographies, there was the chance that one might seek to define oneself otherwise than what the community expected. This possibility of deviation from the norm was then either purged from the archive or literally ripped out of the family album, or it was subsequently enlarged to serve as an icon for posterity of the new and better as it was emerging.

THE SUBJECT OF PHOTOGRAPHY

The idea of the camera as a recording device that can capture moments in time for an anticipated future is as old as the medium itself. In 1839, Louis Jacques Mandé Daguerre announced his invention of the physical and chemical process that gave nature "the power to reproduce herself." Curiously, the periphery offered one distinct advantage over the metropole: "The imprint of nature would reproduce itself still more rapidly in countries where the light is more intense than in Paris, such as Spain, Italy, Africa, etc." Brighter conditions would permit sharper images, and hence southern climes were more amenable to nature's reproduction of herself in images. Beyond the physics and chemistry of his new technology, Daguerre also identified its democratic potential: "Everyone, with the aid of the DAGUERREOTYPE, will make a view of his castle or country-house: people will form collections of all kinds, which will be the more precious because art cannot imitate their accuracy and perfection of detail. Even portraits will be made."[18] Anyone could make a picture of her dwelling. Anyone could collect these images. And the daguerreotype process could be used to make a likeness of any person or people. Thus from the start, Daguerre recognized that "writing with light," as Henry Fox Talbot described the new technology in 1844, was inherently political and that this invention would open up who could represent others and be represented themselves.

The Harvard savant Oliver Wendell Holmes took the logic of photography several steps further, famously predicting that images were "henceforth divorced from matter." The thing-in-itself no longer mattered; all that was needed were photographs of things. Yet what has been overlooked is that in conveying this archival desire of encyclopedic proportions, Holmes reached deep into Latin America with a violent metaphor: "Every conceivable object of Nature and Art will soon scale off its surface for us. Men will hunt all curious, beautiful, grand objects, as they hunt the cattle in South America, for their *skins*, and leave the carcasses as of little worth. The consequence of this will soon be such an enormous collection of forms that they will have to be classified and arranged in vast libraries, as books are now."[19] Shooting a picture was like shooting an animal that could be mounted and displayed as its substance was left to rot. But what happened when those whom imperial, corporate, and state power considered neither curious nor beautiful nor grand harnessed the democratic potential of the medium? Could such an archive of "their skins" enable the retrieval of possibilities and aspirations that were left as carcasses, as forgotten futures, potentialities aborted by a capitalist project that summoned the violence of two different nation-states to discipline labor and reshape landscapes?[20] Some photographs, I will argue, capture a moment in which a newness was produced, thus indexing historical openings that were only subsequently foreclosed. Such photos enable us to recover something of the subjects who created those forgotten possibilities.

In 1989 Alan Trachtenberg eloquently recast the "photographer as a national historian, one who keeps records of the famous and eminent, as well as the run-of-the-mill citizen."[21] Trachtenberg focused on the role of famous American photographers—Mathew Brady, Timothy O'Sullivan, Alfred Stieglitz, Lewis Hine, and Walker Evans. Although the importance of such photographers continues to be studied, in the years since Trachtenberg's landmark work was first published, art historians, anthropologists, and historians have become increasingly interested not only in photographic genres outside of the United States, Britain, and France, enabling the description and theorization of the ways that various photographies are created and sustained in China, India, Indonesia, South Africa, Egypt, Brazil, and Mexico, but also in vernacular, amateur, and popular photographic practices.[22]

Despite the fact that the study of the visual has exploded in recent years, it has been late in arriving in Latin American and Caribbean history per se. Over the past two decades, scholars in academic departments of literature, anthropology, and art history have written the most important works in this field, contributing the analytic of visual economies, rethinking the performance of state power as a mode of seeing, tracking down the flow of tropicalizing images, and demonstrating how photography was made to err by Brazilian and Mexican modernists.[23] In 2004, the *Hispanic American Historical Review* (*HAHR*) published a special issue with three articles by historians who were sensitive to the specificities of visual culture; but what looked like a promising start has yet to be built upon. What each of the contributors to that special issue took for granted—and what historians should continue to insist upon—is that photographs are a unique kind of historical document.[24]

In one of the *HAHR* essays, Greg Grandin put a twist on literary theorist Gayatri Chakravorty Spivak's question "Can the subaltern speak?" by asking, "Can the subaltern be seen?"[25] One scholar problematized the speaking subject; the other, the seeing historian. In Spivak's foundational essay, she examined the conditions under which a subaltern subject is inscribed into the historical record as well as the limits on the intellectual's ability to read the contaminated inscriptions that actually made it into an accessible archive. But, Grandin wondered, how might photographs as historical sources affect her argument?

Spivak had compellingly argued that subalternity is a structured place from which an individual's capacity to access power is formally obstructed, necessitating that such subjects express themselves through dominant and mutually reinforcing ideologies, whether colonial, patriarchal, religious, or national. This "marking out" of the subject of systemic and intersecting forms of oppression effaced whatever signs of their agency had managed to make it into the historical record. The camera, with its monocular Cartesian perspective, is perhaps the technological equivalent of the discursive filters through which each and every photographed subject inevitably passes on its way into the archival record.

Yet Grandin's examination of portraits of K'iche' Mayans in Guatemala prompted him to conclude that "the subaltern can not only be seen, but they can also see and act, at least as well as anybody can from where they find themselves."[26] Historical methods, he argued, are best able to track the uneven accumulation of wealth and the transformation of institutions, habits, and tastes over time. But at a certain point, traditional source material and official archives, to say nothing of widely circulated artistic productions, begin to swallow up popular actors, rendering them either unknowable or readable only through dominant colonial and national ideologies. This is the most important reason for turning to the visual archive, for it offers the possibility of reworking historical methods and historiographical problems.

Beyond the structural barrier to the inscription of subaltern subjectivities into the historical record, Spivak described a further limit to our ability to understand the lives of people who had been subject to imperial rule and patriarchal religious ideologies. This epistemic constraint had less to do with the site of the subject being studied and more to do with the location of the historian, cultural critic, or political theorist who attempted to offer an account of that subject's speech. In a direct challenge to Michel Foucault and Gilles Deleuze, among the most critical voices of French thought in the early 1980s, Spivak argued that neither of these intellectuals was capable of recognizing the nonuniversality of his own subject position, which he rendered transparent while purporting to convey what the oppressed thought and felt. But in carving out a privileged space for "the postcolonial woman intellectual," Spivak supplanted the critical Euro-American thinker with a different kind of elite knower. The problem is that Spivak presumed that a certain vanguard must pull back the curtains of ideology so that workers and rebellious students might see past their own illusions to get a glimpse of a reality that only the properly situated critic can reveal.[27] There are several reasons to reject this position. But with respect to my immediate concerns as a historian-spectator, I would lean on theorist Ariella Azoulay's recent work to insist that photographs result from always unfinished encounters in which no one has the power to fully dominate another. I would thus suggest that treating photographs as historical documents entails reworking Spivak's claims about the ways that marginalized subjects are (and are not) inscribed into the historical record as well as the issue of which subject positions might enable one to access subaltern self-representations.

To build from the most self-evident of premises, the photo is not a pure and immediate representation of a subject prior to structure, ideology, or discourse. It is not the subject in itself, an unmediated being, unaffected by historical and place-specific formations of capitalist production and regimes of gender, nationalism, and religion. Rather, I maintain that the photo always indexes a subject in her place or in the place that she pretends to be. Hence if a given photo happens to index a subject in itself, it is always also marking the split between the subject-in-becoming and the society, norms, ideals, and material culture in which that subject finds herself.[28] That is, the photograph registers not only a depicted person but also the place in which that person finds herself. In some rare photographs, the force of the subject may overwhelm the structures acting upon her. In such images, the subject creates herself and her place in the world as something positively new. But in most photos in which people are depicted, what registers is either the placing of the subject or the subject placing herself in a specific scene.

The photo and the subject it depicts are, moreover, known from a particular standpoint. To reckon with how and what we can know through the photograph, I again draw on Azoulay in asserting that photography mediates relations between people such that no single participant in a photographic encounter—neither photographer, nor sitter, nor viewer—has sovereign authority over how the resulting image will be used and interpreted. Azoulay's notions of "the civil contract of photography" and "the event of photography" can help us to extricate ourselves from what Latin American studies scholar Gareth Williams has called "the active implementation of center-periphery thinking," in which the subaltern becomes difference itself, located in a periphery to be accessed, and the intellectual becomes self-transparent, accessing the subaltern from the center.[29] The special characteristics of photography, and of the encounters that it enables, can shift this debate and level the playing field in ways that even testimonial literature cannot.

Azoulay argues that everyone who engages with photographs—producing, posing, storing, and looking at them—is a citizen in what she calls "the citizenry of photography." The citizenry of photography is not governed by a sovereign or limited by territoriality; it includes anyone who addresses others through images or who takes the position of a photo's addressee.[30] Furthermore, by entering into what Azoulay calls "the event of photography," anyone can attempt to reconstruct the broader situation within which marks were made on photographic paper, analyzing what happened within the frame and what may have been going on outside it. But the mere presence of visual traces of subaltern agency does not guarantee that they will be recognized as such. As we look at the uncaptioned photograph that Platero Paz took of the Chinese merchant who had been beaten in El Progreso, we have to risk actively speculating on what could have led to this man's injuries and his decision to document them. In doing so, we are exercising what Azoulay calls "civil imagination," reversing the image to think back to the moment when the picture was taken and to the circumstances that resulted in the depiction of this man's wounds.

For thinking both within and outside of the photographic frame, I employ philosopher Jacques Rancière's notion of "the distribution of the sensible," which provides a broad framework for analyzing the underlying historically constructed facts of sense perception that effectively limit what can be seen, said, and done in particular social arrangements.[31] The distribution of the sensible is the set of historically sedimented preconditions

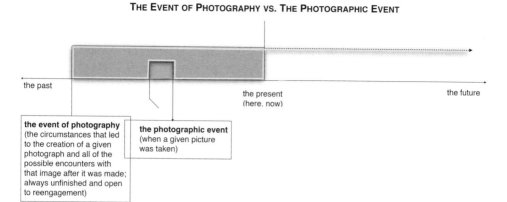

Fig. 1.4. Diagram of Ariella Azoulay's distinction between the event of photography and the photographic event. *Diagram by the author.*

that govern what counts as speech in a specific situation as well as when and where certain kinds of people can be seen and heard. A given distribution of the sensible is disrupted, according to Rancière, when members of a community that has been excluded come forward and point to their exclusion. In this regard, anyone at any time can disrupt an arrangement of positions and sensibilities. Adapting these concepts, I explain how the presence of the United Fruit Company and the hierarchy of general managers, engineers, overseers, and plantation workers came to seem appropriate and even natural. But by denouncing a wrong, the workers disrupted this distribution of places. The denunciation of low wages in the general strike of 1954 produced a dispute in which those who had been excluded from political, economic, and cultural decisions voiced a demand that presupposed a fundamental relation of equality with their putative superiors.

Bridging the theoretical space between Azoulay and Rancière, I conceptualize photography as a technical means of enacting new ways of seeing, thinking, and doing that are never fully controlled by the operator of the camera, the subject of the picture, or the viewer of the image. But whereas both Rancière and Azoulay focus on the social power of photographs and the ethics of spectators who encounter these images, I attempt to keep the subject before the camera in tight focus. My emphasis on the role of the subject of the photograph is, in large part, an accident of circumstance.

As I conducted research into the politics of images in El Progreso, I never gave up searching for ways that photographs circulated and for the ways that people received and consumed these image objects. But what I found instead were splendid private archives and frustratingly few venues for the mass circulation of photos in early twentieth-century Central America. Circumscribed by what I could infer about the reception and distribution of images in neocolonial Honduras, I came to focus more on the subjects of the pictures. Photos can help us understand the naturalization and production of economic impoverishment. But they can also beckon us to pause to contemplate the lives and loves of others. Platero Paz's photographs of the 1954 strike captured and extended a moment when workers changed what could be seen, said, and done in their banana-company town.

In posing for a photo, subjects make individual choices about who they are and who they want others to believe they are. Photography allows individuals to make subtle attacks on existing psychosocial conditions and on the reigning allocation of privilege. Hence some photos must be understood as nano-assertions through which the photographic subject stages, practices, and embodies a new way of being. Thus I think of photography as a specific kind of trace-making mediation that produces self-awareness in the sitting subject.

In a word, I have come to think of a broad range of photographic genres—from disciplinary to documentary to studio—as social practices of self-forging. My notion of these photographic practices as purposive, repeatable exercises that slow down the act of looking and the interior reflection on the fact that one is being looked at is capacious enough to allow for photography to be understood both as a means of surveillance, discipline, and classification and as a tool for self-sculpting. What photography as surveillance and photography as self-presentation have in common is that both are modes of practice that are consciously undertaken and gradually improved upon.

In the pages that follow, I offer a visual history of forgotten banana workers and their families, in an attempt to recover something of their projects and aspirations. I seek to retrieve these moments of individual and collective self-fashioning through the photographs that inscribed, in Azoulay's phrase, "an inalienable point of view" that cannot be fully controlled or negated by corporate or state power and which any potential spectator, now or in the future, may attempt to reactivate.[32] I thus treat photographic images as historical documents that enable the reconstruction of events and subjectivities that have otherwise remained misunderstood or inaccessible.

To get from the studio to the street, from the private assertions of self-respect to the collective demands of worker-citizens, we will first need to explore the founding of El Progreso by a group of local farmers and traders of tropical hardwoods. Soon their vision of citizenship would collide with the identificatory and instrumental gaze of the United Fruit Company, creating an exceptional space out of which bananas were extracted and local identities forged.

Along the way, we will consider the transnational icons of the "banana republic"—Sam "The Banana Man" Zemurray, Carmen Miranda ("The Lady in the Tutti-Frutti Hat"), and even the awkward lovers in Woody Allen's *Bananas*. After reveling among publicly circulated images, we will be able to better appreciate the private image economies of El Progreso and the intimate practices of self-fashioning that photos from those local archives encoded. An unpublished photograph from the 1930s of our photographer, Rafael Platero Paz, embracing a white North American man in the nude provides us with a vantage point on his entire archive as one of contact, over and against the images of separation produced by the United Fruit Company. For their part, Palestinian merchants facilitated connections among the racially and ethnically diverse consumers of this busy banana-company town. Their family photographs signal the multilayered nature of the banana republic: a juxtaposition of national and global sovereignties and forms of visual citizenship, registered and exhibited through the camera. The protections of citizenship are precisely what were withdrawn during the seventeen-year-long constitutional dictatorship of Tiburcio Carías Andino, a political strongman installed by the company.

Fig. 1.5. The Ulúa River, as light painted it in Rafael Platero Paz's camera obscura, before the days when the arch of a bridge spread across the mighty river and when only an infrequent ferry connected its banks. *Courtesy of the Rafael Platero Paz Archive.*

With the setting of this exceptional space sketched out—from the founding of a town called "Progress" to the coming of the United Fruit Company, from the photographer who depicted the townspeople to the pariah entrepreneurs who connected various local groups to each other and to the world—the event of the 1954 banana workers' strike emerges as the coming into being of a new visual subject: the worker-citizen. Platero Paz, *Life* magazine, and *Bohemia* were all there to capture and extend the moments in which these new agents gathered in their stained and ragged work shirts in front of the company's American Zone, threw up collective kitchens, and brought the local Catholic priests into the Ramón Rosa Plaza to celebrate an outdoor Mass. Such photographs reveal and help to consolidate the will of a subject trying to escape the place to which she or he had been socially assigned. As spectators, we are called upon to reflect on lives that were and lives that could have been.

TWO

Visualizing Progress

In the early 1920s, Rafael Platero Paz took a picture of people walking on a road being built in the town of El Progreso (figure 2.1). The late-afternoon light cast long shadows across the scene, creating a stunning chiaroscuro effect. Off to the side of the men dressed in white linen, the United Fruit Company would subsequently set up its regional headquarters in a two-story building with an extensive annex that included a swimming pool for the company's "first class" employees. On the other side of the dirt road, near the three women in white dresses, the company would build the American Zone, an exclusive, racially segregated neighborhood to house its US personnel: a superintendent, engineers, accountants, teachers, and plantation overseers. By 1963 this road would round the corner toward the Ulúa River and lead to a bridge that was inaugurated as Democracia by Ramón Villeda Morales, the country's first president to address the needs of the banana workers.

In 1927, workers erected a kiosk in the center of El Progreso's main public square, the Ramón Rosa Plaza.[1] The structure architecturally supported the clock that the city had imported from Hamburg, Germany, in 1925.

Fig. 2.1. *Courtesy of the Rafael Platero Paz Archive.*

When Platero Paz took this picture of a civic space being built, he stood in front of the offices of the municipal government of El Progreso and captured, in the background, the store of Salomón (Selim) Mahchi Lorenz, a prominent local merchant who had emigrated from Palestine in 1913 (figure 2.2). Decades later, it was in this plaza, around this very kiosk, that tens of thousands of striking banana workers in their tattered long-sleeved shirts and frayed trousers would gather for an outdoor Mass as they prayed that the Honduran government and the United Fruit Company would recognize their needs for higher wages, better living conditions, and the right to join together to make their collective voice heard.

The photographs of the road and the kiosk seized and extended the early twentieth-century architectural program of a town with ambitions of becoming a small city. The pictures and the construction that they document were bets placed for the kind of modernity that local planners envisioned for the future of their increasingly urban space. Platero Paz arrested this local process of modernization as it was happening. In picking up his camera to make a record of the two projects, he was acting as a local historian of his present. His images are laden with temporality, providing motifs of change, of self-conscious, future-oriented, shared undertakings of horizontal and vertical construction. Many years later, workers too would organize outward, approaching fellow laborers in other divisions of the company, as they simultaneously organized upward, to the president of the country, the CEO of the corporation, and the US secretary of state. The two movements—sideways and ascending—were premised upon prior and parallel interior movements along both axes, as *progreseños* aspired to a future that they themselves would have to usher into being.

In the aestheticization of their own spacetime, Platero Paz's pictures search for and summon a particular version of modernity for El Progreso. Modernity in these two images is about a road and a railroad through town, but it is also about late-afternoon walks with friends and family and the way the light hit Mico Quemado when it was shrouded in clouds. Modernity is about the clock tower and the men who climbed up ladders to build it, around the corner from Platero Paz's studio. Modernity, in these photographs, is about construction, about building, about sculpting oneself and one's community in the present to build the future that one desired.[2]

Fig. 2.2. *Courtesy of the Rafael Platero Paz Archive.*

But to get to these stories of local self-fashioning, of encounters between banana plantation laborers and US managers, of a general strike and a model of economic imperialism in crisis, we should start at the beginning. The founding of a town called Progress, before the advent of the banana companies, seems like the right place to start.

FOUNDING A TOWN CALLED PROGRESS

On the north coast of Honduras, in the village of Río Pelo, a motley crew of farmers and mahogany traders erected what would later become a booming banana town. Nearly 250 years earlier, Franciscan friars from Guatemala had come on the backs of mules and baptized the village with the biblical name of Santa María de Canaán de Río Pelo, linking this New World cultural geography to the Land of Canaan, which encompassed ancient Palestine and, over the second millennium before Christ, was gradually conquered and occupied by the Israelites. Hence the indigenous men and women tending to their crops and fishing on the banks of the Pelo and Ulúa Rivers would not have been wrong if they felt a sense of foreboding at the sight of these men in cassocks. If they were the New World's Canaanites, they would soon disappear. A couple of centuries later, on the first day of the year 1893, a Sunday, no less, the village of Río Pelo, situated on a river that wended through the community like a silky braid of hair, was legally reconstituted as the town of El Progreso. The very renaming of the town indicates something of the future that its latter-day leaders envisioned.

"Progress" was the new metaphor for the place. The name itself condensed the larger processes and ideals that swept through late-nineteenth-century Central America and were adopted, with varying degrees of success, by modernizing political strongmen (caudillos) in capitals from Guatemala City to San José. In contrast to the vast majority of villages and towns in Latin America, this town was named after neither a saint nor a virgin. Instead, "El Progreso" embodied the notion of liberal secularization promoted by elite politicians—like Justo Rufino Barrios, Marco Aurelio Soto, and José Santos Zelaya—who sought to reduce the economic and political power of the Catholic Church in their respective Central American republics.

Setting a precedent for the neocolonial relationships to come, the first mayor of El Progreso was William "Guillermo" Bain, an Englishman who had migrated from Britain to help build the Honduran Inter-Oceanic Railroad.[3] From his florid signature and from documents he prepared for the construction of the railroad, it is clear that Bain was a literate man. Other prominent members of his cabinet, including Raimundo Panchamé, were much less comfortable with pen and paper; so rather than sign their names, they left digital copies of their official authorizations: their thumbprints. On that same first day of the year 1893, Juán Blas Tobías, a native of Mexico who had come to Honduras for precious hardwoods, was sworn in as a judge. "I promise that I will perform and I will uphold the Constitution and laws, according to their text," he solemnly stated.[4] The newly constituted municipal authorities immediately sought to establish a system of local taxation and create a budget.[5] The next order of business was to attract permanent settlers. They created a legal framework in which families who came to the municipality with the intention of becoming residents would be granted plots of land with the understanding that they were then obligated to construct their own houses on those lands within two years; single individuals were given seven months. Municipal trustee Julio Flores was named judge of property measurements, and he swore to verify and document the allocation of land.[6] Next, on Wednesday, February 15, the founding fathers of El Progreso agreed that a city hall and town jail needed to be built. "Whereas there is a need to build a council house [*cabildo*] and likewise a piece that serves to jail; considering that for such purposes is suggested the popular vote of the neighbors [*vecinos*], they simultaneously agreed to build a house 12 yards [*varas*] long and eight wide. One side will be for the *cabildo* and then a 'double wall' to separate the jail from the *cabildo*."[7] Law and force were thus the foundation upon which the town was built, separated only by a double wall. The landscape was seen abstractly, as property lines were delineated and maintained by a local community instituting its own laws. The founders also created a constitutional arrangement in which the governors sought the consent, through the vote, of the governed, who were inclusively figured as *vecinos*, neighbors. Thus through *vecindad*, a form of local citizenship available to respectable and rooted men, this "new" town rested upon a Hispanic political tradition that dated back to eleventh- and twelfth-century Castile.[8]

In an ellipse whose path took 116 years to travel, from the founding of the town in 1893 to the coup d'état that would oust the democratically elected president of the country in 2009, the family of the British railroader-turned-settler William Bain curiously reappears, as if following Kepler's laws of planetary motion. Upon taking power on June 28, 2009, Roberto Micheletti Bain, grandson of the founding father of El Progreso, promptly suspended the constitutional protection of civil liberties in an effort quash the largest movement to restore popular sovereignty that Honduras had seen since the 1954 banana workers' strike. In El Progreso, neocolonial desire and the will to self-govern have been in constant tension, from 1893 to the present.

Towns and cities, like photographs, are physical records of distinct moments and choices. But whereas photography results from an encounter between a subject, a photographer, and a spectator, cities gradually accumulate from the everyday encounters between residents, political officials, and the outside currents that circulate through them. More so than photographs, cities are artistic objects that have been and continue to be collectively constructed. "The city," Adrián Gorelik has written, "is time recorded in stone."[9] In late-nineteenth-century El Progreso, it was not stone, but lumber and adobe in which the memory of a people building a new town was recorded.

In graduating from being a village to becoming a town, El Progreso's first generation of leaders established a municipal government, systems of taxation and land distribution, and an incentive program to attract settlers, demonstrating their keen awareness of the connection between building up a critical mass of *pobladores* and commercial development. Ramón Llecet and José Melesio Velásquez paid the first eighty pesos of tax revenue received by the municipal government for "imports, exports, and the right to operate a store and cantina."[10] In 1898, the municipality improved the road to the port at Tela and was promoted in the *Directorio comercial* that G. R. Perry was seeking to publish.[11] In short, before the banana companies came, *progreseños* had already put in place the institutions and mechanisms of their local government.

Unsurprisingly, the early leaders of El Progreso sought to symbolically link their new town to the Honduran nation. On June 22, 1893, they met to vote on congratulating President Domingo Vásquez for having just defeated a rebellion by a rival caudillo, Policarpo Bonilla. The founders of El Progreso ratified the following statement:

> Considering that our pueblo, only recently born, has marched and will always march observing proper obedience to legitimacy.
>
> Unanimously, we agree:
>
> We will adhere in every way to the Government headed by the Benemérito General Vásquez, offering our services to sustain his government and legitimacy.[12]

By referring to "legitimate" government, the founders of El Progreso explicitly subscribed to a democratic discourse of civic participation and civil liberties. "Legitimate" governments, they assumed, were not dictatorships but were instead made up of elected officials who represented the people. The first generation of *progreseños* were also good publicists who sought to endear themselves and their municipality to the federal regime, whose tenuous existence depended on support from local governments. And while national politics was being pursued with guns and ammunition, local politics in El Progreso was carried out in town meetings at which each resident voted aloud, a type of proclamation that was very common in Mexican and Central American political culture after independence.[13] Here again, the *vecinos* of El Progreso were replicating a particular kind of political culture—it was a new town guided by some old rules and customs.

TIME RECORDED IN LUMBER

Honduran hardwoods first attracted the founders of El Progreso to the region. On December 1, 1906, the Waller Lumber Company requested permission to cut down trees on *ejido* (public or communal) lands. The request was granted to cut stands "of mahogany, cedar, San Juán, Laurel and Santa María, upon payment of five silver dollars for each mahogany and cedar tree, four for each San Juán, and three for each Laurel or Santa María, in the *ejido* of this town."[14] The cutting down of the fragile forests of northern Honduras continued unabated throughout the early twentieth century as the descendants of the English founder continued to harvest lumber for the municipality. In 1909, for instance, Mayor Manuel Moya Amaya acknowledged the receipt of 624¾ feet of milled lumber from Carlos R. Bain, son of the town's first mayor and owner of a prominent import-export house.[15] Likewise, Señor Gustavo Panchamé "completed the work of dragging three thousand feet of milled lumber that was contracted on behalf of the Municipality, at a rate of six pesos a thousand."[16] Thus while several members of the Bain and Panchamé families served at various times in the municipal government, their private businesses benefited from the municipal contracts they were granted. The municipality of El Progreso was constructing roads, bridges, schools, and a community butcher stand, all of which required lumber.[17] The cleared forests, in turn, were converted into agricultural lands, which were rapidly gobbled up by new agricultural entrepreneurs.

As these examples illustrate, Hondurans invested in their infrastructure (including public buildings, roads, bridges, and agricultural land), created public institutions (including municipal governments, legal codes, police, and schools), and developed mechanisms for generating revenue and financing public services. This fact of local governmentality belies the ideological claims that were subsequently repeated as a justification for the actions of the US fruit companies in Latin America. In El Progreso, the United Fruit Company found not a blank slate, but rather the social, agricultural, and political infrastructure needed to establish one of its bases of operations.[18] The founders of the town had already begun transforming the forests and communal holdings into square lots (*manzanas cuadradas*), a grid that was intelligible to capitalists and the marketplace.

The early twentieth century was a time of great optimism for people living and working in the alluvial plains of northern Honduras. Small producers were able to sell their fruits and vegetables at a reasonable price. US fruit companies were buying, transporting, distributing, and marketing tropical fruits, primarily bananas, but they were not yet producing these commodities in significant quantities. Thus local producers had a high degree of autonomy. The municipal government of El Progreso sought to bolster the production of agroexports. On January 9, 1910, the governing members and the town's *vecinos* met as a community.

The ninety *vecinos* present received the mayor's proposal to dedicate public lands to the prosperity of the town with "applause and enthusiasm" and unanimously agreed to "adopt agriculture as patrimony and to choose for this the banana, coffee, cocoa, sugarcane, and rubber."[19] Those who had recently renamed the town had done so in the imperative mood: "Progress!" By growing crops "suitable for export," they understood that it was their task, as well as that of capitalists everywhere, to convert substances into flows.[20] As more bananas and sugarcane flowed out from El Progreso, more money would flow in. As an early experiment in communal agriculture, the comparatively better-off joined forces with the impoverished but hardworking peasants to produce agricultural exports. Welding their local material efforts to the national project of modernization, they immediately put El Progreso's agricultural and livestock zones into production and then inaugurated them on Honduran Independence Day: "It was agreed that on September 15, the immortal date of the month of the emancipation of our Country, a public work should be inaugurated, and the Division of the Agricultural and Cattle Zone is one that deserves recognition for the beneficial results it offers."[21]

So, nearly a decade before the United Fruit Company became a legal business entity and more than two decades before North Americans began producing bananas in the Sula Valley, *progreseños* had already built the key institutions and the mechanisms of administration that were the very pre-conditions for subsequent economic exploitation by private enterprise. Such local collective agency and governmental capacity would soon be effaced by the cheerful imperialist naiveté of the fruit companies and their boosters.

FROM LOCAL PRODUCERS TO BANANA REPUBLIC

The era of the smallholder and communal agriculture was soon to be eclipsed by an alliance between US capitalists and pliable Honduran political elites, both of which were forcefully backed by US gunboat diplomacy, as geographically illustrated by Hermann B. Deutsch in *The Incredible Yanqui* (map 2.1).

In 1899, three investors in Boston and Costa Rica—Lorenzo Baker, Andrew Preston, and Minor Cooper Keith—founded the United Fruit Company. Lorenzo Baker was a ship captain who in May 1871 had sailed the *Telegraph* into Boston with the first cargo of bananas and by the 1890s had founded the Boston Fruit Company. Highly perishable and "exotic" to North Americans, bananas were risky business. Andrew Preston had barely an elementary school education and worked as an assistant to a produce

Map 2.1. Map of banana imperialism. From Hermann B. Deutsch, *The Incredible Yanqui: The Career of Lee Christmas* (1931), inside cover.

dealer, but he saw a potential market for bananas and persuaded nine men to give him $2,000 each, without the hope of profits for at least five years. With this capital, Preston succeeded Baker as president of the Boston Fruit Company. At a cost of $8 million and four thousand lives, Minor Cooper Keith built a railroad that linked Costa Rica's Meseta Central to its Caribbean coast. By 1893, he was exporting bananas from four Central American republics.[22] In 1899, Baker, Preston, and Keith consolidated their businesses into the United Fruit Company.

During the early years, the company purchased fruit from independent smallholders (*poquiteros*), then transported it to North America and Europe. Gradually, several North American entrepreneurs established banana plantations throughout the Caribbean Basin. In Honduras, one fiefdom began to emerge in the area around La Ceiba, as the Vaccaro brothers and Salvatore D'Antoni founded a business that would be known, as of 1924, as the Standard Fruit Company, now Dole Fruit.[23] At the other end of the coast, in the Sula Valley near Puerto Cortés, other entrepreneurs were creating separate banana colonies. In 1902, the Honduran government gave William F. Streich of Philadelphia a large land concession. In return for the land, Streich was charged with building a five-mile stretch of railroad from Cuyamel to Vera Cruz so that Honduran producers would not be dependent upon river barges to transport their commodity to the port of Omoa. In addition to the railroad, he began planting bananas on the land that had been granted to him in the railroad concession.[24] Although he failed to successfully establish his plantation, he had hit upon the large-scale banana production that would come to displace the independent growers.

Short on funds, Streich was looking to sell his land. Onto the scene walked an Eastern European with the Anglicized name of Samuel Zemurray. This latter-day titan got his start, so goes the myth, by selling bananas from a pushcart in Mobile, Alabama.[25] Buying ripe bananas at this United Fruit port of call, Zemurray shipped them upcountry to railroad towns, a practice the company resented as soon as Zemurray began to cut into its profits. Soon United Fruit offered Zemurray a deal he could not refuse. In exchange for relinquishing his contract to sell ripe fruit, the company would give him the capital that he needed to buy Streich's property and rights. It helped him organize a partnership with Ashbel Hubbard. The two men purchased a battered old banana steamer, which they conducted to and from the port of Omoa. Zemurray's business grew rapidly. He sold 336,000 bunches of bananas in 1903, nearly 600,000 the following year, and 1.75 million in 1910, the year he bought the Cuyamel Fruit Company.[26]

In early January 1911, US Secretary of State Philander C. Knox negotiated the refinancing of the Honduran national debt, which had accrued as various unscrupulous US entrepreneurs, Honduran politicians, and British financiers vainly pursued the hope of building an interoceanic railroad. The Paredes-Knox Convention would guarantee the customs receipts for payment of the loan while also restricting Honduras from increasing its import or export duties without the permission of the United States.[27] One person unhappy with the prospect of customs duties being paid to J. P. Morgan and Company was none other than Zemurray, who stood to lose if Honduras taxed his imports of railway materials. Zemurray's friend, ex-president Manuel Bonilla, led the charge against the offending president, Miguel R. Dávila.

On Christmas Eve 1910, a yacht called *The Hornet*, which Bonilla had purchased with money from Zemurray, sailed just outside of New Orleans, where it rendezvoused with the Banana Man's forty-foot cruiser and took on board the US soldier of fortune "General Lee Christmas and his lieutenant, Machine Gun Molony, a case of rifles, 3,000 rounds of ammunition and a machine gun."[28] The rebel ship then sailed to Roatán and Trujillo, which it "captured" on January 10, 1911. By January 28, President Dávila was sending urgent cables to President William Howard Taft, agreeing to the convention and the loan and pleading for US intervention to stop the banana mercenaries. Meanwhile, in the United States, the Senate rejected the Paredes-Knox Convention, and J. P. Morgan and Company declared that they were not prepared to purchase the old bonds.[29] Soon afterward, the US consul at Puerto Cortés was mediating between the various factions aboard the USS *Tacoma*, where he settled upon Dr. Francisco Bertrand Barahona, who was favored by the Zemurray-backed rebels, as Dávila's successor. Less than a year later, elections were held and Bonilla was returned to the presidency. Lee Christmas was appointed US consul to Honduras. Thus the era of the "banana republic" began.

CONCESSIONS AND LAND TRANSFERS

All the while, *progreseños* continued to successfully solicit titles to plots from their municipal government, finding that they could sell their agricultural products to Samuel Zemurray and the Cuyamel Fruit Company. There were two ways that land was distributed to private petitioners. The first was *dominio útil*, which gave the petitioner the right to use and improve public land; it often was granted with the understanding that the petitioner might later be granted full private ownership of that plot. The second was *dominio pleno*, in which the petitioner immediately acquired full ownership of the land, along with the right to sell it for his or her own benefit. On July 1, 1913, Quintín Juarez gained *dominio útil* to twenty-five *manzanas* (17.25 hectares) of prime agricultural land, the northern boundary of which abutted one of the town's *ejidos*.[30] The municipality also granted Juán J. Meza *dominio útil* to twenty-five *manzanas*, seven of which were already cultivated with bananas.[31] The Tela Railroad Company, a local subsidiary of the United Fruit Company, would soon displace many of these mestizo cultivators.

At the national level, President Bonilla rewarded his benefactor Zemurray with a number of generous concessions, reversing long-standing legal protections designed to keep Honduran land in Honduran hands. Charles Kepner, one of the first scholars to critically examine the work of the United Fruit Company, found that the agrarian law of 1898 stipulated that "the nation should retain the legal ownership of the national lands assigned to villages and towns, and prohibited the alienation of lands within eight kilometers of the sea and, unless authorized by a new law, of alternate lots surveyed in connection with land distributions and reserved to the state." Meanwhile, Decree 36, issued by the Honduran Congress in February 1902, "prohibited the permanent alienation of national lands within the Tela district, and Decree 50 of the same month arranged for the division of these lands into lots, the *dominium utile*—but not the *dominium directum*—of which could be acquired by Hondurans or foreigners."[32] By January 1906, the Congress extended this protection to all national lands within thirty miles of the coast. Finally, Decree 63 of March 4, 1909, reserved legal ownership of land to the Honduran state and ordered that only *dominio útil* (and not *dominio pleno*) would be granted for unused national lands.

The port of Tela, famous for its beautiful white beaches and vibrant Afro-indigenous Garifuna community, was situated between the spheres of influence of Zemurray's Cuyamel Fruit Company in Puerto Cortés and Vaccaro Brothers and Company in La Ceiba. The multiple concessions granted by Bonilla and the Honduran Congress in 1911 and 1912 helped cement the relationship between Zemurray and the United Fruit Company, which had for some time sought a foothold in Honduras. And while these fabled concessions have been frequently opposed, it is extraordinarily difficult to determine the actual terms of the agreement between Honduras and the fruit companies. So it is worth including a lengthy extract from one of the original concessions granted to the Tela Railroad Company (TRR):

Article 1.—The concessionaire [United Fruit as parent company of TRR] undertakes to build a pier on the point that it chooses between Cape El Triunfo and Puerto Sal in the Bay of Tela and Puerto Sal, Department of Atlántida, and a railway, which, beginning at said port and connecting to it, will end in El Progreso, Department of Yoro.

Article 16.—The Government will grant the concessionaire, in property, six thousand hectares of free public lands, with the trees of all kinds that they contain, for every twelve kilometers from the main line and branches that the concessionaire builds. These lands are given in alternate lots, for the concessionaire and the Government, of four thousand hectares on each side of the railway.

Article 20.—The operator may introduce, for the work of its company, the workers that it deems appropriate, with the exception of Chinese, coolies, and blacks; but the latter [blacks] may be introduced with permission from the government.

Article 21.—The concessionaire will pay the Government an extraction tax of an American gold penny per bunch [racimo] of bananas to be exported by rail and dock built.[33]

With a few strokes of a pen, the Tela Railroad Company gained ownership to thousands of acres of land, as well as the timber on it, in exchange for agreeing to build a port and a railroad line from Tela to El Progreso.

The transfer of vast swaths of public property from Honduras to the United Fruit Company was enabled by a mode of instrumentally apprehending land and labor. The north coast was envisioned and mapped as an abstract visual space that could be geometrically carved up into alternating lots of four thousand hectares each. The natural history of the place was thus enfolded into the goal of building the coveted railroad—"the trees of all kinds" were expendable and exchangeable. So too were the human beings. Labor would certainly be needed to build the railroad. No mention is made of Honduras's own population, made up primarily of mestizos, indigenous peoples, and the Garifuna. Instead, the concession gave the company the right to decide what "workers it deems appropriate" for its needs. The Honduran government, for its part, reserved the right to exclude "Chinese, coolies, and blacks," racializing the development of the railroad and the plantation system that it was designed to stimulate and serve. Thus, in the alternating lots, we see the beginnings of two sovereign gazes—that of US-based capital and that of the Honduran state—supplanting local allocations of land with their externally agreed-upon divisions of the landscape and labor.

By 1912, United Fruit had two subsidiaries in Honduras, the Tela and Truxillo railroad companies. The fruit company vertically integrated to control not only the transportation and marketing of bananas, but also their production. In 1918, United Fruit had 14,081 acres under cultivation; by 1929, that number had risen to 95,300 acres. The company purchased from local producers only 15 percent of the fruit it exported from Honduras; in contrast, it purchased 75 percent of the fruit it exported from Costa Rica.[34] Given that producers maintained more autonomy and reaped greater economic benefits than the wage laborers the company employed, this discrepancy is significant and points to future economic and political divergences between these two Central American nations.

On October 23, 1914, William C. Akers entered the offices of the municipal government of El Progreso. Akers noted that his employer, the Tela Railroad Company, benefited from a generous concession that gave it easements across several strips of land, some of them assumed to be property of the municipality and the rest in the hands of private individuals. Akers must have been happy as he left city hall that day. The municipal officials of El Progreso agreed "to transfer communal rights from the *vecinos* to the company."[35] In laying the tracks, the Tela Railroad Company stretched across properties of the politically and economically important as well as the humble.

The municipal archive bears no record of protest on the part of the former owners. They might have felt that allowing the company's railroad and canals to cross their properties would benefit them personally while also serving the greater ends of local and national development. In any case, efficiency, geometry, and the concessions awarded by a small group of politicians who owed their influence largely to their ties to the US fruit companies trumped the heterogeneous, organic, and local. Besides, most who granted the company the right to cross their land could not have anticipated that, a few short years later, vast expanses of the north coast would become the property of one of the first multinational corporations.

Meanwhile, the city of El Progreso continued in its drive to modernize. New tax laws were written to keep up with an increasingly diverse array of imports and exports. Small businesses were being opened at a fast clip. And the city continued to pull itself away from its village origins and closer to the "modern" ideal of a rationalized, ordered, and surveilled space. Censuses were taken. Procedures for administering *ejidal* land were adopted.[36] Rules and consequences were drafted to control the movement of animals, prostitutes, beggars, unlicensed *curanderos* (practitioners of indigenous medicine), and habitual drunkards. "For good maintenance of the zone," the police were put in charge of punishing people for these infractions and ordered to report back to the municipal government on progress made in curbing undesirable behaviors.[37] The increase in administrative control dovetailed with the economic aims and modernist aesthetics of the United Fruit Company. Yet to everyone's frustration, the gap between ideals and reality was painfully wide: "Reviewing the Book of Police Sentences, it is severely distressing to find only seven convictions. The lack of compliance with the Civil Laws in this population is disgracefully palpable; there are numerous people loitering, much public drunkenness, a lot of scandals, and many lapses in the Police and hygiene."[38]

By 1916, the town of El Progreso had three schools, one for girls, in a rented building, and two for boys, in buildings of their own. None of the schools had furniture, and attendance at the girls school was abysmal. "Malaria is rampant," the local government reported, "but given the climate and the conditions of the place in which we live, the lack of hygiene and good water, we don't suffer many disruptions." On top of all this, many bemoaned the town's lack of "ornateness."[39]

In this era of modernization, a time in which administrative minds projected toward an ordered future, the early eighteenth-century notions that linked climate and race resurfaced under a sovereign malaria to be overcome by enacting higher standards of cleanliness and hygiene.

Just as the Tela concession (Decree 113) gave the company new rights and exemptions, some of the Tegucigalpa wheeling and dealing was not honored at the local level. For instance, in 1917, the municipality of El Progreso was having a difficult time getting the company to pay some of the taxes it owed. Mayor Raimundo Panchamé sought counsel from the governor of Yoro and the mayor of neighboring San Cristobal. Ultimately they cited Article 128 of the Municipal Law of Honduras and resolved to send Colonel Manuel M. García to the local offices of the Tela Railroad Company to collect the taxes due for the months of January through June 1917. The local governments were owed one gold penny for each bunch of bananas exported.[40] But the national government had already stipulated that the company would pay that much in federal taxes and explicitly exempted the company from paying any further taxes on imports or exports.[41] Taking issue with the federal government and the company, the local government of El Progreso was reluctant to relinquish its right to tax its most important industry.

The audacity of this small municipality's challenge to United Fruit is remarkable. El Progreso lacked even a small fraction of the power of the Honduran state, yet it pursued the company for taxes due. United Fruit was being extolled for its "conquest of the tropics." It was already deemed a corporate empire. Yet El Progreso tried to keep the company's voracious appetite in check. While it failed, this failure demonstrates how United Fruit worked within geographic and political spaces that it could easily dominate. El Progreso's experience also illustrates how the company used its influence at different levels—from the national government, to the city council, to the individual landowner.

Haggling over municipal taxes was one thing, but stopping the company was quite another. In the Department of Yoro, in just twelve days in July 1924, there were a whopping 122 transfers of land from many dozens of Hondurans and several North Americans to the Tela Railroad Company. Some of these transfers were large. Ernesto Lázaro sold 368 hectares in Camalote to the company for 3,750 gold coins. For 12,000 gold coins, Manuel Garcia, a wealthy immigrant from Mexico, sold 552 hectares of La Bolsa ranch near El Progreso. Eligio Bautista sold seven plots of land, one of which included an adobe house about thirty feet from a railroad station. The largest of the Bautista plots was 580 hectares, which he sold for 4,000 gold coins. Much national land was also transferred to the Tela Railroad Company, apparently as part of a railroad concession: 1,606 hectares of national land "5A" in the jurisdiction of El Progreso; 2,523 hectares of national land "3A" in the jurisdiction of El Progreso; 2,297 hectares of national land "6A" in the jurisdiction of El Progreso. In just nine transactions, ownership of 11,678 hectares (45 square miles) of Honduran national land in the municipality of El Progreso was transferred into the hands of the Tela Railroad Company. Curiously, a certain Lewis M. Thornburgh sold several small parcels of *ejidos*, public lands, in El Progreso to the company for $50,000. Many of those who received land for free from the municipality later profited by selling it to the Tela Railroad Company, among them William "Guillermo" Bain, Raimundo Panchamé, Nicolás Gabrie, and J. Milecio Velásquez.[42] By May 1925, the company was offering to install an electrical generating plant and power lines throughout the city of El Progreso in exchange for excusing the company from $37,747 that it owed in local taxes.[43] Perhaps the municipality's earlier pursuit of the company, together with the later massive appropriation of land, compelled the company to offer a goodwill gesture.

After the stock market crash of October 1929, United Fruit reached a deal with Sam "Banana Man" Zemurray to purchase the Cuyamel Fruit

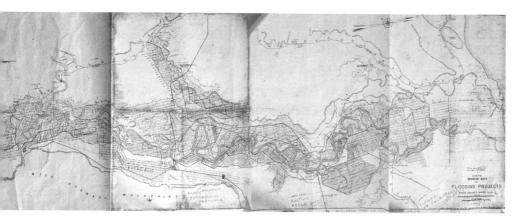

Map 2.2. Visualizing the landscape. Tela Railroad Company flooding projects on the banana plantations around El Progreso, 1951. *Courtesy of the Rafael Platero Paz Archive.*

Company from him in exchange for 300,000 shares. The deal was valued at some $32 million.[44] The United Fruit Company also owned several companies that sold consumer products in the domestic markets of Honduras, Nicaragua, Guatemala, Costa Rica, Panama, Colombia, Ecuador, Jamaica, Cuba, and the West Indies. By 1930, United Fruit was the largest employer and private landholder in Central America. In addition to bananas, the company produced sugar, cocoa, and Manila hemp, which was used as rope on US battleships. The Tela Railroad Company was exporting record amounts of fruit and reaping unparalleled profits, while the Honduran government and people were losing their land in quick, glancing blows and seeing few benefits from increased production.

OVERSEERS AND TIMEKEEPERS

Just as independent and locally controlled production had given way to wage labor, by the mid-1920s, local visions of progress gave way to the United Fruit Company's visualization of the banana plantation. The iconic figure of this new regime was the *mandador*, or overseer. In his 1968 book *Empire in Green and Gold*, Charles Morrow Wilson celebrates the role of the overseer:

> Only the banana plants seem large. Men seem puny and incidental by comparison. But browned men, most of them equipped with the broad-bladed machetes, work almost incessantly to perpetuate the harvests.

The overseer, who is usually assisted by a timekeeper or assistant overseer, is directly accountable for the entire farm and its labor force of 125
to 200 workers per thousand acres of cultivation.

Ordinarily banana farmers work in the forenoon, from dawn until
nearly midday. While the laborers take the afternoons for *siestas*, the
overseer and his timekeeper must fill out interminable reports and
records—weather reports, fruit estimates, pay rolls, harvest tabula-
tions, reports of acreage and livestock, work contracts, requisition slips,
sick lists and hospital records, over-all farm budgets, and an individual
account for every worker on the farm.[45]

Wilson's juxtaposition of the lazy siesta-loving fieldworker with the industrious overseer reflects the cultural stereotypes that underwrote banana
imperialism. More pragmatically, the company joined oversight with the
regimentation of tasks. Together, the overseer and the timekeeper controlled the life and productive capacity of vast and precisely delineated
spaces. With payrolls, weather reports, and hospital records, the United
Fruit Company overseer was merely the intensification of the overseer on
the seventeenth-century slave plantation that Nicholas Mirzoeff so inci-
sively describes.[46] With his unitary gaze and through a racialized regime of
wage labor, each United Fruit Company overseer was at the top of the pay
scale for agricultural work and commanded 125 to 200 workers per thousand hectares on the company's plantations.[47] Under the prior regime, each
smallholder was his own sovereign, ruling over his dominion of twenty-five
manzanas in the manner that he saw fit. But as a wage laborer, he was subject to the oversight of a North American sovereign and his deputy *mandador*, both of whom served as the local surrogates, "accountable for the entire
farm," of executives in Boston. The line of authority on the banana plantation was thus straight and vertical and transnational, originating in Boston,
passing through New Orleans, and terminating in the company's plantations in Cuba, Jamaica, Guatemala, Honduras, Colombia, and Ecuador.

But given that workers continued to nurture historical memories of
autonomy, dignity, and plots of their own that they cultivated for subsistence and a surplus to sell to the shippers, United Fruit also relied upon
a network of national and regional authorities to maintain a disciplined
workforce. In El Progreso, the workers' "countervisuality," to use Mirzoeff's
term for a subaltern regime of classification, separation, and aestheticization, would not materialize until the general strike of 1954.[48]

Against Charles Morrow Wilson's celebration of the overseer, we might consider an article entitled "The Repressive Apparatus of the Tela RR.Co.," in which the Tegucigalpa newspaper *Vanguardia Revolucionaria* analyzes the mutually reinforcing elements of the United Fruit Company's regime of oversight:

> This apparatus constrains in different ways. Military commanders, watchmen, deputy commanders, corporals, and railroad guards are aided by a corps of paid spontaneous spies, all of whom are entrusted with the right to punish.
>
> The head of each department can apply economic sanctions, promotions, layoffs, and salary cuts.
>
> To this we must add the legal department and the political department.
>
> The commanders of various categories are the contact point between the banana trust and government agencies. Special accounts from the monopoly's private budget are used to maintain complete armed convoys, with their respective bosses, in addition to guards it maintains in Tela and La Lima.
>
> Sergeants are in each field. All manner of authority is concentrated in their hands: civil, military, legal. They arrest, imprison, fine, and deport workers who are no longer pleasing to the powerful of the plantations. In their respective jurisdictions, the commander of La Lima, El Progreso, Tela, and Puerto Cortés appoints them, by choosing, preferably, audacious and unscrupulous men.
>
> The vigilante corps is a military legion of special use to the company. The director is in Tela. The corps knows about complaints, fines, and even marital discord. They have a small private jail, a few meters from Tela Viejo.[49]

This editorial was published in 1950, after nearly two decades of the United Fruit–backed dictatorship of Tiburcio Carías Andino and during the early days of democratic opening permitted by the administration of President Juan Manuel Gálvez. In the enforcement mechanism of the company's production hardware, the figure of the vigilante—he who keeps watch—is crucial. He informs, he reports, he conveys information to superiors, he slips in unnoticed, and he gets into the private lives of workers. The regulation of the plantation workforce rested upon a force that was not so much legalized as performed and enacted through a million glances. The looks from this technologically armed will to discipline carried threats of economic coercion and physical punishment. The Honduran military, the police, and a network of spies supplemented the company's stern, photographically reinforced gaze.[50]

A table created by the Tela Railroad Company in 1931 schematized the line of sight and oversight within the company's hierarchy of command. Titled "Unit Prices Paid for Farm Work," the table of salaries and wages systematically displays a chain of authority that ran from the overseers and timekeepers at the top, to the office clerks and foremen in the middle, to the day laborers and housegirls at the bottom. This enumeration of positions and wages did not include the salaries of the superintendent, the division manager, or the higher-level managers in the corporate offices in Boston. Their physical presence was not needed on the plantations. The local crew could be counted on to carry out the orders.

The very term *overseer* is worthy of etymological analysis. But for our purposes, it is enough to briefly note the ordinary meanings of the noun *overseer*—"a person who oversees; supervisor—*the overseer of a plantation*"—and the verb *oversee*—"to direct (work or workers); supervise, manage; to see or observe secretly or unintentionally; to survey or watch as from a higher position; to look over, inspect."[51] Thus the word *oversee* conveys the tight connection between sight and power. The Spanish translation of *overseer* is *mandador*, and *to oversee* is *mandar*, words no less eligible for etymological study. Here again, the dictionary definition alone will allow us to travel a great conceptual distance in very little time: "Mandar: 1 Ordenar o imponer como obligación o como tarea. 2 Gobernar o dirigir. 3 Enviar, hacer ir o hacer llegar."[52] So while the English *overseer* emphasizes ocular power, the Spanish emphasizes the power to command. To command is to govern, to direct, to send. A command given may not result in obedience, but power can still issue commandments, tolerating degrees of disobedience and transgression while remaining in its position of authority.[53]

Bearing in mind the divergent semantic charges of the English and Spanish names for this key figure in the banana plantation, we can proceed to the lower rungs on the ladder of oversight and command. Within the United Fruit Company, the farm foreman was below the overseer. The foreman, or *capataz de finca*, was a deputy overseer who exercised many of the powers of the overseer but in a more limited domain. It is worth pausing to reflect on the visual impact of the *capataz de finca*. Many of them were quite proud of who they were and what they did. Complete with the material trappings of their trade, they loved to pose for the camera.

In El Progreso, Rafael Platero Paz photographed many of the company's employees, including the overseers and farm foremen (figure 2.3). Platero Paz's daughter, Profesora Aída López de Castillo, married a timekeeper who worked for the United Fruit Company. When I showed her husband, Oswaldo Eloy Castillo, this photo of a foreman, he explained,

> The *capataz de finca* always rode on a mule. Mules are better than horses. The Company owned the house. The firearm, at that time, was used to establish authority. It says, "I command" ["Yo mando"]. He carried a small notebook in his pocket with a list of the jobs to do.[54]

Fig. 2.3. North American foreman, *capataz de finca*, in El Progreso. *Courtesy of the Rafael Platero Paz Archive.*

The foreman always rode above the fieldworkers. In the first few decades of United Fruit's operations, he was a white North American. The company gave him better pay and a nice house and positioned him, literally and racially, above the workforce he commanded. His firearm was there to ensure that the ordered people and plants that the company envisioned, and which he oversaw, would become a reality. The foundation of his authority was thus buttressed by race, language, national origins, social status, access to force, and, crucially, the latitude to decide when to use that weapon. His job was to watch over and command various teams of workers, sending some to dig drainage ditches, others to clear brush, prune, or spray pesticides. He was the lieutenant, in charge of seeing, knowing, and transforming a given area, reporting up to the general, whose task it was to oversee the entire battlefield of people, plants, pests, and prices.[55] These quick-response, mule-mounted, dispatching, detection, and destruction cyborgs roamed throughout the plantations. Like the hand near the revolver, the analog of the company's apparatus of surveillance and violence could be found in the US Marines and gunboats that often hovered off the coast of Honduras.

Fig. 2.4. Overseer's house. *Courtesy of the United Fruit Company Photograph Collection, Baker Library Historical Collections, Harvard University.*

Even after the company began employing more locals as foremen and overseers, it maintained the hierarchy between the North American and non–North American crews. In the company's Bocas del Toro Division, for example, a Panamanian with eleven years of service was earning only $100 a month, as compared to a North American with seven years of service who was earning $165 a month.[56] While they may have earned less, Hondurans who made their way into the upper echelons of the company's local operations were considered, as Don Eloy put it, "empleados de confianza," or "trusted employees."[57] As a timekeeper, Don Eloy worked on all of the company's farms around El Progreso: Guanchías, Finca 10, Finca Cobb, Finca Mesa, and many others. These key employees—the overseer and the timekeeper—were in charge of regulating the space and time of labor. They thus served as the crucial transmitters and translators of management's dictums, wringing perfect bananas out of rationally ordered soil and sweat.

As *empleados de confianza*, they were the protected and compensated middlemen between North American management and tens of thousands of unskilled Central American and Caribbean field hands. For a concise description of the role of the overseer and the special place that he enjoyed within the company's workforce, we can again turn to Charles Morrow Wilson:

> Within their own well-surveyed boundaries the company banana farms operate according to an agricultural master plan. The overseer, or *mandador*, is in charge. He lives in a one-story bungalow with a screened piazza, a living room, dining room, two bedrooms and a bath, a kitchen, a servant's room, and an office. For each overseer's home the company supplies a cook and sometimes a yard boy or other servants. Furniture, silver, and linen are also furnished by the company. It is almost inevitable that flowering hedges, beds of roses, and hibiscus will ornament the open lawns.[58]

But not everyone agreed on the agricultural master plan.

VISUALIZING PROGRESS AS EQUALITY

On November 15, 1929, the general manager of the United Fruit Company's Tropical Banana Division, Arthur A. Pollan, sent the following memorandum to the managers under his direction.

TO BANANA DIVISION MANAGERS

I am attaching a photograph for the purpose of familiarizing you with the appearance of Manuel Calix Herrera. He is the figure outlined in the center. This man is an agitator of the worst type; anti-American, extremist, given to writing and preaching Red, Bolshevist, and Communistic propaganda. He has recently been the principal organizer of a Bolshevist move originating on the north coast of Honduras. It is possible that as his activities have been restricted in that country, he will move to other fields, and you should be on the lookout for him.

His description is as follows:

Single

24 years of age

Native of Olancho, Honduras

Height about 5'10"

Weight, about 125 lbs.

Very slightly stooped

Eyes, grey

Color, white

Hair, dark brown

Smooth-shaved

Small mouth

Complexion, pale, as if suffering from some ailment

Is quick and alert, and rapid in his movements

Usually dresses without coat or necktie, and a straw hat, with one side turned down in a rakish fashion.

Personal habits: drinks occasionally, sometimes to excess, given to frequenting low resorts.

Yours very truly,

[Signed by A. A. Pollan]

Enclosure [Photographs of Manuel Cálix Herrera][59]

This memorandum and the two photographs that accompanied it circulated within a private network of power that originated in Boston and extended south through the Caribbean, in Central America, and into parts of South America. Within this network, the United Fruit Company used photography to identify and regulate the spread of political ideas.[60] In the case of Cálix Herrera, the images are mug shots, with frontal and profile views. The aura of criminality that surrounds photographs of this type frames the subject

UNITED FRUIT COMPANY

GENERAL OFFICES, ONE FEDERAL STREET
BOSTON, MASSACHUSETTS

ARTHUR A. POLLAN
GENERAL MANAGER
TROPICAL BANANA DIVISIONS

CIRCULAR NO. B-31

November 15, 1929.

TO BANANA DIVISION MANAGERS

I am attaching a photograph for the purpose of familiarizing you with the appearance of Manuel Calix Herrera. He is the figure outlined in the center. This man is an agitator of the worst type; anti-American, extremist, given to writing and preaching, Red, Bolshevist, and Communistic propaganda. He has recently been the principal organizer of a Bolshevist move originating on the north coast of Honduras. It is possible that as his activities have been restricted in that country, he will move to other fields, and you should be on the lookout for him.

His description is as follows:

    Single
    24 years of age
    Native of Olancho, Honduras
    Height about 5'10"
    Weight, about 125 lbs.
    Very slightly stooped
    Eyes, grey
    Color, white
    Hair, dark brown
    Smooth-shaved
    Small mouth
    Complexion, pale, as if suffering from some ailment
    Is quick and alert, and rapid in his movements
    Usually dresses without coat or necktie, and a straw
      hat, with one side turned down in a rakish fashion.
    Personal habits; drinks occasionally, sometimes to
      excess, given to frequenting low resorts.

            Yours very truly

Enclosure

Figs. 2.5 and 2.6.
Internal United Fruit
Company memorandum
on Manuel Cálix Herrera,
November 15, 1929.
*Courtesy of United Fruit
Company, Letters, Bocas
del Toro Division.*

for viewers. Even if all the allegations against Cálix Herrera were known to be false, the producers and spectators of mug shots still treat these images as bearers of truth. Once such an image was inserted into the discourses of anticommunism and hypernationalism, the denoted person was successfully linked to a "subversive" and "foreign" political identity. Beyond the conventions of framing and composition that connote the subject's deviance and guilt, the author of the memo sought to impugn Cálix Herrera's character by suggesting that he was given to drinking and "frequenting low resorts."

While contemporary eyes may be confounded by the suit and necktie, similar mug shots abound of equally well-dressed alleged criminals, including John Dillinger, Charles "Pretty Boy" Floyd, and Charlie "Lucky" Luciano. More confounding is Cálix Herrera's slight smile, indicating confidence rather than defensiveness. But even mug shots lacked the narrative capacity to disclose to managers why they should care about the people depicted in them. The text of the memo accompanying the photographs thus stripped Cálix Herrera of the bourgeois respectability that the sports coat and slight smile might have lent him. The words reinscribed the image and the pictured person, situating Cálix Herrera within a reviled international movement that was assumed to be against the company's interests. Within this company-spun web of meaning, the repression directed at "an agitator of the worst type" was not only warranted, it was to be extended.

The circumstances that allowed the photographs of Cálix Herrera to be accessible to the eyes of the public are worth examining. The producers and distributors of the image did not intend for it to be seen by lay spectators. It was meant exclusively for the eyes of those within, to use Carlos Enrique Ramírez's description, "the repressive apparatus of the Tela Railroad Company."[61] The fact that managers circulated this photo reveals that the fruit company officials—from high-level executives in Boston, to division managers scattered throughout the tropics, to the *mandadores* in each of its plantations—understood some of their most important tasks to be policing, conducting surveillance, and deciding which people under their jurisdiction should be targeted for direct violence. The fruit company gathered intelligence on its workers and even on people who did not work for the company but whose ideas could influence the behavior of the company's peons. For instance, in September 1932, the main offices in Boston sent a circular, providing the biodata on two labor "agitators"—Richard Fitzsimmons and Albert Dougherty—to all Tropical Banana Division managers.[62] To cite a second example, after the famous 1928 massacre of striking workers in

Ciénaga, Colombia, the fruit company sent a photograph of five labor organizers and a memo that noted that one of them had already been killed and another, imprisoned.[63]

To further reconstruct the conditions that led to this photographic event, it is necessary to contextualize the life and aims of the subject of the image. Manuel Cálix Herrera was born in 1906 in the Department of Olancho, famous for its timber, cattle ranching, and Wild West culture of masculinity. Pulled by the migratory currents of the banana industry, he moved to the north coast in the mid-1920s. In 1924, he fought in the Honduran Civil War on the side of Tiburcio Carías Andino, future dictator and faithful ally of the United Fruit Company. Disillusioned by Carías and witnessing firsthand the exploits of the fruit companies, "he was filled with venomous rage" and "became a socialist."[64] In other words, he envisioned a very different order of people and plants on the north coast. Such outrage indicates that, at least in the eyes of labor militants, the United Fruit Company had failed to aestheticize its program for progress. People like Cálix Herrera continued to struggle for more egalitarian social and economic relationships.

In 1927, with the publication of various agitprop newspapers and pamphlets, Cálix Herrera began to enter into the historical record. According to historian Rina Villars, the US consul in La Ceiba reported that Cálix Herrera and Zoroastro Montes de Oca were "creating a Socialist Party in La Ceiba and publishing a radical weekly periodical."[65] The consul's description is consistent with Cálix Herrera's own comments in a letter that he wrote to A. Herclet, a syndicalist in Paris:

> Following the publication of *El Forjador*, our newspaper of revolutionary propaganda, the scourge of state violence was unleashed upon us. The bourgeoisie of La Ceiba and the gringo consul complained to their ally, the government; some said that we were Bolsheviks, and the representative of the BEARS OF THE NORTH, that we have injured the North American government; they carried us off to prisons, they scraped the hair off our heads, and they held us practically without food (this was in the port of La Ceiba), they brought us on foot to the capital, making us walk long stretches of the path.[66]

Soon after, the mutualist Federación Obrera Hondureña (FOH) expelled Cálix Herrera from the organization, saying that he had "tried to introduce communist theories": "The Board of Directors cannot accept this for

Honduran labor, since he continually seeks to instill that there is no Homeland for the worker; that everything is for everyone; that the property of others should be shared."[67]

Cálix Herrera sought to challenge this multinational corporation, which played one country off another and the workers of one race or nationality against their brethren of another, with a vision of solidarity that stretched beyond the boundaries of the nation-state, race, and gender. Just a few months after the fracture of the Honduran labor movement and from his prison cell in San Pedro Sula, Cálix Herrera penned *Verdad*, a communist tract with an initial print run of five thousand.[68] In August 1929, as secretary of the Unión Ferrocarrilera, he sent a note to the US consul in Tela: "Before you, a legal representative of Yankee imperialism, the Railroad Union energetically protests the assassination of Sacco and Vanzetti, victims who were sacrificed to satisfy the Yankee Bourgeoisie's thirst for blood." He also protested "the U.S. invasion of Latin American countries and the brutal procedures of the Yankee marines in the Latin American sister countries that defend the liberty of our peoples." In Cálix Herrera's eyes, the enemy could be identified as the self-designated overseer of the hemisphere. He signed off, "Without any consideration and for the social revolution."[69] The *mandador* can issue commands, but the subaltern gets to decide whether or not to obey.

Communist organizers like Manuel Cálix Herrera were the voluntary counterparts of the United Fruit Company's overseers. The labor organizer envisioned a new social reality and sought to reinterpret the dominant ways of thinking about the relationships on the plantations. Organizers could not issue commands, but they could denaturalize the reigning order and put forward an alternative vision for the future. This countervisuality had the potential to be forcefully instantiated in a general strike.

In April 1931, workers struck at the ports and on the banana plantations of the Tela Railroad Company. A prominent Honduran newspaper reported on the strike:

Observers believe that the propaganda and the recent Bolshevik activities in the north coast are connected to the revolution that has found fertile ground because of the large number of unemployed and the financial crisis. The [USS] *Trenton* and the [USS] *Marblehead* are expected this morning in Tela and Trujillo.[70]

The workers protested a 15 percent reduction in their pay and demanded better living quarters and food, as well as fixed shifts. Cálix Herrera was one of the key organizers of the strike. Meanwhile, the United Fruit Company found immediate support from the light cruisers of the US Navy. The authority of the company's overseers did not rest on mystical grounds but instead could be seen just offshore from the Port of Tela. Ultimately, the Honduran military stepped in and put an end to the strike. But the incipient labor movement continued to gain ground among the workers in the company's plantations. In 1932, Cálix Herrera was put forward as the presidential candidate for the Bloque Obrero-Campesino, but his defiance cost him. He died on July 11, 1939, at the age of thirty-four, from a tuberculosis infection that he contracted while in prison.[71]

Yet capital could not subordinate his vision. Even as the ghost of Cálix Herrera lay sleeping during the dark days of the Carías dictatorship, it would return unexpectedly to haunt the company and to inspire a new generation of banana workers who dreamt of individual and group autonomy and the ability to decide on how to care for each other in their own hospitals and community kitchens. These aspects of freedom and self-government, experienced in the early years of the banana industry by *poquiteros* and the founders of this town called Progress, were both a historical memory and the horizon toward which workers and other *progreseños* strived. These notions of local autonomy were also the ever-present friction that oversight tried in vain to overcome.

Vaudeville and Empire

Consider the term "banana republic," or *república bananera*. What does it conjure up? Trendy "tropical" clothing that can be purchased at a high-end shopping mall? A small Central American country, prone to military coups and presidents who carry on lusty love affairs only to be toppled by the more powerful banana-company executives who rule them? Or perhaps one's own country, ruled by a corrupt plutocracy that is bought and sold by multinational corporations bent on pushing aside local businesses, exploiting their own workers, and racking up public debts for private profits? Each of these widely available and somewhat mutually exclusive sets of meanings can be ascribed to the same term, testifying to the fact that the notion of a "banana republic" is deeply embedded in the public cultures of both the United States and Latin America. The specific meanings it evokes reflect, as do responses to all images, prior identifications of race and class, gender and nation that shape individual subjectivities and one's politics of location. Widely circulated and recognized, the term appears in novels, songs, movies, photographs, posters, graffiti, and newspaper editorials warning that "the US is becoming a banana republic."[1]

The notion of a banana republic is indeed iconic. It is a constellation of public and private works of art and mass culture that create a composite image of an ignoble country, dependent upon a single agricultural export—the banana. Conceptually, the term links economic dependence on large-scale plantation agriculture with an endemically undemocratic polity, often ruled by a servile dictator. The American writer O. Henry created such an image (and in fact used the term "banana republic" to refer to it) in his 1904 fictional romp *Cabbages and Kings*. As he drafted the story of the fanciful Republic of Anchuria—a supposedly Central American republic that can only be Honduras—O. Henry himself was accused in the United States of embezzlement and chose to hide out in that same "grocery and fruit stand that they call a country."[2] Later, the image was given a new valence by Carmen Miranda in the 1943 musical film *The Gang's All Here*, which depicted a sensual and extravagantly exotic Latin American temptress known as "The Lady in the Tutti-Frutti Hat." Banana workers throughout Latin America refigured the metaphor to shift the emphasis away from the country and onto the corporation, creating a new icon in the process: the United Fruit Company as an octopus with its arms stretched around the world, holding it in a death grip. These are just a few of the ways that this distinctive iconography has been taken up by various producers for widely divergent reasons.[3]

But the hierarchical social relations of workers on the north coast of Honduras were sustained not merely through the deft use of images and the rhetoric of modernization. Rather, these images, and the exploitative relationships that they variously masked and unmasked, depended upon a powerful corporation that cultivated "cooperative" political regimes and was underwritten by a visual complex of disciplinary oversight. By the early twentieth century, the Boston-based United Fruit Company was seen as an integrated corporate empire. Wielding enormous economic, political, and cultural power, it controlled the cultivation, distribution, and marketing of the most widely consumed fresh fruit in North America. It was the challenge that power posed to the sovereignty of the countries in which the company operated that gave rise to the notion of banana republics. As a metonym for Honduras, the aspersion cuts in opposing directions, serving at times to justify the technologies of production, control, and public health deployed by the fruit companies and at other times to condemn those same companies' exploitative practices.

The United Fruit Company was an enterprise that knew how to repress labor organizers and reward compliant workers, how to wield the microscope as well as the crop duster, while successfully producing, advertising, and distributing its blemish-free, ripe yellow mainstay. By transitioning away from purchasing nonstandardized bananas grown by smallholders in favor of industrial production of a single variety, the United Fruit Company initiated a concurrent cultural process through which the global travel of this merchandise generated fetish images of its production, intensifying the demand for land and labor in El Progreso. The term "banana republic" now no longer simply referred to a particular country; it had morphed into a global political, commercial, and cultural formation, intertwining land, labor, and politics in El Progreso with O. Henry, Josephine Baker dancing topless in a banana skirt, the Lady in the Tutti-Frutti Hat, and choosy consumers in the United States.

EMPIRE IN BLACK AND WHITE

In *Conquest of the Tropics* (1914), Frederick Upham Adams boldly asserts, "There was no native agriculture in the American tropics to 'exploit,' and it may astound the reader to know that there never has been and that none exists today. These tropics are productive just about in proportion as American initiative, American capital, and American enterprise make them productive."[4] This mix of praise for the United Fruit Company and disdain for the "tropical natives" runs throughout his now widely criticized book.[5]

"Grim necessity," Adams writes, "had ever forced the natives to cultivate the plantain, but the banana was considered more of a luxury, and tropical negroes and Indian tribes spend little time or effort in the quest for things not absolutely needed."[6] In Adams's book, the same narrative unfolds visually in 194 photographs, each with a caption to steer the viewer toward the desired interpretation of the image. With its lush green cloth binding and gilt lettering, *Conquest of the Tropics* was designed to appeal to a broad readership. The photograph on the cover depicts the tropics through the iconic palm tree. The neat rows of trees lining a path made for human travel underscore the conquest: these trees are not growing willy-nilly; they show how the company created ordered spaces in the tropics.

The endpapers in the 1914 hardbound edition feature a sketched map of the region from southern Florida to northern Peru (map 3.1). There are no words or labels on the map to designate particular countries; only symbols are used—the most obvious of which are the US flags waving above Puerto Rico and the tiny Cayman Islands and flying high over the Panama Canal. Great ships steam from the banana enclaves along the Caribbean coasts of Guatemala, Honduras, Costa Rica, Panama, and Colombia. Radio antennas beam their signals from high above the banana plantations toward

Map 3.1. The endpapers of *Conquest of the Tropics*, by Frederick Upham Adams.

the United States. The plantations themselves are already set in firm relief against a barren, unremarkable, nearly indistinguishable, and unproductive vastness that for many an early twentieth-century entrepreneurial imagination in the United States was the very epitome of Latin America. These were, as Adams never tired of saying, "the American tropics."

The map starkly depicts territorial possession and human agency. The only signs of life are the eighteen steamships whose courses are charted directly from the banana enclaves to their US ports, the radio antennas, the banana plantations, and a sugar plantation and refinery on the north coast of Cuba. There is no indication of any human activity in the expanses of the "American tropics" left untouched by the United States, only smoke billowing from Latin American volcanoes and an occasional, nearly imperceptible palm frond. This map is meaningfully constructed and conveys the publishers' idea of how their US audience imagined, or should have imagined, Latin

Fig. 3.1. Six years after Emanuel Leutze painted his epic *Westward* mural in the US Capitol, Frances Palmer took the same title to make a more explicit picture of western expansionism, *Across the Continent: "Westward the Course of Empire Takes Its Way,"* 1868. *Courtesy of the Amon Carter Museum of American Art, Fort Worth, Texas.*

America. The tropics were seen as a vast, unpopulated, and unproductive frontier awaiting American ingenuity and industriousness.

This was a well-trodden path with clear markers in North American thought. In 1862, when the painter Emanuel Leutze created a 20 × 30–foot mural on the walls of the US Capitol and titled it *Westward the Course of Empire Takes Its Way (Westward Ho!)*, the fact that the North and South were locked in a bloody conflict over slavery and the future of the Union was excluded from the frame (figure 3.1). Instead, the West was imagined as a place of national healing and reunion. Similarly, when Oliver Wendell Holmes found the carnage of the Civil War too gruesome, he locked Mathew Brady's pictures in a drawer. As he later recalled the unskilled women who had never seen a negative developed yet toiled on an assembly line preparing wet plates, Holmes wished away the alienation of labor. In each case, violence was disavowed in favor of rallying cries for westward expansion, triumphant celebrations of the miracle of photographic reproduction, and the poetry of the pioneer spirit.[7]

Once the project of internal colonization stretched from sea to shining sea, many in the United States worried that modernity was robbing their country of its unique strengths. Restless, they began to look for new frontiers. *Conquest of the Tropics* linked "the taming of the West" to what some thought needed to be done in Latin America:

> Our school-books and our histories dwell with pride on the records of the pioneers who braved the wilderness and paved the way of our empire from the Atlantic to the Pacific. Our national prosperity is founded largely on the achievements of those who risked their lives in the conquest of nature. These men did not stop at a river because it marked the then existing territorial limits of the United States. [. . .] We praise them in story and song, and teach our children that much of the glory of the Republic is due to their conquest of the then Unknown West. The instinct which lured them to plant the flag of progress in new fields still exists. [. . .] Mexico, Central America, and the West Indies beckoned to others, and they responded.[8]

Just as explorers and white settlers colonized the American West under the banner of a nationalist and racially inflected notion of progress, Latin America, imagined as tropical jungles and populations mired in animist myths, afforded a masculine race an opportunity to reinvigorate itself by conquering nature and methodically redirecting an undisciplined and still

Fig. 3.2. "Small growers bringing in bananas." From Adams, *Conquest of the Tropics*, 60.

latent labor force. In celebrating the United Fruit Company, Adams extolled the conquest of nature by a scientifically minded private enterprise that could draw inspiration from what was euphemistically referred to as "Westward expansion."

Words were not sufficient to convey the marvelous deeds of the United Fruit Company. Adams used pictures to make the point more powerfully, as the truth-producing authority of the photographic medium was harnessed on behalf of US business. With unrelenting visual force, these images construct "the tropics" and "backwardness" as coterminous. The United Fruit Company, in contrast, is represented as the paragon of modernity, industry, scientific achievement, and benevolence. Like machine-gun rounds, the images come in dyads: tropical backwardness always precedes, and cedes to, the US banana industry.

Some of Adams's images show the tropics and the "backward." Palm trees. Thatched huts. Curved paths. Donkeys. Men with donkeys. Ancient ruins. Marimbas. Colonial-era churches. Babies on the backs of Mayan women. Volcanoes. Jungles. Streams. Tropical storms. Women washing clothes in a river. People carrying goods on their heads. Coconut trees. Swamps. White men posing at "the edge of a tropical jungle." Black families with barefoot children near thatched huts. Shoeless adults. Unshod mule drivers. "Ethnically" clad women. A young man shimmying up a palm tree. A house of sticks and mud with a "typical" family sitting in front of it. A tropical fern bank. A dugout canoe with a boy propelling it—and for contrast, the luxurious

Figs. 3.3 and 3.4. "Conditions before United Fruit Company began its sanitary work in Guatemala" and "One of the smaller hospitals of the United Fruit Company." From Adams, *Conquest of the Tropics*, 266 and 269.

Figs. 3.5 and 3.6. "Washday in Costa Rica" and "Stateroom in modern fruit boat." From Adams, *Conquest of the Tropics*, 93 and 95.

Figs. 3.7 and 3.8. "Site of Almirante. These native huts have disappeared and a massive sea wall insures the safety and health of the town created by the United Fruit Company" and "Residence of a banana plantation official." From Adams, *Conquest of the Tropics*, 151 and 157.

Figs. 3.9 and 3.10. A letter on a landscape, to begin a chapter with these words: "Every reader of the preceding chapter must be aware that the United Fruit Company started its career without any of the advantages which conduce to monopoly." On the facing page, a picture captioned "The modern fruit ship" depicts a woman in a white dress reading comfortably. From Adams, *Conquest of the Tropics*, 86 and 87.

Fig. 3.11. "On the edge of a tropical jungle." From Adams, *Conquest of the Tropics*, 52.

setting in which a woman reads on "the modern fruit ship." Nature. Water-falls. Beaches. Trees. "Guatemalan Indian Musicians." A "Guatemalan Indian dandy." Ornate carvings.[9]

Other images show the modern fruit industry. A hospital amid palm trees. A hospital on a hilltop. Clearing of jungles. Laying of railroad tracks. Bananas. "Record bunches of bananas, with 22 'hands' and 300 pieces of fruit." Steamships of the Great White Fleet. Ports. Orderly rows of banana plants with railroad tracks extending from the viewer to the vanishing point. Locomotives. "Small growers bringing in bananas," their path inter-sected by a United Fruit Company train. Women at the beach wearing hats and long, black, Victorian dresses. Power lines. Upholstered furniture. Wood molding. Plush carpet. The exposed steel and symmetry of the hull of a modern banana ship. Industrial machines to load and unload bananas from ships and railcars. Steel-truss bridges. United Fruit Company ships at harbors in New York, New Orleans, and various Caribbean ports. Pan-oramic views of "a sea of bananas."[10]

There are also images of the tropical fruit industry: Workers loading railcars and carrying bunches of bananas on their backs. Women washing clothes at home, with water streaming out of a tap. Railroad tracks with banana fronds arching over them. White men being chauffeured by black men in hand-cranked railcars. Well-tended gardens. Plantation houses. Superb monoliths—with white men leaning against them.

Lost in this staccato burst are the innumerable local contributions to the success of the banana industry, from the pseudo-stems used to pad the bananas during transport to the muscle, sweat, and local knowledge of banana-plantation laborers. One tool that repeatedly intrudes as a sort of *punctum* in photographs designed to portray US ingenuity amid tropi-cal backwardness is the machete, an emblem of the Central American peas-antry.[11] In retrospect, it becomes clear that Adams had already put into practice what Martin Heidegger would subsequently describe as the axiom of the modern age: "The fundamental event of modernity is the conquest of the world as picture. From now on, the word 'picture' means: the collective image of representing production."[12]

Adams was not alone in creating a story of the virgin tropics, a place and a people during a time before the Fall of Man, a time out of joint with what many considered to be the modernizing forces of the US fruit, mining, and railroad companies. The logic of westward expansionism so eloquently por-trayed by Emanuel Leutze and Frances Palmer and popularly accepted in the nineteenth-century United States was redirected southward, as many Americans' well-cultivated stereotypes of Indians on "free land" were easily adapted to map onto tropical "Latins." In 1871, Henry Adams referred to the yet-to-be-conquered American West as "the interminable, uninhabited, hideous region of the Great Basin." With studied detachment, Frederick Upham Adams applied the same template nearly a half century later: "The lower classes are Indians of innumerable tribes and varying customs, but a considerable portion of them obey the latent instinct of hatred for physical labor. In this particular they differ in no essential respect from the Indians with whom we are familiar save that the Central American Indian lives in a land whose soil and climate removes much of the incentive to work."[13]

This second discovery of Latin America was itself in keeping with the first epochal discovery of American abundance that had to be wrested from purportedly indolent natives. The earliest European explorers—Columbus, Vespucci, and Raleigh—described America as a primeval land, an available, Edenic world outside of time—until, that is, they wrote it into history. Mary Louise Pratt has shown that as Spain watched its empire decline in the early nineteenth century, Alexander von Humboldt made use of his privileged vantage point as a mobile, observing subject journeying through the "new continent" to copiously characterize South America as a spectacle of primal nature whose future and exploitable resources he could envision in the hands of European industry. That same year, Venezuelan Andrés Bello replayed Humboldt's appropriative gesture as part of a larger process of creole self-invention that was taking place throughout Latin America following independence. "Let the axe fell the tangled forest and fire consume it," he wrote, "open in long streets the darkness of its unfruitful pomp." In calling for agricultural development over mining or industry, Bello sought to found a new America based on a patently colonial notion of progress.[14]

Likewise, Honduran liberals of the late nineteenth century saturated their speeches and writings with equally transculturated notions of liberty, civilization, and progress that would force the jungles and indigenous peoples of the north coast to yield to the locomotive. The creole elites who provided the ideological justification for the Honduran Reforma Liberal saw the country, of sparse population, as virgin and vast, with enormous natural resources that made anything possible. So just as North Americans spun myths of the American West as a blank slate upon which to inscribe their future, Honduran politicians imagined the dense forests and alluvial plains of their Caribbean coast as spaces in which the transformative future of the country would be realized. Like liberals throughout Latin America, they saw Europeans as the ones who would connect their country to the world economy. In 1882 Ramón Rosa wrote, "The Latin American republics need to be populated by European immigrants. . . . We need them to come to our soils in great currents of immigration, and to bring with them the work ethic and commitment to liberty that they have created in the United States of America." However, Rosa continued, "to these enormous interests, the Latin American states should not sacrifice the dignity of their autonomy and power."[15]

EMPIRE WITHOUT AN EMPEROR (AND WITH ONLY AN ENGINEER)

Another chronicler of the United States in Central America saw the tropics not as a pre-Fall paradise but as a post-Fall, pre-Christian hell in which nature ruled over man and men incessantly and bloodily sought to rule over each other. "For four and a half centuries the white man has battled against nature and against his fellows in that region between Cancer and Capricorn which forms the American tropics," Samuel Crowther proclaims in his 1929 book *The Romance and Rise of the American Tropics*. "And nature until lately has always won. Only now is man gaining a measure of mastery." Nature, Crowther explains, ruled over the Native Americans as it ruled over the peoples of the tropics: "The Indians had to take what nature gave. But we are no longer mere serfs." Whereas the indolent people of the tropics succumbed to nature, the North Americans subjugated it. The nature-conquering "we" was white and Protestant and embodied in "the American engineer" who was guiding the transition from chaos and poverty to order and bounty. Like Adams, Crowther retooled the logic of westward expansion and Manifest Destiny to push southward into Central America. In taming distant lands, the pioneers, settlers, and explorers were now being replaced by "the American engineer."[16]

As the landscape of the tropics became a compelling subject for photographers and writers in the late nineteenth and early twentieth centuries and as the romance and drama of the US capitalist overseas came to warrant mass-marketed books, the notion of an informal empire was gradually embraced by broader currents of North American thought. Crowther swelled with pride at extracontinental US imperialism:

> In and about the Caribbean Sea, a new kind of empire is rising. . . . This empire has no sovereign. It has a leader. That leader is the United States. That leadership has been gained not by armed force, but by a power greater than can be exerted by arms—the power of mutual interest.[17]

This new empire had no emperor but was led by the United States. It was decentralized and rested on force, but not brute force (never mind that when Crowther's book was published, the US military had already occupied Nicaragua for seventeen years and Puerto Rico for thirty-one). It was an economic empire whose centrifugal power was drawn from the mutual interests of the actors involved. Those shared interests were expressed in contracts and loans, engineering and science, culture and an increasing capacity to dominate nature. This empire without a sovereign relied, in part, on engravings, lithographic prints, photographs, and textual pictures of itself interacting with its colonial other.

The Romance and Rise of the American Tropics is graced with 175 images. Each photo, together with its caption, visually narrates and expands upon the imperial exegesis. The illustrations invite the viewer to relate to the tropics in different ways, but each pretends to dispassionately offer information, which is the secret of its persuasive technique. In the frontispiece, for example, next to the Classical Mayan stone carvings stands a peasant with his mule loaded down with bananas (figure 3.12). He confronts the viewer directly, but he is sandwiched between the camera and the other members of his party, who are watching the photographic event unfold. Visible beyond them, in the rear plane of the image, are a palm tree and

Fig. 3.12. "Aspects of two civilizations. A banana pack train among the Mayan monoliths of the fourth century, at Quiriguá, Guatemala." From Crowther, *The Romance and Rise of the Tropics*, frontispiece.

Fig. 3.13. "Running the lines through the jungle—1850."
From Crowther, *The Romance and Rise of the Tropics*, 95.

dense jungle. This image does not simply convey information; it was set up
to relay a particular story of two "ancient" civilizations. The American tropics were rising out of a stubborn Mayan past still clinging to the embodied
backwardness of the Guatemalan present. Elsewhere in the book, engravings from 1594 illustrate "the adventures of Columbus" planting the cross
and accepting tribute from nearly naked, well-sculpted natives. Lithographs
from 1850 depict land surveyors brandishing their scientific instruments
in a resolutely tropical space, complete with a dark "native" holding a spear
and a monkey hanging from a palm tree overhead (figure 3.13). Like Timothy O'Sullivan's photographs of Clarence King's survey of the American
West in the late 1860s, these images offer a double point of view. Observation is itself under observation. The viewer of the image becomes a witness
to nature being translated into knowledge, into picture and survey.[18]

The meanings of the pictures in Crowther's book are held in place by their captions: "The unchanging Indian women of the highlands of Guatemala and their characteristic weaves" and "Momotombo, the volcano that dominates Nicaragua. Lake Nicaragua, which would be part of the canal route, may be seen beyond." And in his three-piece suit against a black studio backdrop stands "Minor C. Keith, a pioneer in the American tropics and now Chairman of the Board of International Railways of Central America." Throughout, the reader is treated to a visual celebration of "the methods of American enterprise," such as "the pier at Puerto Castilla, Honduras. United Fruit Company office and store at Tela, Honduras."[19] One of these images features a silhouetted car parked at a port. As the sea and sky fade into the distance behind them, two monumental ships of the Great White Fleet occupy the center of the compositional space. The mutually reinforcing aspects of this phototextual narrative are clear and unambiguous: the romance and rise of the tropics is due to North American ingenuity.

Just as captioning was integral to making sense of photographs, photography was integral to creating and reinforcing the storyline that sustained US business, military, and cultural ventures in Central America. Lithographs and photographs testified to a Central American "need" for US intervention, illustrating poverty, unchanging indigenous people, and dense jungles. Images paired with these stories of lack showed the US way forward: massive machines, fashionably dressed engineers leaning on cars or peering into microscopes, and cleared rows of monocrop agriculture. Not only was US ingenuity needed, it was portrayed as visibly good and morally right.

For nation-forming Latin American creoles, this supposed need for someone to guide nature could be seen in the "tangled forest" that Andrés Bello envisioned as "long streets." For the United Fruit Company and its boosters, "tropical negroes and Indian tribes" had been forced by nature to cultivate the plantain, as Frederick Upham Adams explained, so they "spend little time or effort in the quest for things not absolutely needed." As Adams and Crowther subsumed these peoples into nature, they simultaneously constructed in both the people and the landscape a need for US capital and ingenuity to guide them into more productive ways of being. Like the Christian who helps God to complete His creation, the engineer helps nature and dark natives to fulfill their purposes. By this logic, creation, on its own, is assumed to be imperfect and incomplete. In early twentieth-century Honduras, everything remained to be done, and creation had just barely begun. In fashioning itself as a co-creator, the United Fruit Company presented itself as a necessary agent of progress, intervening in a timeless, unclaimed primitive terrain. The lithograph captioned "Early engineering" makes this neocolonial relation clear. The white surveyor acts. He is the seeing man, the knowing subject, the mobile observer. The half-naked, spear-bearing black native and the monkey hanging from the palm tree are passive representatives of Central American backwardness and virgin nature in the presence of an active observer who is "running the lines through the jungle." The native and the monkey are there in the lithograph, but it is the surveyor who makes observations, takes notes, and creates knowledge that can be acted upon to reshape this landscape. The image as metaphor is perfect. Unable to act, unable to generate knowledge, nature is passive before the engineer. But civilization is making science out of jungles and barbarism.

Condensed in this lithograph is yet another idea: if America first needed explorers and adventurers, now it needed land surveyors and engineers. To be discovered, America needed Columbus. To be developed, it needed to harness Newton for commercial and industrial ends. As the surveyor looked through the telescope and the United Fruit Company carved out enclaves of "progress" from what was being represented as swamps and jungles, US neocolonial scientists and engineers disclaimed domination by portraying their work in Latin America as the dispassionate deciphering of the essence of things—from the malaria that beset its workforce to the sigatoka that attacked its bananas—to manipulate them so that the American tropics might be made more productive. But instrumental vision blinds the engineer to the person standing before him and directs him to focus on what he can build in, through, and sometimes in spite of the other. As the surveyor in the lithograph peers through the telescope, he looks in order to build a railroad across the isthmus. He cannot even see the native in his blind field. Instead of the other as a being in and for itself, he sees nature as there for him, as the raw material that he can use to realize his own goals. That such backward, irrational material needed the US engineer to fulfill its own telos made the conquest of the tropics that much more noble a pursuit.

THE SERPENTARIUM

So just was the cause, so cheerful was the can-do attitude, and so systematic was the approach that even temptation could be studied and controlled. Temptation, that Hydra, came literally in the form of the legless creature slithering across the earth, through the banana plantations, and into human habitations. In Christian doctrine, it was the one that beguiled Eve. It was the devil in disguise.

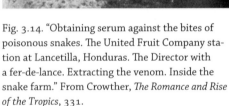

Fig. 3.14. "Obtaining serum against the bites of poisonous snakes. The United Fruit Company station at Lancetilla, Honduras. The Director with a fer-de-lance. Extracting the venom. Inside the snake farm." From Crowther, *The Romance and Rise of the Tropics*, 331.

Fig. 3.15. *Courtesy of the United Fruit Company Photograph Collection, Baker Library Historical Collections, Harvard Business School.*

In addition to installing pliant political regimes that granted land concessions, the fruit companies sought to maximize their profits by understanding and controlling nature. In 1941, at the Thirty-Seventh Annual Meeting of the American Society of Tropical Medicine in St. Louis, Missouri, Herbert C. Clark reported on a snake census of the coastal plain of Honduras. "Snake accidents," he noted, "had never been a subject of great importance in these plantations yet occasional tragic accidents did occur and we were not prepared to offer modern treatment nor did we have scientific information regarding the species of snakes responsible for the accident."[20] Clark's locus of enunciation at the meeting of the American Society of Tropical Medicine underscores the role that the North American public health community played in attempting to make the tropics safe for the foot soldiers of US empire. From the perspective of big business, the desire to know the area, and to control every possible aspect of it, was a practical concern. The discourses of science and modernity provided further justification for spending time and money on what was, by United Fruit's own admission, not a problem of great importance.

As part of the snake census, the company created multiple enclosures to bring serpents under the gaze of spectators and scientists. Each serpentarium was situated under a canopy of palm fronds, with walls about five feet tall enclosing eight octagonal terrariums with four openings and a removable roof. It was a modified panopticon. The handler could see the snakes wriggling through the open space or simply pick up the lightweight roof to expose them. The fact that others should be able to see this instrumental gaze in action was considered as important as actually looking at the snakes. The United Fruit Company Photograph Collection at Harvard University contains dozens of pictures of "serpentariums" in Honduras. For popular consumption, the images were republished in Samuel Crowther's *Romance and Rise of the Tropics*, in the context of a discussion of the benefits of American capital investments in Guatemala. For a scholarly audience, the images were printed in the company medical department's annual report, to which the most important medical libraries in North America subscribed for the benefit of their researchers. As the knower and the known were inextricably bound up in the photographic event at the serpentarium, the observer—the subduer of serpents, the manipulator of nature—was coded as superior to the observed.[21]

As reported on the page preceding images of the serpentariums, Guatemalan president Lázaro Chacón González told Crowther, "We would welcome more capital and must look to the United States not only for it but for guidance."[22] US readers of the book were led to see this photo literally and allegorically: a white North American man in a necktie poses with what the caption identifies as a fer-de-lance (*Bothrops asper*), or lancehead pit viper. The snake is in the center of the pictorial space, positioned between the viewer and the man, who calmly holds it in his bare hands. The image is nicely composed, as the ascending stairs and handrails frame the man and the snake. The man looks squarely into the camera, a mode of identification that is direct and immediate, fostering the viewer's uptake of the ideological message of control over nature. The other two images of the serpentarium support this first and most important picture, which appears in a chapter proclaiming to refute "The Propaganda of Imperialism." In a second picture, the photographer has zoomed in tight to explicate how venom is collected from these dangerous snakes. Thus, in the first image, the scientist takes the snake in his hands; in the second image, only his hands are present as he dominates the snake, forcing it to surrender its venom into a collecting vial. The third photograph is an achievement of modernist aesthetics, framed by three white walls and shadows that form inverted triangles whose apex is at the hero's head. The image is geometrical. Only the curves of the snakes and their handler disrupt the ordered lines and shadows. As the herpetologist calmly squats down among so many snakes, as he acts upon them rather than they upon him, the viewer is reassured that this is normal and that he is in control. The hierarchy of applied science over nature, of a fruit company taming jungles, is restored. With the snakes having been taken out of the jungle and made safe for lay spectators, a woman is invited to see the serpentarium. In this photograph that did not make it into Crowther's book, a woman in a white dress and a hat is escorted by a man in leather, knee-high boots.[23] This is a leisure activity for her. The work boots, the lab coats, the snake laboratory: these are in the domain of the banana men.

As miniature spectacles of power, the serpentariums were just one of the many means for making visible the limitless curiosity of the missionaries of modernization. In the context of an intercultural encounter structured by inequalities, controlling snakes had the practical value that the fruit company ascribed to it: the need for good antivenins. It also resonated in the mythological registers of local Protestants and Catholics in these rural Honduran spaces. But as company scientists brought snakes under their clinical gaze, seeking to neutralize or extirpate an occasionally deadly menace to members of their workforce, they simultaneously stripped the creature of its mythical value. The snake being handled and forced to give up its venom could hardly be seen as a full and specific representation of the devil. Instead, the scientists transformed snakes into specimens, each made up of knowable and controllable elements.

Yet even as Latin America was portrayed by North Americans as a land of poisonous snakes, so too could Hondurans attribute the Fall of the north coast to the US-run banana companies. Literary historian Leticia de Oyuela has captured this popular way of thinking through the figure of a beggar who is making his way from the north coast to Comayagua. The beggar has only the useless nickel coins distributed by the fruit companies and recognized only in their commissaries; he wants to trade a pile of them for one small coin of gold or silver. In a conversation with the moneychanger, he describes the "hell into which the north coast has been transformed." Part of the problem, according to the beggar, known only as the *costeño*, is that "in a few days the entire zone had been disgraced by the arrival of blacks from Jamaica, who worked on the construction of the iron pathway." He goes further: "In trying to clear the fallow lands, those deadly snakes called yellow beard [pit vipers] began to emerge. Women began to shack up with the overseers and abandoned their children and houses and, worst of all, they paid in the camps with those nickels, which weren't accepted in any store."[24] In this telling, like that of Gabriel García Marquez in *Cien años de soledad*, the fruit companies have converted the pre-Fall paradise into viper-infested wastelands.

The beggar links the coming of the train to racist feelings of resentment toward the West Indian migrants whom the company has brought in as laborers. The moral decay of the women who shack up with the overseers fits closely with the creation myth of Eden, in which God, "the inflexible gardener," tries to protect the unaltered paradisiacal landscape from the guileful serpent.[25] Oyuela narrates: "In this way, as if by magic, the old cattle pastures were lost, converted into huge puddles in which only snakes, parasites, and toads can live, humming a sad song to communicate with each other at night."[26] In this account, the serpents slithered forth as a result of the devastation, wrought by the giant fruit companies, of forests and grasslands. Pit vipers were metonyms for the United Fruit Company in the whispered stories of workers, ex-workers, and figurative beggars in places far removed from the banana plantations.

Yet the company's widely circulated photographs of its attempts to control snakes and harvest their venom encode the company as the stern and systematic gardener. Honduras was framed as the land of snakes. The angels who put the Honduran snakes into boxes and forced them to yield their venom were zoologists from the United States who held them nonchalantly. Once this threatening land was tamed, it was safe for tourists and the snapshot photography that vouched for "Kodak's conspicuous consumers abroad."[27]

"DONKEYS AND YOUNGSTERS ARE ALWAYS LIVELY SUBJECTS FOR YOUR CAMERA"

After the completion of what a cruise-line brochure dubbed "Uncle Sam's New Ten Mile Strip of Empire," the Panama Canal Zone was marketed as having undergone a process of full Americanization.[28] Similarly, in a twenty-four-page booklet produced by the United Fruit Company Passenger Service, the cruise ship was shown as if it were a floating US suburban country club, headed to exotic but carefully managed tropical locales. The brochure

Fig. 3.16. "Great White Fleet Cruises from New York to the Caribbean and West Indies, Winter 1939–1940." Equipped with outdoor swimming pools, library, gift shop, lounge, barbershop, hospital, smoking room, and various classes of rooms, the ships carried North American tourists to Guatemala, Havana, Costa Rica, Honduras, Jamaica, Colombia, and the Panama Canal Zone. *United Fruit Passenger Service brochure.*

was organized around the tourist, featuring "Cruise Close-ups" with passengers photographing other attractive white North Americans: playing shuffleboard on the deck, walking hand in hand in bathing suits, dancing to the music of a live band, drinking martinis, and smoking cigarettes. This image is part of a large-format, six-page spread that portrays camera-wielding tourists taking pictures of "the natives" shoveling coffee beans, burdened by cargo, and tying up a donkey, along with views of colonial-era churches and volcanoes. The caption reads,

> 'CLOSE-UP' travel is the keynote today. And on a Great White Fleet Cruise you will see the charms and beauties of the Caribbean. Consider the scenes pictured here: A flash of the old-and-new in Havana—a grim turret on the historic sea wall of Cartagena—the velvety lawns of the Myrtle Bank Hotel, Kingston, Jamaica—agricultural scene in sunny Costa Rica—stunning cathedrals and devout Indian worshipers constitute a picturesque background for Guatemala's famed Lake Atitlán—donkeys and youngsters are always lively subjects for your camera—the Ruins of old Panama. Rich in human interest, beauty and history—these are the lands you will visit on the Great White Fleet.

On my copy of the brochure, pencil marks made by the original owner are still visible on the map of the "Ports of the Great White Fleet"—lines drawn from New Orleans to Havana to Tela to Puerto Limón to the Panama Canal and back through Havana. United Fruit not only had made the tropics safe, it offered a growing white middle class in the United States new ways to flaunt their spending power by jaunting through exotic landscapes. Kodak enabled them to return home with pictures to demonstrate how they had spent their leisure time: gawking, posing next to ruins, drinking, and dancing. The cruise ship and the camera, North America and the tropics of the Caribbean and Central America, the natural and the national: all became intertwined as recreational space and time expanded with the racial nationalism of the United States.

AMERICAN ZONES

United Fruit housed its North American employees in suburban enclaves called "White Zones," a term that was later changed to "American Zones." For decades, these planned communities were exclusive and strictly segregated by race. Like upscale country clubs and gated communities in the

R. HOSPITAL F.C. DE. TELA, HONDURAS.

Side view of hospital, showing native wards, another wing back of this one. The front of building has the white ward and private rooms and the dispensary below. The kitchen and stoves are in the wing directly back of the entrance. Operating room at this end.

Fig. 3.17. Tela Hospital, constructed in 1914. *Courtesy of the United Fruit Company Photograph Collection, Baker Library Historical Collections, Harvard Business School.*

United States, these corporate compounds had private golf courses, social clubs, swimming pools, paved roads, and single-family homes that varied in size according to rank. On the frontiers of what North Americans considered their expanding empire, engineers, doctors, teachers, and managers enjoyed certain privileges that came with an obligation to maintain social boundaries. Company wives were at the rearguard in maintaining US hegemony abroad, as Ronald Harpelle has argued: "The realm of the company wife was the home, where cultural identity and common values were maintained as a safeguard against the moral degradation of the men who were leading the campaign."[29] Outside this landscape of privilege, the company sought to create a working class with middle-class aspirations and consumption habits that could be satisfied at one of its local commissaries. Besides, it made economic sense not to have the banana boats returning empty from their US ports.

American Zones were enclave communities in the strongest sense. They were bounded and locatable, enabling a particular vantage point on the banana plantations, the workers, and the towns in which they were situated. The enclave as a vantage point can thus be associated with a particular kind of photographic gaze, one that facilitated closeness and detachment simultaneously. The enclave as a visual regime authorized oversight of the community while regulating what could flow in and out of the protected space. The American Zone was an architectural arrangement that enabled ideas, orders, and commands to flow out from the superintendent's house, while only provisions, servants, and permitted guests were allowed to flow in through the guarded gate. The American Zone was not intended to be a contact zone. It was a space in which only company-sanctioned types of social interaction could take place. It was the most locally visible on-the-ground manifestation of the US component of the banana republic.

Just across the river from El Progreso sits the town of Lima, where United Fruit set up one of its largest tropical research facilities. Inside the American Zone (in which North Americans no longer reside) lived Billy Peña, son of the company's former general manager, William Arthur Peña Souza. William Arthur was born to a Portuguese-American mother who had accompanied the US Marine Corps in their 1912–1933 occupation of Nicaragua. His wife was the great-granddaughter of General Francisco Ferrera, the first elected president of independent Honduras.[30] I interviewed Billy in 2009. Even though he was the son of a former division manager and a descendant of a founding father of the republic, and despite living deep inside the gated and guarded American Zone, he was scared to set foot outside his house, much less venture from the dilapidated corporate enclave. In the 1970s, when the fruit company drastically scaled back its direct production of bananas, it also reduced Peña's social power. He sat alone inside his shuttered house, chain-smoking and gazing nostalgically at a picture of his deceased mother: seated on a pedestal, she was elevated like the Virgin Mary in a flowing white dress, holding a scepter and wearing a crown. The Zona Americana, while still behind "a high wall of woven wire," continued to close in on itself, architecturally asserting its superiority while betraying its fear of social miscegenation.[31]

THE BANANA REPUBLIC AND VAUDEVILLIAN REPRESENTATION

The banana republic was originally a literary image, invented by O. Henry. In writing his 1904 book *Cabbages and Kings*, a novel that pushes reality to its most absurd limits, O. Henry incorporated one of his experiences in Honduras into the story: "At that time we had a treaty with about every foreign country except Belgium and that banana republic, Anchuria."[32] From 1896 to 1897, O. Henry lived in Honduras so that he could avoid being extradited to stand trial in Houston on charges that he had stolen money while working as a bookkeeper for the First National Bank of Austin. His metaphor of the Honduran political economy stuck, proliferated, and morphed into an icon.

As historian Héctor Pérez-Brignoli points out, the banana republic is, first, the frame through which the United States and Europe have seen and continue to see Honduras, Central America, and even the larger countries of Latin America. Moreover, Central Americans, especially intellectuals, tend to perceive their own countries as banana republics. Finally, this representation colors how people in one Latin American country tend to see people in another—as residents of a banana republic, something that their own country, fortunately, is not. Part of what made this image stick, Pérez-Brignoli argues, is that there is a degree of truth to it, especially in the case of Honduras. The country's rapid succession of presidents and its dependence upon banana exports, as well as the cameos of Guy "Machine Gun" Molony and General Lee Christmas, make the history of the country as tragically comic as *Cabbages and Kings*. And this, it seems, is another reason the image has attached itself to Honduras: the form and content of the story are consistent.[33]

One of the central protagonists in *Cabbages and Kings* is Billy Keogh, daguerreotypist, photographer, and modern-day plunderer of tropical wealth.

> In the midst of the hullabaloo a man stepped to the door of a small wooden building and looked out. Above the door was a sign that read "Keogh and Clancy"—a nomenclature that seemed not to be indigenous to that tropical soil. The man in the door was Billy Keogh, scout of fortune and progress and latter-day rover of the Spanish Main. Tintypes and photographs were the weapons with which Keogh and Clancy were at that time assailing the hopeless shores. Outside the shop were set two large frames filled with specimens of their art and skill.[34]

Keogh's fictional gallery was not unlike Mathew Brady's gallery on Broadway. It was a gathering point, a meeting place, as Alan Trachtenberg put it, "a place of putting on and encountering appearances, a place of illusion and recognition, a place where the very making of illusion could be witnessed."[35] Keogh's gallery and photo studio were, in that regard, a microcosm of the banana town and the larger vaudeville theater of the Republic of Anchuria—that is, of fictionalized Honduras. "Not much of a town," Frank Goodwin tells the woman he believes to be an opera star and the dictator's lover. "A banana town, as they run. Grass huts, 'dobes, five or six two-story houses, accommodations limited, population half-breed Spanish and Indian, Caribs and blackamoors." This was a gathering place for "knots of women with complexions varying from palest olive to deepest brown," ardent revolutionists, mestizo workers, and white southerners who were looking to earn a quick buck and to Americanize a new frontier (and sometimes to escape justice in the United States).[36]

Keogh's gallery, the fictional town of Coralio, and the banana republic of Anchuria: each corresponds to an idea of Honduras that was shared by many in the United States and by important segments of Honduran society. It is an idea that preceded O. Henry, but it was he who gave us the lazy shorthand, and a powerful metaphor, for comprehending it. It is a particular notion of a distant place that stands as a marker of social evolution, a simple description that fixed how many North Americans understood the people and politics of Central America. That shorthand, that stereotype within which the diversity and aspirations of a country were deformed, is the notion of a banana republic. The banana town itself was envisaged by fruit-company officials and Honduran liberals as the concrete, material reflection of that progress. Workers, merchants, engineers, accountants, and managers embodied the prosperity that bananas generated for the region. Images—literary and visual, fruity and melodious—were hurled into the world as emblems of an ideology that found validation and reinforcement in each mechanical marvel that came as precious cargo on the Great White Fleet. In each moment of political instability, in each fruit-company hospital or school, in each "native" photographed by the Kodaking tourist, the ideology of the banana republic was fixed and naturalized.

"[Carolus] White set up his easel on the beach and made striking sketches of the mountain and sea views," writes O. Henry in a chapter that trenchantly satirizes the power of both the grand-style history paintings of the nineteenth century and the photographic images of the twentieth. "The native population," O. Henry continues, "formed at his rear in a vast, chattering semicircle to watch him work. Keogh, with his care for details, had arranged for himself a pose which he carried out with fidelity. His role was that of friend to the great artist, a man of affairs and leisure. The visible emblem of his position was a pocket camera."[37] Thus begins an elaborate heist. The idea was to appeal to the vanity of the dictator of Anchuria, to lure him into paying ten thousand dollars for a portrait by Keogh's friend Carolus White, who was to pose as a distinguished American painter. The two agreed, and soon the autocrat requested that White paint his portrait. But White could not betray the muses:

> I can't paint that picture, Billy. You've got to let me out. Let me try to tell you what that barbarian wants. He had it all planned out and even

a sketch made of his idea. The old boy doesn't draw badly at all. But, ye goddesses of Art! Listen to the monstrosity he expects me to paint. He wants himself in the center of the canvas, of course. He is to be painted as Jupiter sitting on Olympus, with the clouds at his feet. At one side of him stands George Washington, in full regimentals, with his hand on the president's shoulder. An angel with outstretched wings hovers overhead, and is placing a laurel wreath on the president's head, crowning him—Queen of the May, I suppose. In the background is to be cannon, more angels and soldiers. The man who would paint that picture would have to have the soul of a dog, and would deserve to go down into oblivion without even a tin can tied to his tail to sound his memory.[38]

There are some depths to which the reluctant swindler will not stoop—for Carolus White, it is producing kitsch propaganda. Although O. Henry could not have known that this would be the kind of kitsch that would later glorify General Tiburcio Carías Andino, who ruled Honduras at the behest of the United Fruit Company from 1932 to 1949, he perceived the potential for this possibility to be concretely realized.

"Down with the traitor—Death to the traitor!" echoed through the streets of Coralio.

Fig. 3.18. Photograph by Rafael Platero Paz of a public works project in El Progreso with an image of Tiburcio Carías Andino superimposed above it. *Courtesy of the Rafael Platero Paz Archive.*

The cause of this demonstration of displeasure was the presence in the town of a big, pink-cheeked Englishman, who, it was said, was an agent of his government come to clinch the bargain by which the president placed his people in the hands of a foreign power. It was charged that not only had he given away priceless concessions, but that the public debt was to be transferred into the hands of the English, and the customs-houses turned over to them as a guarantee. The long-enduring people had determined to make their protest felt.[39]

O. Henry not only captured the essence of Dollar Diplomacy, he also prophesized the proposed Paredes-Knox Convention of 1911, which spurred Zemurray to fund the mercenaries aboard *The Hornet*. Sarcasm and parody highlighted the outrage of ordinary Anchurians toward their treacherous political class:

On that night, in Coralio and in other towns, their ire found vent. Yelling mobs, mercurial but dangerous, roamed the streets. They overthrew the great bronze statue of the president that stood in the center of the plaza, and hacked it to shapeless pieces. They tore from public buildings the tablets set there proclaiming the glory of the "Illustrious Liberator." His pictures in the government office were demolished. The mobs even attacked the Casa Morena, but were driven away by the military, which remained faithful to the executive.[40]

Iconoclasm ruled the night. The banana republic was contested by shattering pictures of its despotic Anglo-backed stooge. The people of Anchuria made a brief, dramatic claim to local sovereignty, protesting a situation in which a foreign power had surreptitiously acquired a legal claim to their natural and economic resources through a puppet ruler. But "the greatness of Losada was shown by the fact that by noon the next day order was restored, and he was still absolute."[41] Thus the local dictator squashed the popular denunciation of corruption to reconstitute Anchuria as an exceptional space in which local laws could be subverted by outside powers.

Losada, the president and dictator of fictionalized Honduras, publicly denied that he had entered into any negotiations with England. But by the middle of the afternoon, Billy Keogh rushed back to share some big news with his partner in crime and principled fabricator of illusions, Carolus White.

He [Billy Keogh] retired to the little room where he developed his pictures.

Later on he came out to White on the balcony, with a luminous, grim, predatory smile on his face.

"Do you know what that is?" he asked, holding up a 4 × 5 photograph mounted on cardboard.

"Snap-shot of a señorita sitting in the sand—alliteration unintentional," guessed White, lazily.

"Wrong," said Keogh with shining eyes. "It's a slung-shot. It's a can of dynamite. It's a gold mine. It's a sight-draft on your president man for twenty thousand dollars—yes, sir—twenty thousand this time, and no spoiling the picture. No ethics of art in the way. Art! You with your smelly little tubes! I've got you skinned to death with a kodak. Take a look at that."[42]

Keogh had captured on film the president signing a huge concession over to the Englishman. He would accept a $20,000 bribe from Losada "to keep it [the picture] out of circulation."[43] The photograph as evidence, the significance of public culture, an icon of national and economic betrayal: each of these visual problems is posed as the status of photography as art is ridiculed.

Just as O. Henry wrote Central America into the fictional time of theater and meditated on the ways that exploitative political and cultural relations could only be represented in literature, art, and tintypes, the images and rhetoric of the fruit companies take Honduras out of real space and time and etch the country into mythic time—the Garden of Eden, timeless natives, and prehistoric creatures meet machines, modernization, and scientific progress. In this register, Hondurans could not live in the present but could only inhabit an ancient past or a promised future of modernity. As a 1920s cruise-line brochure declares of the Americanized Panama Canal Zone, "The quarters, the hospital, the jungle, the slackness and demoralization of life near the equator. Here the humblest American will feel some of that imperial pride aroused in the citizen of ancient Rome or of modern Britain by the sight of his race carrying light to the darkest places of the world."[44] The tropical present had to be surrendered to the US imperial state and its private enterprises, both of which are also inscribed into the historical time of "great" civilizations. The literary and visual images that emerged through this unequal encounter became allegories of the neocolonial relationship between the United States and Honduras. Both valences of the banana republic—that of US-driven modernization and that of US-backed exploitation—dulled the capacity of those who accepted the metaphor, leaving them less able to critically understand the present as well as the lived experiences of those represented. The form and content of US-Honduran encounters were simultaneously illuminated and confused. Just as photography freezes a passing moment, rescuing it from oblivion while missing the vast majority of other important moments and experiences, so too did the fragmentary images of Honduras as a banana republic denote an important aspect of the country's political culture, which could then be used to denounce exploitative fruit-company practices even as it besmeared a range of subjectivities and life paths under the totalized will of US agents.

The epilogue to *Cabbages and Kings* strips down this philosophy of history:

> Vaudeville is intrinsically episodic and discontinuous. Its audiences do not demand dénouements. Sufficient unto each "turn" is the evil thereof. . . . Therefore let us have no lifting of the curtain upon a tableau of the united lovers, backgrounded by defeated villainy and derogated by the comic, osculating maid and butler, thrown in as a sop to the Cerberi of the fifty-cent seats.[45]

Vaudeville, the comic opera, the satirizing short story—these are the media that O. Henry enlisted to entertain readers with a tale of swindling gringos, hapless natives, and vain dictators. And just as there is truth in a vaudevillian Honduras, so too is there exaggeration, irony, and self-reflective artifice. *Cabbages and Kings* makes no pretense to being anthropologically realist. It is, instead, a black comedy. It is a burlesque of US diplomats, adventurers, entrepreneurs, and businessmen—none of whom comes across as a modernizing savior. It is also a blistering caricature of Hondurans, or more broadly "Latins," who are portrayed as hopelessly gullible, undifferentiated people who "yearn for music and color and gaiety."[46] After spending only eight months in Honduras and with only rudimentary Spanish-language skills, perhaps O. Henry, a shrewd observer of people, could seek to achieve only this: a potent distillation and ridiculing of prevalent US assumptions about the small countries of the Central American tropics.

From the very first page of the novel, the reader learns that the innocent people of the tropical town of Coralio believe that a grave tended to by an "old Indian, with a mahogany-colored face" contains the body of Anchuria's former leader President Miraflores, who was supposedly killed while trying to escape "that volatile republic" with the contents of the country's treasury and a young opera singer from New Orleans, Doña Isabel Guilbert.[47] In fact, however, Miraflores is still very much alive. When the two arrive in the port town of Coralio, "Shorty" O'Day, a detective with the Republic Insurance Company, arrests them and whisks them off to New York. But the detective is really after J. Churchill Wahrfield, the fugitive president of the insurance company, and his daughter. An American expatriate, Frank Goodwin, and his revolutionary friends are seeking to capture President Miraflores and ensure that the country is not bankrupt when they seize power, but they unwittingly capture Wahrfield and his daughter instead. In the confusion, Wahrfield commits suicide and his daughter marries Goodwin, fooling everyone in Coralio into believing that she is Isabel Guilbert. At the end of the book, in one official company letter and three scenes from "The Vitagraphoscope," the reader discovers that it is actually the body of the fugitive gringo Wahrfield that lies in the grave with a headstone honoring President Miraflores.

Thus the core of the story rests on multiple problems of mistaken identity: the corrupt dictator and the fugitive North American, the opera star and the daughter of the fugitive. The Republic of Anchuria is thus a funhouse mirror held up to the faces of North Americans. Far from progress and prosperity, people of the United States bring tintypes, phonographs, and deceit countenanced by "Saxon honesty and pride and honorable thoughts."[48] The last line of the book calls attention to itself as a set of representations, not unlike the banana republic that it invented: "After all, what is the world at its best but a little round field of the moving pictures with two walking together in it?"[49]

The novel suggests that cinematic representation, which is characteristically less capable than written language of dealing with abstract ideas but better able to denote concrete detail, is superior to lived experience. *Cabbages and Kings*, with its literary representation of Honduras as the quintessential banana republic, flattens Hondurans. The "Indians," the Afro-indigenous Garifuna communities, and mestizos become props, minor characters in a story about modern-day US pirates. But set in firm relief are the mechanisms of US neocolonialism, which the book humorously undermines, on the one hand, and tacitly domesticates, on the other.

CHIQUITA BANANA

Toward the middle of the twentieth century, it was in television and cinema that the icons of the banana republic proliferated. The Lady in the Tutti-Frutti Hat, Carmen Miranda, appeared in eight highly successful Hollywood musicals and several Broadway revues. As part of Hollywood's contribution to Roosevelt's Good Neighbor Policy, Miranda was, as scholar Shari Roberts has argued, "a spectacle of ethnicity." With her thick accent, zany malapropisms, sexual excess, and outrageous performances, "the Brazilian Bombshell" provided a complex pleasure for homefront audiences entertained by the soft-sell wartime propaganda of Fox Studios. In each of the Miranda musicals, the US fantasy of unity was enacted, leading some reviewers in Latin America to complain about Hollywood's homogenization of widely varying cultures. Upon the release of *Weekend in Havana* (1941), the Argentine magazine *Sintonia* complained that the "United States' goodwill drive [. . .] has taken on the characteristics of a spiritual blitzkrieg prepared in the arsenals of Yankee advertising."[50]

With Miranda's hats bearing products imported from Central America, these popular musicals performed a pernicious displacement. The signifier of a banana republic was set in Havana, Buenos Aires, and Rio. But neither Miranda nor her audience was totally unsophisticated. Roberts has compellingly shown that Miranda was in control of many aspects of her costumes, characters, and persona. Furthermore, Roberts concludes, "Busby Berkeley's number 'The Lady in the Tutti-Frutti Hat' in *The Gang's All Here* [1943] lampoons *both* U.S.-Latin American trade relations and notions of feminine sexuality through the casting of Miranda as the overseer of countless enormous, swaying phallic bananas buoyed up by lines of chorus girls who dance above other girls who have oversized strawberries between their legs."[51]

Only one year after the lucrative run of *The Gang's All Here*, the United Fruit Company launched a wildly successful advertising campaign built around a half-banana, half-woman cartoon character. Based on Miranda's signature carnivalesque Afro-Bahian market-woman costume, Chiquita Banana performed a calypso that established the singing commercial:

I'm Chiquita Banana
And I've come to say
Bananas have to ripen
In a certain way.
[. . .]

But bananas like the climate
Of the very, very tropical equator.
So you should never put bananas
In the refrigerator.

With Miss Chiquita, United Fruit marketing executives sought to brand a generic fruit, as historian John Soluri has shown. For the middle-class North American housewives who were the intended audience for this advertising jingle, a bouncy, popularly understood phallic symbol in a skirt linked their domestic setting of household appliances (radios, on which the jingle was heard, and refrigerators, into which bananas should not be placed) with the tropics in which the fresh fruit was grown.[52]

There are still other iterations of the banana republic that could be traced, but in the spirit of *Cabbages and Kings*, let us conclude with an ironic stance that ridiculed the paternalism of late-twentieth-century US imperialists. Woody Allen's 1971 film *Bananas* took Miranda's lampooning of North American stereotypes of Latin Americans a step further by drawing attention to the malevolence of US interventions into the sovereign affairs of other countries. The story begins with Howard Cosell playing himself, a sports broadcaster from the American Broadcasting Corporation (ABC):

Fig. 3.19. (left): Josephine Baker, Folies Bergère, Paris (1930s). *Postcard, author's collection.*

Fig. 3.20. (above): Carmen Miranda in *The Gang's All Here* (1943).

Fig. 3.21. Consumer culture is often driven by commodity fetishism, a cultural process that effectively erases the labor that goes into making a given product, whether a banana or an iPhone, by transforming it into a fetish object. In a marketing campaign that made working conditions invisible to the consumer, Miss Chiquita invited North Americans to consume the tropics by identifying the image with the product itself, which was emptied of the meaning of its production and the labor that went into growing it. *Chiquita Banana advertisement, circa 1954.*

Fig. 3.22. Poster from the 1971 film.

Good afternoon. Wide World of Sports is in the Republic of San Marcos where we're going to bring you a live, on-the-spot assassination. They're going to kill the president of this lovely country and replace him with a military dictatorship. Everybody is about as excited and tense as can be. The weather this afternoon is perfect and, if you've just joined us, we've seen a series of colorful riots that started with the bombing of the American Embassy, a ritual as old as the city itself.[53]

US soldiers fight on both sides, for the dictatorship and for the guerrillas ("The CIA's not taking any chances"). The story concludes with Howard Cosell reporting on live TV, as the rudderless character played by Allen consummates his marriage with a caricatured 1960s feminist. The movie suggests that from the political to the intimate, US mass culture has turned everything into a public spectacle, a process that is both colonializing and alienating. *Bananas* concludes with a news bulletin moving across the bottom of the TV screen: "The astronauts have landed on the moon and erected the first all-Protestant cafeteria." Woody Allen's spoof took the logic of the banana republic to its furthest point, as the moon became just another space upon which the United States could reenact its technological dominance and reproduce its discriminatory social spaces.

The banana republic as an iconic visual formation stands for a country that is not a country. It is a terrain awaiting development, a republic with no other law than depredation and whose only institution is exploitation. It is one giant spatial exception that expands out from the nucleus in the enclave, that visual form of progress that is simultaneously a legal caesura in which no formally written and adopted law applies, other than that decided upon and enforced by the company. While Frederick Upham Adams and the United Fruit Company juxtaposed the "before" of jungles and disease and the "after" of rationally ordered productive spaces made safe for American tourists, it was not Central American backwardness that caused Honduras to become a banana republic. Rather, Honduras became a spatial exception that could be plundered because it was envisioned that way. The company and its apologists adopted what Nicholas Mirzoeff might term an "imperial visuality," one that assumed that Central America was lost in mythic time and that with US capital and industrial agricultural practices, its idle people and worthless plants could be made productive and profitable.

This is the "empire without an emperor" that Samuel Crowther described as dependent upon US naval power. In contrast to this discursive practice whose material effects were keenly felt in El Progreso, O. Henry's *Cabbages and Kings* named and satirized imperial visuality as the creation of a "banana republic," a term that has since provided an emblem for understanding how local sovereignties can be usurped by meddling foreign capitalists. In this countervisuality, the banana republic is always an effect, and not a cause, of imperial power. O. Henry also pointed out the self-consciously ascetic disposition of "the scouts of the gentle brigade of *fakirs*" who "carry on the work" of retaking "the historic 300 miles of adventurous coast." It was the self-denying modern fairy prince who took it upon himself "to awaken the beautiful tropics from their centuries' sleep."[54] Where there were small-scale producers and tropical nature, the company saw only untapped resources, and as a result of that seeing that was also a willful blindness, where there could have been a country, a collectively owned US business created a banana republic that the US military "to some extent, polices."[55]

FOUR

An Egalitarian Optic

It is the 1930s. Both men are stark naked and cover only their genitals with leaves. They stand enclosed by dense foliage that opens into a clearing in the foreground, where the camera is set up. With his right hand on his hip, local photographer Rafael Platero Paz holds a couple of branches from a tree resembling a flowering dogwood, with its smooth, broad leaves that fall a bit too low to fully cover his pubic region. And the other man, whom I have not been able to identify but who was in all likelihood a US citizen employed by the United Fruit Company, stands with his left hand on his hip. He is wearing a wedding band and holds a single huge, sheathing leaf that is tucked between his crossed legs. Their eyes look directly into the lens of the camera. With the corners of his mouth slightly raised and the beginnings of crow's feet around his eyes, Platero Paz has a slight Duchenne smile. The North American squints a little from the brightness of the midday sun but self-assuredly holds his head back and sticks his chest out. Each man is turned toward the other at a slight angle, the vertex of which is right between them at the ribs. In their nakedness and with their arms, the two men are physically connected to each other by overlapping signs of intimacy. The homosociality, if not homoeroticism, of this image reminds us that multiple modes of cross-cultural encounter were possible in the banana-growing regions of Honduras.

In *Cabbages and Kings*, O. Henry wrote of a US consular officer who reclined as "he gazed dreamily out upon an Eden."[1] But what kinds of local responses did the tropicalizing notion of the country as an unspoiled paradise elicit? The unpublished Edenic image in which an unclothed Platero Paz embraces a white man near a river in El Progreso might help us consider this question while also thinking about the possibilities that are opened up, in Jean-Paul Sartre's terms, by the possibility of being seen by another person.

Fig. 4.1. *The Garden of Eden. Courtesy of the Rafael Platero Paz Archive.*

INTERPRETATIVE INDETERMINACY

Whereas Platero Paz's traditional self-portraits are pasted into family photo albums and hang on the walls of his daughter's living room, the photo that I will refer to as *The Garden of Eden* appears to have circulated in neither private nor public image economies. The North American in the image most likely took a copy of it. But that raises the question of its significance, given that before I discovered this image among other negatives in the Platero Paz archive, perhaps only two people had seen it. Its first order of significance is thus as a record of an event, which all photos are. This photo is evidence of an encounter between two people and a camera. But its greater significance is that it is a record of a particular kind of unexpected encounter, one of intimate equality in a site characterized by violent hierarchy.

Much of the analysis of visual culture appropriately focuses on images that circulated in public economies. The idea is that from the ways in which these images were produced, marketed, and consumed, researchers can draw inferences about the values and beliefs of those who made and viewed them. This hermeneutic, which moves between images and the records of the public cultures within which they circulated, is methodologically and epistemologically sound. This is precisely the presupposition that guides my interpretation of the photojournalistic images featured in chapter eight.

In contrast to the usually legible and intentionally produced meanings of images that circulated publicly, the meanings of photographs plucked out of an archive without any accompanying text are simultaneously less full and more open to a wide range of interpretations. The interpreter of such pictures is constrained by the archive itself, which operates according to its own logic. But once an image has been taken out of its repository, the semantic cargo of that picture is there for the taking, held in place only by the concrete referents that it depicts and by the very materiality of the image-object.[2]

It is worth comparing the archive of Rafael Platero Paz to that of the United Fruit Company. The Platero Paz archive is property not of an institution like the Baker Library at Harvard Business School but of a significantly less well-heeled individual, the photographer's daughter, Aída López de Castillo. And if the United Fruit Company was a capitalist creator of images, then Platero Paz was a proletarian of creation. The first contributed to the production of the banana republic as a visual formation that is readily understood throughout the Western Hemisphere, while the second helped to produce a local *progreseño* imagescape that sometimes undermined the instrumental realism of the corporation. Furthermore, just as the company introduced industrial agriculture, displacing the small-scale banana farmers who had thrived in late-nineteenth-century El Progreso, Platero Paz practiced a craft of mechanically reproducing likenesses, displacing artisanal modes of visual expression. The United Fruit Company and Platero Paz were both representational machines of modernity. And both of their archives provide resources for remembering the past and for making certain futures possible. But in listing the similarities between these two archives, we have already begun to enumerate their significant differences.

The logic of the Platero Paz archive is indeed incommensurate with that of the United Fruit Company Photograph Collection. Unlike the company archives and family photo collections, Platero Paz specialized in producing the kinds of images that his clients—banana workers, campesinos, and young families—paid him to produce. He put his craft at their service. He primarily made images for them, photographs that they would want to purchase for their own purposes, which were most often sentimental, holding meanings that were certainly social but whose complexity only those in an intimate circle of family and friends might understand. The United Fruit Company produced images for itself and for its own purposes of research, governance, and advertising. Meanwhile, the Palestinian merchants had images made that would preserve their ancestral history and perpetuate their memories. They used photography like most of us do, as mementos, and were among Platero Paz's most faithful clients. Thus the Platero Paz archive operates according to the demands of self-representation that his customers made of him. At variance with the accretion of a subaltern image archive, the United Fruit Company Photograph Collection resulted from the steady application of photography as an instrument of realist representation put to use in managing its workforce, extracting bananas from tropical soils, and marketing them to consumers in the United States.

Two men posing nude together in early 1930s Central America was not typical. But insofar as *The Garden of Eden* photograph ironically advances a vantage point on Platero Paz's entire archive, this image is also emblematic. The banana republic photos that we just examined were what I would like to refer to as "enclavic" images that assumed a binary between barbarism and civilization, Latin America and the United States, the jungle and the railroad, lazy natives and industrious engineers, the backward malarial outside and the ordered and disease-free inside of the American Zone. In contrast, the Platero Paz archive shows how this local photographer worked modern visual citizenship onto the everyday cultures of El Progreso, proposing new articulations between modernity and local practices. If the enclave was a bounded, tightly regulated space that was to serve as a US-engineered model of progress in the midst of primitivism, then *The Garden of Eden* as a historical document and as an aesthetic object suggests some of the ways in which the Platero Paz archive was not determined by the same logic of exclusion. This single picture invites us to reconstruct a moment of intimate equality that was not subjected to the binary reason of the American Zone. This photograph is an emblem of a logic that is utterly heterogeneous to that of the enclave. The photograph, like an exceedingly rare pottery shard, demands interpretation because it seems to serve as evidence of an inter-cultural act that contested the enclavic arrangement of who could be seen doing what in El Progreso.

RAFAEL PLATERO PAZ'S OTHER

In 1898, a boy was born in the thriving coffee town of Santa Tecla, El Salvador. His parents, Florencio Platero and Andrea Paz, were small-scale coffee growers in a region of the country that was connected to the world economy by railroads, ports, and roads. They named him Rafael Platero Paz, and he was only twenty years old when he left home in search of a wider world. From his birthplace in El Salvador, Platero Paz headed north to Mexico City, where he found work in a pharmaceutical laboratory called El Aguila. While there, he measured the dosages of medicine and quantities of the various chemicals that the company sold, providing him with the rudiments of the technical understanding that he would later draw on to develop film in a darkroom.[3]

It was not long before Platero Paz made his way farther north. His first job in the United States was as a salesman in New York City, where he summoned his gifts as a conversationalist and artist to sell Parker pens to the passersby whose faces he sketched as he stood on the sidewalk. His daughter Aída nostalgically remembers the stories that her dad used to tell her of how the store would fill up with people watching him draw. As an indication that he had talent as well as desire, this memory takes us from his attraction to artistry to a first public recognition of his skill.[4]

By the time he was twenty-three years old, he had enlisted in the US Army, in which he served as a private specialist sixth class with the medical detachment of the 41st Squadron. In the Army, Platero Paz worked as a pharmacist, never carried arms, never entered battle, and was never wounded. (The know-how required to work in a pharmacy seems to have been perfect training for running his own darkroom; at any rate, he had this background in common with a better-known portraitist, Nadar.) His physical condition was listed as good, and his character was noted to be "excellent." On May 21, 1921, the Army paid him $37.70, and his superiors noted that his "service was honest, 'faithful,'" and that he had "no time lost to be made good."[5]

Platero Paz's passport was stamped on September 24, 1926, for passage through Guatemala to Honduras, where he would soon arrive at his final destination in El Progreso, a town that lies a mere 150 miles from where he was born. After passing through the burgeoning industrial city of San Pedro Sula and then continuing on to Tela, he stopped in a small eatery next to the Hotel Ulúa in the city of El Progreso. The woman who prepared his warm victuals that day, Adelina López Pinet, was a single mother. She was also the woman with whom Platero Paz would spend the remaining fifty years of his life, suggesting that the way to a man's heart really is through his stomach.[6] Her young daughter was Aída López, future guardian of a massive collection of photographs.

A PORTRAIT OF THE ARTIST

In addition to the thousands of images that he took for clients, Rafael Platero Paz left a series of remarkable self-portraits. With the camera, he created images of himself. He probably made some of the self-portraits simply because, as a model, he was available on those slow days when few customers were walking through the doors of his studio. He also may have taken pictures of himself for the reason that we look in the mirror—just to see what he looked like. In other images, the carefully arranged settings and the clothes that he wore suggest that the intent behind making those self-portraits was to offer images of himself as he wished to be seen by others. By contrast, in the image of himself as an old man whose face shows signs of disease, he is not using self-portraiture as a projection of himself to raise his social status. Instead, he looks inward and feels comfortable documenting his own physical decline.

Yet, through many of his self-portraits, Platero Paz showed himself to already be who he wanted to become. In the photo that I have named *The Thinker*, he reenacts this logic of self-portraiture (figure 4.4). Platero Paz depicts himself looking off into the distance. The viewer's position is designed to be on his front porch and with enough distance so that his entire

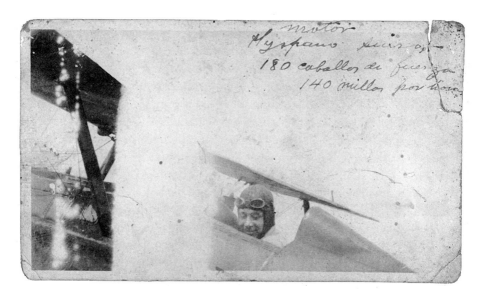

Figs. 4.2 and 4.3. Rafael Platero Paz in an airplane. Like the railroad, the telegraph, and Platero Paz's own chosen instrument—the still camera—the airplane was and still is a symbol of modernity, bestowing upon the traveler an aura of belonging to a larger, more cosmopolitan community. Platero Paz was a man on the move, and he found the whole thing exhilarating, as reflected in his handwritten note on the back of this photo sent back home to family: "SE-5 [a World War I fighter built by the Royal Aircraft Factory]. This photo was taken from another airplane while flying—note the expression on my face due to the terrible wind produced by the vertiginous course of the plane—140 miles per hour." We can imagine the planning, effort, and resources that went into producing this memento. As if this photo could not speak for itself, he literally wrote across it, making explicit in words what had already been visually encoded. He, Rafael Platero Paz, is participating in the vertiginous flight of modernity. *Courtesy of the Rafael Platero Paz Archive.*

body can be taken in as an object. In making himself the subject of this photograph, Rafael Platero Paz has made himself the object of the viewer's gaze—he does not look at us, we are to look at him, to objectify him, to see him as that which he wishes to become. With his back toward the house, he looks out into the distance. He is on the porch and is thus predicated by the domestic setting. But he also hangs his leg into the space beyond the house, explicitly connecting himself to what lies beyond his front porch. The declaration that he is of this world and that he is willing to get his hands dirty is accentuated by his rolled-up sleeves. Nature, given by trees and shrubs, is his backdrop. Thus he situates himself right on the point that separates his home from the world beyond it. While he is firmly rooted in the domestic, inside which he literally sits, he is oriented outward, toward the horizon.

He is contemplative, not active. As he stares off into the distance, the viewer sees him as a subject, as a being with projects and aims, as a man who looks at the horizon and thinks about what is possible. In this way, he makes himself known to us as fully human. Yet we know that he is constructing who he wants to become, and in so doing, he has certain roles and paradigms in mind.

While Platero-Paz-as-Thinker is certainly one possible interpretation of this image, another is of the movie star. He could be seen as the leading man, the hero on a Hollywood movie poster, another Clark Gable or James Cagney. But in this image, he was not playing the part of the caudillo or a campesino, both of which have their own distinctive iconographies. Here he can be seen as a new urban type, an up-and-coming Latin American man anchored to his home and family but with an outlook and sense of self-madeness that rejects restrictively local identities. While he sits contemplating the horizon, he does so in a posture that connotes the potential for intentional action. In this self-portrait, Platero Paz uses his body to form several triangles, including the two pronounced ones that are formed by his left arm, which points back toward his house, and his right leg, which points outward. His gaze doubles the strength of this vector that connects him to the world beyond his house, enabling him to visually narrate his own role as a mediator between his home and the world beyond it.[7] Thus the identity he fashions for himself is not that of a transcendental, decontextualized authentic and essential self; rather, it is one that is rooted in a place, perched on a boundary between nature and domesticity. In this photograph, Platero Paz narrates the contingent, still-unfolding story of his own becoming.

Platero Paz most often photographed himself as he wished to be seen by others. By linking himself to particular cultural artifacts—an airplane, the

Fig. 4.4 (top left): *The Thinker*, a self-portrait made by Rafael Platero Paz in 1938. *Courtesy of the Rafael Platero Paz Archive.*

Fig. 4.5 (top right): Self-portrait by Rafael Platero Paz. *Courtesy of the Rafael Platero Paz Archive.*

Fig. 4.6 (middle right): *The Photographer*, self-portrait by Rafael Platero Paz. *Courtesy of the Rafael Platero Paz Archive.*

Fig 4.7 (bottom): *An Old Man*, self-portrait by Rafael Platero Paz. *Courtesy of the Rafael Platero Paz Archive.*

camera, a suit and tie—and striking formulaic poses, he repeatedly reaffirmed his status as a modern, cosmopolitan individual. Yet these iterations might also suggest that the Other to which Platero Paz addressed himself photographically may have never recognized him as being who he represented himself to be.

ENCOUNTERS WITH OURSELVES THROUGH OTHERS

In creating a self-portrait, I, as an artist, make myself into both the subject and the object of my own work. Yet it is structurally impossible for me alone to make myself into an object. To objectify myself, I must always posit the possible presence of another being who is capable of seeing me. Hence, far from being indulgences, self-portraits always and inevitably connect us to other people; they reaffirm to us that we are beings in the world and that an essential aspect of our lives is what Jean-Paul Sartre referred to as the "permanent possibility of being seen by the Other."[8] Thus I paint myself, or take a photograph of myself, aware (however vaguely) that despite my ceaseless attempts to define myself, to become what I am, there are two epistemic limits that I cannot cross: I can never be an object to myself, and I cannot know myself as others know me.

Self-portraiture is one way that we get around this problem of self-knowledge. We start by recognizing that there are other points of view. We then write, paint, or photograph ourselves by throwing ourselves in the direction of the Other. By projecting ourselves onto a screen that others may view, we start to become what we aim to be. In this way, we set up a situation in which the Other can catch us using our freedom to depict ourselves as we wish to be depicted. The Other can still objectify me and my goals (we can imagine someone saying, "He painted himself in that way because he wants to appear to be smart, or anguished, or caring"). Thus it is in the very indeterminacy of the self-portrait that I experience the Other's freedom and she experiences mine.

To put it another way, Sartre reasoned that to see another person, it has to be possible that that person can see me. In his words, "'Being-seen-by-the-Other' is the *truth* of 'seeing-the-Other.'" By extension and much more concretely, we note that a self-portrait is not merely me staring at my own reflection held in place by a mechanico-chemical process, yielding a result not unlike what I see as I stare into a pool of water or in what is reflected back to me from the tain of the mirror. We can even say that self-portraiture is not only considering oneself in the mind's eye and trying to represent the imagined image. On the contrary, in an important way a self-portrait allows me to cease being the center of my world, because in constructing a particular image of myself, I acknowledge the importance of the viewer that I would like to have recognize me in this image. So I create an image of myself knowing that another may look at it and that I, in fact, need another to see and recognize me in it.[9]

Furthermore, I need the Other to accept me as I show myself to be in the picture. If the person whose acceptance I wish to earn looks at the photo and says that I am just putting on airs, then the Other has actualized the very possibility that I most feared. For in not recognizing me as being authentically the person I portrayed myself to be, the viewer has declared that there is a disconnect between my appearance and my essence. Indeed, the gaze of the Other creates new possibilities of being—and some of them may cause us to tremble. "It is not that I perceive myself losing my freedom in order to become a *thing*," Sartre reasons, "but my nature is—over there, outside my lived freedom—as a given attribute of this being which I am for the Other." We are who we portray ourselves to be only to the extent that others recognize us as being that person.[10]

In short, there are two steps in our encounters with ourselves through others. First, I can be seen, and that creates the possibility that I can be the object of another's look. But this subjective operation remains incomplete until, second, I obtain the recognition of the Other.

We have thus struck upon a formal aspect of photography. The camera, which can substitute for the "two ocular globes" of another person, is an apparatus that reminds us that the Other may see us in the mechanically reproduced image it captures.[11] But eyes are not, Sartre reminds us, the other's look. That person could be looking at something else. More importantly, as I see the other's look as an object, I miss the new ontological possibility it creates. For Sartre, to apprehend the look is to be conscious of being looked at. Thus the camera stands for the look that we apprehend when we are conscious of being looked at or the mere possibility that we may be looked at as we are right now, at this moment, which will be stopped in time.

In short, self-portraiture is a highly complex act that may be undertaken for multiple reasons: to explore who one is and is not, who one was but is no longer, and who one wishes to be. Self-portraiture can certainly allow one to represent herself as the other while also allowing the artist to meditate on issues and ironies of identity, relationships, being, and technique. Self-portraiture, especially in photography, which cannot escape its own indexical nature, also allows the artist to attempt to represent herself as herself for the other. That is, through the look, the other and I mutually constitute ourselves.

This is so even though photography is always one-way viewing. The beholder of the photo sees an image of a subject. But the subject of the photo cannot see the beholder of her image and can never see herself as her beholder sees her. So the subject of the photo is being-seen-by-the-Other without being able to see the Other.

As a relational being, only if others see me can I be what I want to be and become what I want to become. In a curious way, then, self-portraits validate the importance of the Other, of the viewer. Self-portraiture, by my analogy, is a Sartrean cogito. Like the Sartrean "I think" that necessarily happens in the presence of the other, the self-portrait not only implies a distance between subject and object, it also posits the necessary presence of an Other who must be there to recognize me as I wish to be seen and known by others and myself. It is this new ontological possibility that will allow me to become what I want to become. In self-portraiture, the artist cannot apprehend the look of the other, but he or she is conscious of being, or potentially being, looked at.

The Other is necessarily outside the subject. But the Other is also inside the subject. It is when the Other recognizes the subject as she wishes to be seen that the subject is externally validated.

RAFAEL PLATERO PAZ'S OTHER AND RAFAEL PLATERO PAZ AS THE OTHER

In posing for a photo, the subject always does so, whether she realizes it or not, with the gaze of the Other in mind. Even though a different viewer can always come along to look at the image, the sitter comports herself with tacit reference to the eyes of a potential ideal viewer. By "ideal" I mean "archetypal" on the one hand and "imagined," "ideational," and "hypothetical" on the other; but I do not mean that this imagined Other is somehow perfect. In the photographic act, a subject sits imagining a particular person, or type of person, looking at the picture of herself as she is now.

Who was Rafael Platero Paz's implied viewer? Who was the Other to whom he visually addressed himself? Who was this, imaginary or present, ideal viewer toward which he directed these images of himself? Given that there are strong links between a style and an outlook, which stylistic tokens in these photographs can be used to describe the archetype that Platero Paz projected?

From the poses and the cultural trappings employed in his self-portraits, it is evident that Platero Paz posited local viewers who would understand the more general rhetoric of US-inflected notions of progress and modernity. He visually and textually linked himself to specific technologies, such as the airplane and the camera, and to the purveyors of these technologies. Thus, Platero Paz's second persona—the Other toward which he projected images of himself—was a particular brand of social and cultural modernity, epitomized not only by his camera but also by his poses.

As we have seen, Honduran experiences with capitalist modernity began in the late nineteenth century. Liberal intellectuals and political leaders— most notably Antonio R. Vallejo, Ramón Rosa, Rómulo E. Durón, and Marco Aurelio Soto—initiated various projects of societal modernization, including increasing the bureaucratization of the state and linking Honduras to the world economy by providing generous incentives to North American mining, fruit, and railroad companies. Likewise, they sought to elaborate a cultural modernity based on the specificity of Honduras, knowable through its history, territory, ethnology, traditions, and language. The very name of the town where Platero Paz lived and worked inscribed a Honduran appropriation of the rhetoric of modernity.[12]

Building on the social and cultural infrastructure created by local townspeople, the United Fruit Company enacted what Charles Taylor might term an "acultural" developmentalist notion of modernity. Wielding the camera, Platero Paz was himself a historical agent of capitalist development and cultural modernity in this dynamic region.[13] Yet this acultural notion of modernity was not simply North American or European. Indeed, as we will soon see, the merchant-industrialists of Palestinian descent exercised growing economic power on the north coast. In their stores, they sold the very goods that indexed a consumer's social status as well as their participation in the project of national progress.

It was within this terrain of intersecting national and transnational discourses that Platero Paz visually inserted himself into a racialized and strongly developmentalist modernist project, one that largely excluded the indigenous and black communities of Honduras. Thus, even as Platero Paz attempted to join this community of modernity on the basis of his mode of being and not his *ladino* bloodline, within the gaze of his ideal viewer, particular strains of nationalism, race, and social class comingled.[14]

To reiterate, in each of his traditional self-portraits, Platero Paz attempts to affirm that he belongs in a place of wealth, progress, and refinement. He accomplishes this by linking himself to cultural artifacts of high symbolic yield, investing in what Roland Barthes has referred to as the denotative power of photography to naturalize the connotative messages built into each image.[15]

Yet Platero Paz as-he-appears-in-photos is concealing a part of himself that is stubbornly stable and that he is attempting to negate and overcome. That stable aspect of his identity is his identifiable and locatable social, cultural, and class position in the "Third World," on the periphery of US empire, as a Salvadoran immigrant and artisan-entrepreneur in Honduras. Accordingly, these self-portraits are not lies, but doors opening into the symbolic world of his consciousness. More modestly, these portraits reflect various aspects of his identity and the code switching necessitated by turning in multiple worlds.

So, what of the real or, rather, what traces of Platero Paz's unsymbolized self remain, not fully excluded from this racially and geographically stratified story of progress and modernity? To put it simply, did Platero Paz ever attain the recognition that he desired from his Other?

From these photographs, taken at various points throughout his long life, we might conclude that he never managed to be recognized as actually being who he wished to be seen as. Thus the continual need to photographically reassert his membership in a broader community of modernity, displayed through specific items of consumption and the pursuit of his craft.

But in 1969, the tranquil surface of Platero Paz's belonging was suddenly rent by the armed conflict between Honduras and El Salvador. Beginning in 1963, he served as the Salvadoran consular officer for El Progreso. As a surrogate for the Salvadoran government, he submitted hundreds of legal requests to the Honduran state so that Salvadoran workers and their families could remain in Honduras. The mandatory ID cards allowed the police and military to identify citizens and noncitizens, an especially important task as border disputes with El Salvador became more frequent. These identity-card pictures were a mainstay of Platero Paz's business, providing a steady stream of income for the duration of his career. Besides, as an upstanding citizen who organized the Salvadoran community to help out in times of crisis, he likely felt that he was providing a valuable service to his adopted country and to his compatriots.

Yet, as the number of landless peasants multiplied, due in part to decades of migration from El Salvador, Salvadorans who had lived and worked in Honduras for generations came to serve as the constitutive Other, especially during the brief 1969 conflict between the two countries. It was then

that Platero Paz, a man who had served since the 1930s as the most important photographer in El Progreso and had married and raised children with
a Honduran woman, had to hide in fear for his life. His daughter, Profesora
Aída, recounted the experience of seeing her father hunted by a mob:

> In the war with El Salvador, in 1969, they entered the houses of Salvador-
> ans and dragged them away. There was a neighbor who was, as they used
> to say, "an ear of the DIN [National Investigation Department]," a spy for
> the police. They came to take him [Rafael Platero Paz] out of our house!
> They came at midday to take him as a prisoner to the stadium in San
> Pedro Sula! Because it was in the stadiums that they put all the Salvador-
> ans. But when I went to the police to find him, my sister was calling me at
> the school, so I went to the police. But he was on a bus. His friends, they
> got him out. It was terrible. They destroyed the houses of the Salvador-
> ans. There, a block over, there was a photographer from El Salvador; they
> destroyed his entire business. That man had to flee and never returned. It
> was horrible.

The Salvadoran photographer who had his studio burned to the ground was
Gerardo Flores. He was among those rounded up in the Humberto Micheletti Stadium, a sports arena named after the man who was the son of the
first mayor of El Progreso and the father of Roberto Micheletti Bain, who
would seize power in the 2009 coup. Although in his daily life Rafael Platero
Paz fit in and served as a cross-cultural bridge for Hondurans, Salvadorans,
and US engineers, priests, and teachers, something remained out of kilter.[16]

A CAMERA IN THE GARDEN OF EDEN

> History, and things of this type, one cannot cover up.
> Profesora Aída

We cannot know for sure whether there was a third person present to
take the picture of this au naturel encounter between two men or whether
Platero Paz rigged his camera to release the shutter automatically. But we
do know that from a technical standpoint, cameras could be set up with a
self-timing mechanism. I also know that he was a professional photographer who had an extensive collection of cameras, lenses, tripods, and other
accessories. Because the negative was found among the thousands of other
negatives that he tucked away in boxes in the back of his studio, I am also

confident that this image was taken with one of his own cameras.

While the question of who clicked the button may seem secondary, this photo, like all photographs, is a record of an encounter. The immediate presence of others changes what happens when two people are alone. The presence of just one other person creates a dynamic different from that of the meditation-like activity of solitary self-portraiture. Given that there were at least two people present during this encounter, interesting and unanswerable questions arise: How did the idea of taking the picture emerge? Was there a campy humor to the act? Perhaps it was a daring move to a new kind of authenticity? Perhaps a show of courage? For whom was the picture taken and why?[17]

It is possible that the picture was taken for the North American, that he who likely came to El Progreso to work for the United Fruit Company pressured Platero Paz to take an image of them mocking the Garden of Eden. After all, he had more power and may have been able to economically coerce the local bilingual commercial photographer into this situation. Moreover, his visible membership in a small group that was there reshaping the landscapes and livelihoods of the tropics can itself be traced, in part, to Abrahamic discourses that still get traction in our public cultures and were first put forward early in the book of Genesis: "And God said unto them, Be fruitful, and multiply, and replenish the earth, and subdue it."[18] Hence this photo could be read as a manifestation of the white gay male tapping into colonial stereotypes of the dark-skinned, tantalizing yet threatening, colonial male Other.

But for several reasons, this reading in which the power of the North American eclipses that of the Salvadoran photographer seems off. First, Platero Paz looks into the camera with the steady gaze and voluntary smile of a person who is not under undue pressure. Second, the two men appear to be collaborating in parodying the Garden of Eden. Third, the children and grandchildren of Platero Paz often recalled how comfortable he was with people from the United States, speaking to them in fluent English.[19] Fourth, the visual codes operative in this pictorial space reveal that neither Platero Paz nor the North American was objectified in any totalizing way. In this photo, Platero Paz and his white companion are not decontextualized essences, ontologically reduced to being pure sexual objects, concrete manifestations of tacit and less tangible neocolonial stereotypes. Instead, they are clearly in nature. They are not abstracted out of time and place to be made into fixed signifiers of some erotic and racialized aesthetic ideal. No, they stand on stones, are enveloped by shrubbery, and the sunlight is intense. Further situating them is the vanishing point of the image, and thus the focus of the viewer: the "fig leaf" as the signifier of a foundational myth of Christianity. The fig leaf repels the gaze, allowing the two subjects to maintain their dignity and to resist the viewer's attempt to turn them into mere objects. Thus the fig leaf hides the sex and thereby resexualizes the two men by placing them into the mythical world of Eden that they are in the act of remaking. In short, while inequalities of race, nationality, and social class certainly conditioned the relationship between the two men, it is unlikely that this image was the result of the Anglo coercing the Salvadoran photographer to pose with him in this manner.

A more compelling explanation is to be found in the way that they bound themselves to each other in this moment. They did so physically and mythically, playfully and photographically.

For starters, the image itself offers a reason to reject the idea that the white man may have dragooned the local photographer into posing nude for a selfie. As a studio photographer, Platero Paz was paid to take "good" pictures. His customers did not want to be rendered out of focus or with their heads cropped out. They wanted to appear neither washed out nor muddy, but perfectly exposed. But in *The Garden of Eden*, Platero Paz overexposed his white companion, limning him as unnaturally bleached, washing out the highlight details of all but the darkest shadows cast by his chin and the broad, strategically placed leaf, the shadow of which suggests a concealed, and perhaps alert, presence. Platero Paz's control over the shutter speed and lens aperture rendered his own skin tone and the shadow details of his body in the harsh midday sun so that they retained their hues in the resulting photograph. Platero Paz's choice of exposure thus reflects, at the most technical level, his location as a Latin American photographer who looked at and photographed people who looked like him. Platero Paz inscribed the place from which he looked—to recall Argentine cultural theorist Beatriz Sarlo's question "¿Cómo armar una perspectiva para ver desde Argentina?"—into this photograph, rendering the white man as unnaturally white and himself as naturally olive-skinned. The light range of his film was too narrow to render both the mestizo Platero Paz and his white companion as properly exposed. If Platero Paz had correctly exposed his companion, the resulting image would have rendered him and the entire scene too dark. Instead, he made the pencil of nature err, to invoke Esther Gabara's notion of Latin American vanguard projects that not only problematize photography's status as a technology of capture but also self-consciously reflect upon the medium as a mode of social critique.[20] Platero Paz's companion in this intimate space of neocolonial contact was rendered as the Other by his skin tone that absorbed less light. So while the pose was one of intimate equality, the exposure of the film was a decolonial choice.

Beyond the details of composition, this image is a clear allusion to the story of the pre-Fall state of humans in the Hebrew Bible. In the beginning, the story goes, God created man and took him to the Garden of Eden to tend to it, giving only one instruction: not to eat from the tree of knowledge of good and evil. Then, taking a rib from the man, he made a woman. But soon after, a serpent sought to convince Eve to eat from that tree, saying, "For God doth know that in the day ye eat thereof, then your eyes shall be opened, and ye shall be as gods, knowing good and evil" (Gen. 3:5). Thus the ocularcentric epistemology of Western civilization is partially nourished by a mythology of competing voyeuristic impulses, of God as all-seeing yet desiring that humankind wander with its eyes closed, and our own human desire to see as gods see. "And when the woman saw that the tree was good for food, and that it was pleasant to the eyes," Adam and Eve fell into temptation (Gen. 3:6). They ate the forbidden fruit. "And the eyes of them both were opened, and they knew that they were naked; and they sewed fig leaves together, and made themselves aprons" (Gen. 3:7). They had been caught in the act. They had been seen. They were not recognized as being that which they wished to be. Embarrassed, Adam and Eve sought to hide their nakedness, covering themselves with fig leaves. Thus one way of interpreting this photograph from El Progreso would be to say that the leaves are the intertextual signifier of human shame before God and each other. But here that shame is feigned and merely conventional. In other words, while the leaves technically situate the allusion as post-Fall, this image evokes the pre-Fall state. The encounter is clearly in the Garden, the natural, unconstructed, precultural site of blissful human experience.[21]

The Garden of Eden reverberates with the religious imagery that Platero Paz strategically inserted into many of his studio portraits. For instance, he produced hundreds of First Communion pictures. Making these images required a two-stage process. He first photographed the child looking up at his hand, as if he were holding the Host (figure 4.8). "Here is where God will appear," he would tell the child. He then double-exposed the film to a picture of Jesus's face, which was superimposed over the photographer's hand (figure 4.9). The final image was of a prayerful child looking up to Jesus. Through the juxtaposition of the boy and the hand on which the youngster has been told to reverently train his eye, the staged nature of these photographic events is evident in each of the negatives. Thus these photos inadvertently depict Althusser's moment of interpellation, in which an individual is hailed by an ideology, and at the moment that the person recognizes that he is being called, he becomes a subject of that ideology in the very act of recognition.[22]

In making these visual religious allegories, Platero Paz repeatedly played priest as he produced hundreds of these pictures for young girls and boys in and around El Progreso. The creation of these magical-realist First Communion images was yet another way that he worked modern visual citizenship into the everyday lives of *progreseños*. Photos of his wife, Julia López de Platero Paz, posing in front of Our Lady of Guadalupe in Mexico also ironically resonate with *The Garden of Eden* (figure 4.10). These more orthodox images made it into the family albums.[23]

Figs. 4.8 and 4.9. First Communions, 1950s, a raw photo and a finished image. *Courtesy of the Rafael Platero Paz Archive.*

Fig. 4.10. Funeral notice for Julia López de Platero Paz. At the age of fifty-four, she died of uterine cancer in the United Fruit Company hospital in the neighboring town of Lima. Platero Paz survived her by fifteen years. *Courtesy of the Rafael Platero Paz Archive.*

The garden motif as a figure for the Honduran north coast was not inherent to the region. Rather, it was part of a regime of representation that began to emerge in the 1880s as the Caribbean was promoted to tourists and businesspeople as a tropical paradise. As Krista A. Thompson has shown in the case of Jamaica and the Bahamas, British colonial administrators hired photographers and artists to create "tropicalizing images" that then circulated internationally on postcards and in illustrated guides. The Caribbean coast of Central America was similarly represented to North Americans as a verdant place of abundance. Postcards created by J. A. Doubleday and P. Maier could be purchased in San Pedro Sula and sent to family and friends in Arizona, Alabama, and beyond. Yet it seems that photos often failed to give North Americans the lush landscapes that they imagined, as so many of these postcards were painted in vibrant colors with more tropical plants than the photographed scenes yielded on their own (figure 4.11). Platero Paz himself painted such a touristy landscape as the backdrop for his studio (figure 4.12).[24]

Fig. 4.11. Postcard by J. A. Doubleday. *Courtesy of the Museo de Antropología e Historia de San Pedro Sula.*

Fig. 4.12. Woman posing with tropical backdrop painted by Platero Paz in his studio. *Courtesy of the Rafael Platero Paz Archive.*

A HOMOSOCIAL CHALLENGE TO MONOLITHIC MASCULINITY

In *The Garden of Eden*, a photograph that was secreted away among thousands of more mundane negatives, it is our own shame that is mocked by Platero Paz and the North American posing with him. The two men did stand together to be photographed in the buff. This photographic event occurred sometime around 1935. As a species of self-portrait, this image shares with the rest his wish to express himself. Platero Paz is again showing us, as the Renaissance humanist painters did, that he has the freedom to choose his own way of life. The embarrassment may not have been his—although he certainly hid this photo from his family—it may be ours.

The relationships between social nudity, nature, and eroticism are fraught with tensions that change from one historical and cultural context to another. David Bell and Ruth Holliday have traced the discourses and practices of naturist movements in the West, demonstrating that the unclothed body in nature has sometimes evoked a secret geography of sites for outdoor gay male sex and, more often, reinforced a heterosexual matrix, as in the case of English nudist colonies. What these different movements share is an embodied relationship to nature, with the countryside romantically imagined as the appropriate place for being naked outdoors, which is figured as a precultural (and thus prehomophobic) Edenic site. For both heterosexual and gay communities, "privacy could be had in public," as George Chauncey describes the irony of the less surveilled, less regulated spaces of contemporary Western societies.[25] I reference these disparate traditions of social nudity to suggest that although some twenty-first-century eyes may see homoeroticism, there is a strong chance that what we are looking at was, for the two subjects of this image, a Platonic friendship. But regardless of whether the two men saw their encounter as homosocial or homoerotic, in this photograph Platero Paz demonstrates his awareness of the accepted conventions of portraiture and visually questions them.

Typically regarded as a Renaissance invention for articulating the rise of the individual, portraiture generally assumes, as Patricia Simons has put it, "a particular kind of modernist, western, autonomous individualism . . . a sense of unique and publicly staged selfhood, so that masculine agency is universalised as the norm." Simons goes on to say that "these approaches also assume a universal heterosexuality for both sitters and viewers, thus repressing more complex subjectivities and illicit pleasures."[26] Platero Paz's *Garden of Eden* challenges the metadiscursive constraints of such a monolithic masculinity. It does so by harnessing the realist quality of photography—this event did occur—to demonstrate unequivocally that men were bonding in ways that contradicted, or at the very least unsettled, the rigid definitions of masculinity that dominated early twentieth-century public and portrait cultures.

DEFINING *THE GARDEN OF EDEN* NEGATIVELY

Another way to get at *The Garden of Eden* is to understand what it is not.

Around 1925, an unnamed staff photographer for *Life* magazine took a photograph of the "fallen" Eve covering herself with a gargantuan leaf (figure 4.13). As in Platero Paz's *Garden of Eden*, the tropes that drive this image are embarrassment and hiding the body before the eyes of the other. Yet the

Fig. 4.13. *Life* magazine image originally captioned "Garden of Eden. A modest Honduran hides behind a giant oar-shaped leaf of a banana tree." Circa 1925. *General Photographic Agency/Hulton Archive/Getty Images.*

"shame" is partial and contrived, as the photographer, with the apparent consent of his subject, has clearly set up this picture. The leaf completely covers her body, but the caption is nevertheless "Garden of Eden" and not "After the Fall." Seeing only her face revealed, the viewer is invited to imagine her concealed nakedness. The scale of the banana leaf—and the woman being used to demonstrate the giant aspect of that leaf—accentuates US horticultural prowess, offering another example of the power of the United Fruit Company in Central America.[27]

The photograph taken for *Life* was clearly not a self-portrait. It was taken for the eyes of US viewers. The woman in the photo was an object of their gaze and fit within the stereotypes that people in the early twentieth-century United States had of Central Americans. She is, to paraphrase Homi K. Bhabha, an authorized version of otherness. This US view of paradise suggests that the image is intended to portray the beauty and innocence not of a single person but of a pre-Fall place and people. And if the young woman is indeed a reflection of the entire country, then Honduras is exotic, modest, innocent, and possibly curious about who is looking at her. She is cautious and does not want to fully reveal herself. Thus we have a tidy allegory for US-Honduran relations, a reenactment of a dominant US gaze and the Honduras that North Americans wished to see. The banana republic is transposed from country to text to icon.[28]

Not only are capitalist and neocolonial relations visually encoded in this botanical and anthropological specimen, but they were repeated and intensified when the photographer left with his negative. It is likely that the subject received neither money nor a copy of the image. Instead, in the magazine's archives, this photograph was joined to other pictures and texts that readers purchased and that can now be rented from Getty Images. The photo became part of a larger imagescape that nourished a growing US appetite for imperialist adventures.

In spite of the intended messages conveyed by the editor's choice of caption and the photographer's arrangement of the represented participants, an unintended anti-imperialist reading of this image is also plausible. While nature and lost innocence are intended meanings communicated textually and visually, if we look closely, these meanings are contradicted by the house or building that is blurred by the use of a large aperture setting. Even though they are blurred, the squared edges and eaves of the roof suggest the presence of "modernity" and negate the intended interpretation of a Garden of Eden or "natural" indigenous community. Another detail that upsets the imperialist gaze is the presence of the young woman's skirt peeking out at the bottom of the leaf: she is not the imagined naked Indian. These details highlight the contrived nature of this photographic event, unwittingly revealing that the image was made for US eyes that wanted to see a particular Edenic Honduras. Thus what we see, and what an astute viewer in 1925 could see, was the very process of creating the cultural ideology that underwrote the activities of the US-owned fruit companies in Central America. From whom, then, is the modest Honduran hiding? God saw Adam and Eve transgress. Then they tried to hide their nakedness. In framing and captioning this photo, whom did the editors of *Life* cast in the role of God?

DEFINING *THE GARDEN OF EDEN* POSITIVELY

Platero Paz's rendition of the Garden of Eden speaks the same language as the one published in *Life*. It is a language of looks, of looks before the other. It does not matter whether Platero Paz and his North American companion actually saw the photo published in *Life*, for they had both imbibed the rhetoric of the American tropics as Garden of Eden. Their command of that neocolonial discourse was what enabled them to mimic it, turning what was once the figure of a strong, manly relationship between the United States and its Central American neighbors into a playfully homosocial one. Reflecting on British imperialism in India, Bhabha identified this discursive move: "The *menace* of mimicry is its *double* vision which in disclosing the ambivalence of colonial discourse also disrupts its authority."[29]

An aggressive masculinity governed relations between itinerant workers in the banana plantations. For example, historian Lara Putnam describes a distinction made by a Costa Rican employed by a US company during World War II: "The work was rough and risky," the worker recalled; "we used to say it was work for '*machos y muy machos*.'"[30] The subversive humor comes from the worker's play on the word "macho." Putnam explains: "The bosses might be *machos* because they were blond and light-skinned, with all the privilege their origin implied, but the workers were *muy machos* because they were true males—and did work to prove it."[31] Within the framework of the United Fruit Company's labor force, built from workers it brought from different parts of Central America and the Caribbean, the white man in *The Garden of Eden* would be considered, in his everyday interactions as an employee of the Tela Railroad Company, to be macho. The workers whom he stood above had to show themselves to be *muy macho*, a stance that could unite them in "collective action and demands for the bosses' respect."[32]

But where would the bilingual artisan and entrepreneur Rafael Platero Paz fit into this hierarchy? A diverse clientele called upon him in his studio: North American engineers and managers, priests and teachers, as well as local merchants, entire families, individual workers, and campesinos from the surrounding communities. Platero Paz's respected social position as neither boss nor peon allowed him to furtively transgress the dominant male honor code. In doing so, he and his North American companion made light of the prevailing rules of photographic portraiture, Christianity, and neocolonial rule.

They also offered a new allegory for political culture, one based not on traditional divides between male and female, US and Honduran, but on what might be termed queer cosmopolitanism. The image is cosmopolitan insofar as the two men from different cultures, nations, and races came together for this photographic event to create an image of a single moral community. As such, the image was a potential menace to Christianity, heteronormativity, and hierarchical neocolonial rule. Although both Edenic images originate in the *locus amoenus*, Platero Paz's can be read as a direct reversal of the one published in *Life*. That is the power of being able to represent oneself as one would like to be represented.

Let us now revisit the question posed through our Sartrean reading of this image, namely: Did Platero Paz ever gain the recognition of his Other? After examining his rather conventional self-portraits and recounting the time in 1969 when he was forced into hiding and rounded up by the police, we concluded that he had probably never been recognized as the modern cosmopolitan that he photographically represented himself to be. But *The Garden of Eden* suggests that he did in fact gain the recognition of his Other.

In this image, Platero Paz is accepted by his Other. Furthermore, he is not serving as the negative Other against which Hondurans defined themselves. He photographed himself naked and with his Other, incorporated into his own landscape. The North American Other is no longer gazing at him. Instead, he is assimilated into what Platero Paz is showing us. Likewise, his North American companion leaves behind all of the cultural artifacts that could testify to his inclusion in the dominant symbolic order. Hence this photo explicitly rejects the asymmetrical relations that buttress photography as a philistine art, one that tends to naturalize inequalities. In this image, there is no hierarchical relation of master-slave, subject-object, dominant-dominated. Here, there is no silent narrative of superiority. In this image, the Other—whether manifest and embodied or symbolic and in the form of a cultural ideology—is not looming over us, watching Platero

Paz like an omniscient being, silently mediating our understanding of him and his understanding of himself. What is more, the Other has also been exteriorized by this photo. Platero Paz has taken the Other out of himself, making manifest and concrete his Freudian superego, the law that he had unquestioningly accepted as his own.

Platero Paz's *Garden of Eden* is built around an intersubjective relation through which the "I" becomes "we." In his traditional self-portraits, Platero Paz posed for an eventual Other. He was there, waiting for the Other's recognition and approval. And insofar as the Other was posited as the destination and ideal viewer of these portraits, Platero Paz was declaring, "I am the Other." He was there appearing before the viewer as the Other—progress, modernity, the law incarnate. He appeared as if he did not exist, except in the form of a wish and a desire to be the racialized modern Other. In contrast, in *The Garden of Eden* Platero Paz declares, "I am we," establishing a subject-subject relation in a foreign-local encounter that transgressed reigning artistic, neocolonial, and sexual norms.

As Platero Paz and his North American companion set up this photographic event, each of them saw the other's naked body. Each was both an object for the Other and known by the Other as a subject in his own right. Together, they created an intercultural queer space that transcended, if only for a moment, the hierarchical, heteronormative dynamics of the Honduran banana plantations. With a camera, they framed a new reality, playfully citing an ancient religious text and fashioning themselves as equals.

FIVE

Transnational Imagescapes

If the banana republic is a visual form that subordinated local and national sovereignties to the interests of foreigners, then Palestinian Honduran family photographs index the heterogeneity of that exceptional space. As Palestinians in Honduras posed for the camera, they demonstrated an awareness that they had already been objectified as linguistically and culturally other and that in producing images of themselves, they could fashion new ways of being in a banana-company town.

These migrants lived in a country that marked them as ethnically different and enacted laws to regulate their mobility. In February 1929, the newspaper *Nuestro Criterio* reported on a law being debated in the Honduran Congress:

> Article twelve of said immigration law says that those individuals of the Black, Chinese, Turkish, and Hindu races cannot be immigrants; and in order for them to enter the [national] territory, they need to present the sum of TWO THOUSAND SILVER PESOS and to deposit TWO

HUNDRED PESOS which they will lose if they do not leave the country in two months.[1]

The stated reason for the proposed law was to limit the damage done to "our co-nationals by the immigration of races that are in every sense at odds with our customs."[2]

The legislation adopted a few months later significantly raised the tax on certain categories of immigrants.[3] In a formal statement of racial thinking with the imprimatur of the Honduran National Congress, the 1929 law stated, "Individuals belonging to the Arab, Turkish, Syrian, and Black races, along with individuals referred to as coolies should bring five thousand silver pesos with them to enter the Republic."[4] Slurred as *turcos*, Arab Christian immigrants were largely excluded from the realm of creole power in the interior of the country and from the circles of US power that dominated the Caribbean lowlands.[5]

Palestinian merchants were artists of early twentieth-century capitalism on the economic periphery. To anticipate my strategy for reading their family pictures, I will examine one emblematic photograph before historically contextualizing the immigration of Arab Christians to Latin America. I shall then move more quickly through a corpus of family photos to sketch the broader contours of the transnational imagescape, which I take to be an organized field of visual practices that constructs a community beyond the nation. With the imaginative and social worlds of these improbably successful traders sketched out, I then briefly examine the wider demographics of immigration to the banana zone of northern Honduras. Immigration records prompt me to consider an absence in the Palestinian Honduran family photos that suggests the presence of other in-between subjects, especially Salvadoran plantation workers. These two groups of immigrants, like the smaller group of Chinese merchants and the larger group of West Indian laborers, faced a hostile reception in Honduras. Each group used photographic realism to overcome real discrimination and to imagine, and thereby begin to create, a new reality in which they could be included as citizens.

VISIBLY MODERN

By closely examining the graphic components of the postcard image of a family beside a car, we might begin to see how Palestinian immigrants to Honduras redefined their ethnicity and overcame their status as foreigners

Fig. 5.1. The front of a picture postcard dated August 2, 1930.
From the private collection of Guillermo Mahchi.

to successfully participate as merchants in a booming banana economy (figure 5.1). If we start with the analytical structure of the photo, the primary participants are the men and the woman. This photo is not about what the participants are doing, but how they fit together to make a larger whole, which in this case is essentially a statement conveying their social status and their membership in a community of modernity. The lines of the photo—with the subjects facing the photographer and the car at an oblique angle—underscore that a foreseen spectator is the participants' addressee while also revealing an act of predication, or linking. For just as in school grammar, where the predicate expresses actions, processes, and states that refer to the subject of a sentence, a similar process is realized visually, as the subject of an image is modified, qualified, and described by other elements in the composition.[6] In this photograph of the Mahchi family, the vectors connecting the participants to each other, the car, and the spectator disclose the narrative process at work in the image. The act of predication occurs in the way the people are connected to the car. One man sits in the driver's seat, with his hands on the steering wheel and his eyes peering under the windshield at the camera lens. The two men standing in the back make up the rear plane of the photographic subject; with their eyes focused on their imagined spectator, they occupy the primary field of action. With his hands folded in a "V," the man sitting on the front of the car reinforces the confident and direct manner in which the participants in this photo address themselves to their posited spectator.

In her left hand, the woman in the picture holds a letter or a paper of some kind. She is thus a literate, petit bourgeois woman who is attached to a newly emerging world of human construction, lettered and motorized. The world of grinding corn, cooking on a woodstove in earthenware, and walking from one's village to town is clearly not hers. Hence, in addition to narrating a story of belonging in a world of writing and consumer goods, this photo encapsulates a conceptual process, hardening and crystallizing the participants as members of a particular social class. The story this photo tells is not one of change through time, from backwardness to progress, but one of timeless essence.

From inside and around the car, the four men and the woman attach themselves to what the car represents as an internationally recognized symbol of wealth and a particular version of modernity. The international aspect of this code cannot be understated. The subjects of this photo are linking themselves not to Honduras but to the prosperous and powerful industrial nations in the global North. The act of predication, while clear in this photo, can easily slide out of view. As the participants successfully fuse themselves to the notions and symbols of the mechanical, technological order, spectators can lose sight of the fact that these subjects did so self-consciously for a specific photographic event. In appropriating these symbols of a particular brand of social and cultural modernity—epitomized not only by the car but also by the camera freezing these poses—they obscure the plotting and staging that they used to link themselves to the future-most edge of their present, a series of acts which, if not disavowed, would reveal to others that this vital aspect of their identities was neither given nor natural, but socially constructed.

The buildings that form the backdrop of the compositional space are likewise saturated with meaning. Foreign travelers frequently photographed and commented upon the straw huts, which were particularly well suited to the hurricanes, sun, and locally available building materials of the north coast. Yet these recent immigrants to Honduras chose to be represented in front of a two-story house built of milled lumber. These were the kinds of houses being built by the Tela Railroad Company in El Progreso. Addressing themselves to family back home in Palestine, the people who had this postcard made chose not to be depicted next to the most common style of house in littoral Honduras at that time, but next to a building and around a car that represented their present and a bright future. The electric power lines and the transformer in the background further testify to their non-backward status in Honduras.

Just as photographs do not passively reflect society but actively create new social realities through the actions of individuals and a camera, material culture also acts back and affects the society that uses it.[7] The power pole in the background vertically complements the posts of the house, partitioning the photo into roughly equal fractions. Beyond the spatial connection that the positioned subjects have with the power pole, the transformer, and the electrical lines, this image indicates how they were materially connected to US empire.

On a Friday in May 1925, the municipal government of El Progreso debated a proposal by the Tela Railroad Company. Local officials reported, without fear of redundancy, "The company's engineers are of the opinion that the proposed system, generators, motors, and other equipment, are modern, and of great efficiency to supply the population with an electrical light service from a modern system."[8] The power plant was to use a sixty-horsepower internal combustion engine—Type "Y," Style "VA," with a "47 SKVA generator"—made by the Fairbanks Morse Company. Just as the United Fruit Company had done in the port of Tela, it would use a three-wire distribution system with three transformers to reduce the current from 2,300 volts to 110. The streets of El Progreso would now be lighted with sixty lightbulbs, each 200 to 300 watts, and fixed atop twenty-five-foot cement lampposts. Each bulb would be of the widely advertised Novalux brand. The Tela Railroad Company would also supply the municipal government with the materials to illuminate 150 homes, each getting five light sockets. The company would not cover the cost of installing the electrical systems in private homes. Upon constructing the power station, the municipal government of El Progreso agreed to pay the Tela Railroad Company $34,747. The payments were to be made by excusing the company from paying the taxes and import duties it owed to the municipality, at least until the town had paid off its debt to the company. One suspects that such public and private illumination was not primarily about surveillance by a coercive disciplinary gaze; rather, it fostered the development of liberal subjects who could move freely and safely, day or night, through the streets and, when they could afford it, have electric lights and appliances in their homes.[9] As influential merchants in this burgeoning banana town, the Mahchis were party to the contract with the Tela Railroad Company to electrify El Progreso. Likewise, in this picture postcard, they became party to a photographic pact that prodded spectators to see the family as part of a story of modernity.

Apparently they were not the only ones hitching their wagons to this US-inflected brand of progress. On the wall is a broadside advertising baking flour, an ingredient that is not native to Honduran cuisine but is closely associated with North American, European, and Middle Eastern cooking. The advertisement for Harina El Gallo ran for many decades in several Honduran newspapers. In 1929, this brand-name flour became part of a broader discussion of Honduran nationalism, a sentiment that many recognized as superficially necessary:

> In Puerto Cortés there is a great mill producing flour. The product is called "EL GALLO" and its owners add these words to it: "Superior flour of pure wheat." For its excellence and pure quality and for its eloquent name in pure Castilian this flour is very popular throughout Honduras. They also assure us that the Manager of this Mill is a "Cock" for maintaining in complete prosperity the industry that they have entrusted him with.[10]

The whole point of this front-page article in a leading Honduran daily is to scold foreign companies for not appealing, as Harina El Gallo had, to Honduran sensibilities: "it would be very good and patriotic if these industries were given Honduran names."[11] With the double entendre of "cock," the newspaper pointed to the prowess of the manager while also alluding to his virility, all in celebration of a foreign product with an ostensibly national name.

"United Fruit Company" is not a Honduran name. But "Ulúa," "Tela," and "La Ceiba" are, and these are some of the names with which the Boston-based giant christened its ships. For this, United Fruit earned praise in the 1929 newspaper article, while the Honduran-owned King Bee cigarette manufacturer was derided for having a gringo name. The author of this piece recognized a double movement: foreign companies could adopt Honduran names and have their products recognized as superior, while domestic companies could lend their products an aura of superiority by giving them English names. But while "Harina El Gallo" is a Honduran name, "Mahchi" clearly is not. Nor is it a gringo name.

Yet the picture postcard is not an abstraction. It depicts real people. The woman is Audelia López Moya, who was born in El Progreso in 1902 and died there ninety years later. Audelia López Moya is Guillermo Mahchi's grandmother. She was the granddaughter of a founding father of El Progreso, Juan Blas Tobías, who hailed from a town of the same name on the Yucatán peninsula of Mexico. The man with the mustache is Salomón (Selim) Mahchi Lorenz, who was born in Palestine in 1892, immigrated to Honduras in 1913, and died in El Progreso in 1972. The young man sitting on the front fender of the car was Hanna Mahchi, Salomón's youngest brother, who lived in Honduras for only a few years before moving to Lima, Peru. The man at the steering wheel was the chauffeur.[12] The car was a green 1930 Buick. The house was Salomón Mahchi's, the oldest building in town. To the left is the Ramón Rosa Plaza, site of the municipal government offices.[13]

This picture captures how Palestinian Hondurans, have survived and prospered while remaining ethnic outsiders who never quite fit into the official nationalist imaginary. They became accepted not because they could claim historic ties to Honduras, which they could not do, but by acquiring vast holdings of the currency of progress: consumer goods and fashions from abroad, the written word, and powerful private transportation.

Yet this photo and the Mahchi family itself complicate the generalizations found in the existing historiography on Palestinian Hondurans—contrary to the claims of nearly universal in-group marriage, here we have an example of a Palestinian man marrying a Honduran woman of Mexican descent.[14]

Beyond serving as historical evidence, this photograph also helped to create the modern identity that it depicted. The narrative structure of the image and the referents—the car, the electrical pole, and an advertisement for flour—were part of a visual language of belonging that the Mahchis employed, assuming that it would be understood by others.[15] I am suggesting that in photographs at least two symbol systems are nested within each other. The visual language on which the image relies to communicate its meaning presumes an understanding of the symbols generated by particular sets of artifacts. For example, although the advertisement for baking flour was not consciously placed in the photo, it is significant and requires interpretation. As photographers, subjects, and spectators engaged with images, a community was formed. If we invoke Ariella Azoulay's notion of "the civil contract of photography," this community was bounded by neither national borders nor citizenship status, but only by one's participation as a watcher and/or a producer of photographs. The relation established through photographs is of mutual recognition, and the subjects of this picture postcard posed with the knowledge that their addressees would fulfill their obligation to look. Furthermore, they posed with an awareness that they could not fully control who looked at the photo—surely they could not have known that we would be looking at them. So, with redundant signs, they sought to send a clear message of their own material progress and their membership in an international community of modernity. Yet, ultimately, they released the image to the world and could not control how it was interpreted.

With regard to the separate yet related textual coding, the handwritten note on the back adds another dimension to the encoded messages on the front of the postcard (figure 5.2).

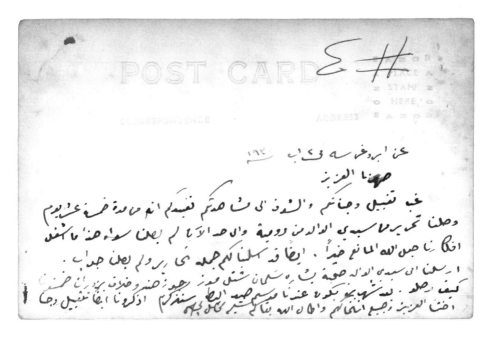

Fig. 5.2. The back of the August 1930 picture postcard.
From the private collection of Guillermo Mahchi.

2 August 1930

　　Dear Son-in-Law,
After kissing your cheeks, and craving to see you, we notify you that
fifteen days ago, arrived from Sir, the father, a letter from Roumieh, and
until now we have not received anything else. That has worried us. God
makes the impediment good. Also, we sent you a series of letters, and we
have not received a reply. We have sent to Sir the father, in the company
of Bechara Salman, banana plants and coconut tree plants, and other
grains, fifty, how did they arrive? In two months, it will be the season of
duck hunting here. We will remember you, and remember us, kiss the face
of our sister and all your sons, and may God give you long life.
　　Salim Mikhaël.[16]

Like the photograph, the message on the back loosely anchors the author
to a place, one where banana plants and coconut trees can be found. Written in Arabic and with physical salutations transcribed, the author writes to
a particular addressee, affectionately acknowledging the familial relationship between sender and recipient. Salim's desire to communicate more frequently is stated clearly, as is his attempt, in spite of the distance, to demonstrate his filial love and concern. By actively seeking to overcome physical
and geographic separation, Salim's message goes beyond the confines of territory and nation to maintain and strengthen family ties that were transnational in nature. In the reference to the seasonal leisure activity of duck
hunting, the author engages in class-specific male bonding. With repeated
invocations of God, the secular symbols of technological progress on the
front of the postcard are tempered with the tender language of family and
popular religiosity. It was this language that provided an interpretive framework for their lives, many generations before the advent of the camera.[17]

IMAGESCAPES AND CIRCULATION

The image of the Mahchi family posing next to the car in El Progreso forms
part of what historians Daniel James and Mirta Lobato refer to in the context of their discussion of Ukrainian immigration to Argentina as a "mem-
oryscape," a montage of images that sustain the memory and identity of
a community.[18] James and Lobato supplement Edward Said's notion of an
"imaginative geography and history," a term he uses to describe how spaces
and times acquire "emotional and even rational sense by a kind of poetic
process."[19] Yet the very materiality of photographs reminds us that family

memories are to no small extent rooted in the artifacts that we imbue with our remembered pasts.

The kindred term "imagescape" alludes to anthropologist Arjun Appadurai's work on global cultural flows, particularly his notion of "mediascapes." The key here is what Appadurai designates by the suffix "-scape," which he uses to describe relations that are "deeply perspectival constructs, inflected by the historical, linguistic and political situatedness of different sorts of actors," from nation-states to face-to-face groups.[20] By appending the adjective "transnational," I would like to draw attention not only to the referents of diasporic images but also to the routes they traveled and to the ties that they bound. For me, the notion of imagescape calls attention to the role of the interpreter of images while still keeping the subjects of those images in view. The analytic of transnational imagescapes allows me to move between privately held and publicly circulated images, between the neocolony and the metropole, while attending to broad discursive practices and local experiments in self-fashioning.

Family photographs are historically situated resources for imagining communities and selves that may not match up with a dominant symbolic order that tends to structure the role that each will play in a given social and, especially, national context. The Mahchis negotiated their ambiguous place in Honduran society by turning themselves into key brokers of early twentieth-century cultural and household goods, allowing them to sidestep the exclusionary regimes of racial discrimination that creoles in Tegucigalpa and the United Fruit Company of the north coast constructed. In international loops of material and symbolic circulation, Palestinian Hondurans carved out their own sphere of less ambiguous belonging.

FROM WHENCE THEY CAME

In the 1880s, some four decades before Honduras received a flood of immigrants, Palestine was a crossroads for European financiers and Christian missionaries, Russian Zionists and Ottoman reformers. The colonizing drive of these groups displaced and dispossessed the indigenous peasantry, changed modes of production, and created new geopolitical units. These transformations empowered a burgeoning urban elite, uniquely positioned to implement the centralizing dictates from Istanbul and to control newly created local governing bodies, including municipalities and regional councils. The nouveaux riches leapfrogged traditional aristocratic and religious hierarchies.[21]

In the revolution of 1908, the Young Turks toppled Ottoman ruler Abdul Hamid II, greatly diminishing the influence of urban Muslim elites in Palestine. The Young Turks instituted policies to counteract the religiously divisive policies of the sultan, whose late rebirth as a fundamentalist Islamist had alienated Christian notables and Jewish city dwellers. At the same time, Istanbul's attempts to force an anti-Arab Turkish identity on all inhabitants of the former Ottoman territories produced a backlash, prompting Anglican-educated Christians to make common cause with an embryonic, more secular Muslim Arab nationalism. And even as associations promoting Arab autonomy were banned and forced underground, a politics from below began to take root, as people held their local officials accountable, demanding better municipal services and price controls on basic goods. Despite these important changes, the lives of the common people of Palestine continued largely unchanged, affected more by annual episodes of cholera and plague than by Turkish secularism, Jewish colonialism, or Palestinian nationalism.[22] This was the Palestine that Salomón Mahchi, a twenty-one-year-old Christian from a prominent family in Bethlehem, left behind when he emigrated in 1913. There was little in their initial exodus from Palestine nor in the antagonistic reception in Central America to suggest that these poor merchants would soon become the principal agents of industrialization in Honduras.

STRAW HUTS

"It was an entire town of brotherhood, without distinctions of class, color or race," wrote Guillermo Mahchi, a US-educated grandson of Salomón Mahchi.[23] In 1992, he published *Archivo fotográfico del ayer: El Progreso, 1900–1965*, explicitly invoking the epistemic authority of the archive to offer a photographic history of what was, by this time, a small but prosperous city on the north coast of Honduras. In his book of photographs, Mahchi paired images with nostalgic commentary and excerpts from an official history, written by a former mayor of El Progreso, Guillermo Enrique Peña Molina.

The very first photograph in Mahchi's book is of four straw huts (figure 5.3). The photograph came from the collection of the Micheletti Bain family, from which the leader of the 2009 coup d'état hailed. It is a photograph of "backwardness," and those who possess it are narrating the story of their own progress, of their membership in a community of modernity. It is the benchmark against which subsequent photos in the *Archivo fotográfico del ayer* are measured. The relation between the participants in the photograph and the viewers is an imaginary one. The distance and angle from which the

Fig. 5.3. "1905—The Ancient Inhabitants of El Progreso."
From Guillermo Mahchi's *Archivo fotográfico del ayer*.

image was taken prohibit the spectator from identifying with the depicted subjects, the effect of which rendered them strangers, objects of curiosity. Such an effect results from a logic of invoking ancient others as forebears while simultaneously denying any direct descent from them or the possibility of their full citizenship in the present. Throughout Spanish America, as historian Rebecca Earle has argued, this process of valuing indigenous heritages worked by consigning them to the remote past and severing them from their living descendants in the present. Following independence, creole leaders accelerated the construction of what Earle called "indianesque nationalism" by proclaiming themselves to be the avengers of vanquished indigenous figures.[24]

The caption below the photograph reinforces the visual messages encoded in the image:

1905—The Ancient Inhabitants of El Progreso
   There around the year 1830, existed on the banks of the Río de Pelo a Village of the same name, inhabited by a tribe of indigenous who had as their Leader the Chief Canaán. They constructed their huts of straw and they dedicated themselves to the exploitation of natural products, like sarsaparilla, plantain and rubber.[25]

In Mahchi's imagetext, an "English photographer" took this picture of the straw huts on April 7, 1905, offering an "eloquent example" of the history of El Progreso as officially related by the town's mayor and chronicler, Enrique Peña Molina. The provenance of the image: the private collection of the Micheletti Bain family, descendants of William Bain, who was himself the augur of a neocolonial onslaught that began in 1872 and would continue through the 2009 coup d'état. Today, just down the street from El Progreso's old American Zone, a bronze statue of the mythic Chief Canaán stands on a pile of rocks in the main thoroughfare.

While Mahchi may have claimed that the El Progreso of the past was a brotherly community "without distinctions of class, color, or race," the reality was that sisters were still not considered full citizens and the indigenous were being displaced by British mahogany traders, Mexican lumbermen, mestizo smallholders, and, as this photo suggests, US-owned fruit companies. The visual representations of the past and Mahchi's appropriation of those images reinforce ethnic and cultural hierarchies by recalling the first inhabitants only as "an indigenous tribe" that was superseded in the march of progress. Consistent with the logic of such strategic evocations of indigenous motifs, the first visual representation in Guillermo Mahchi's book is of what contemporary El Progreso was manifestly not. The original inhabitants are represented as being outside of the imagined community of this city and of the nation that it makes more modern.

Beyond post-independence Latin American discourses and institutions that recalled the native even as their states oppressed actual indigenous peoples, Mahchi's photograph and its accompanying caption also call to mind John Lloyd Stephens's travel narrative, published in 1841. Stephens comments on the peoples he encountered in Trujillo, Honduras:

> Though living apart, as a tribe of Caribs, not mingling their blood with that of their conquerors, they were completely civilized. . . . The houses or huts were built of poles about an inch thick, set upright in the ground, tied together with bark strings, and thatched with caroon leaves. . . In every house were a grass hammock and a figure of the Virgin or of some tutelary saint.[26]

Stephens's racialized gaze saw progress even among "these descendants of cannibals." Mahchi's book begins by locating the narrator and the spectator as outside the community of those who live in straw huts, as foreign voyeurs who have already acquired their modernity and are mobile enough to gaze upon those who are still in the process of making the transition out of the past.

Like similar photos published in Frederick Upham Adams's *Conquest of the Tropics*, the photograph of straw huts in Mahchi's book simultaneously depicts the past of El Progreso and its future. The railroad tracks of the United Fruit Company create an oblique line that states the visual proposition of this image: progress cuts through backwardness. Behind the tracks are straw huts, made by humans but lacking the sharp edges that define the technological order that the railroad tracks and photography itself are heralding. In this sense, the photograph contains an analytical claim that separates these human subjects from modern technology. The huts and their inhabitants pertain to the natural world, to a primal culture that this city on the rise is leaving behind.

Photographer J. A. Doubleday, a resident of the nearby commercial city of San Pedro Sula, produced one such postcard depicting straw huts in a settlement he called Rio Blanco (figures 5.4 and 5.5). In September 1911, R. Muhsfeldt mailed the postcard to his friend W. Jakobsen in Prescott, Arizona, with a short message scrawled on the back:

Dear friends,
Received her safe, but the Brewery is in bad condition cost more than we expected.
Best Regards to All,
R. Muhsfeldt.
  Will send stamps later on. Dick

Four stamps issued by the Honduran postal service show palm trees and a steamship going upriver with smoke billowing from the stack. The image of straw huts that Richard Muhsfeldt sent in 1911 could be juxtaposed with another representation of Honduras, the Tela Railroad Company's symmetrical general office, which appeared on a picture postcard sent to Miss Cora Duffey in Alexandria, Virginia, in 1939 from aboard a United Fruit Company steamship. From the early twentieth-century banana plantations of Central America, people from the United States sent postcards north, visually registering the link between the tropics that they were modernizing and their ties to family and friends in Prescott, New Orleans, New York, and Boston.

Figs. 5.4 and 5.5. Front and back of a postcard
dated August 9, 1911. *Courtesy of Eric Schwimmer*.

But within Honduras, other images often circulated between literate friends, including beautiful halftone pictures of elegantly stylized European women (figs. 5.6 and 5.7). In June 1911, Sara R. Castillo of Trujillo sent her friend Juana Quesada of Olanchito a short note on the back of a postcard depicting a young woman in a flamboyant hat:

> Dear Friend:
> I received the seeds for carnations, many thanks; receive, together with all of your family, an affectionate greeting. Your friend,
>   Sara R. Castillo

Sara Castillo's domestically circulated postcard of a modish woman in profile is far from the picture of the straw huts that is featured as the very first image in Mahchi's book.

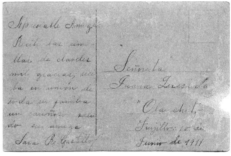

Figs. 5.6 and 5.7. Front and back of a postcard dated June 10, 1911. *Courtesy of Eric Schwimmer.*

Countless pictures of straw huts were not casually taken. In repeatedly circulating images of thatched dwellings, the United Fruit Company, postcard makers, and Palestinian merchants were reaffirming just how far they had come in achieving the impossible: planting the new in the land of the old. The Palestinian Honduran family posing in front of their car in El Progreso narrated the most improbable vertical ascent within a single generation. They had prospered in a land known for its jungles and straw huts.

DONATING THE SEAL OF THE REPUBLIC

The national seal of Honduras is ornately framed and situated front and center in a studio portrait. To the left of the seal sits Salvador Gabrie, who immigrated to Honduras from Bethlehem in 1906.[27] The photograph documents the moment in which the Oriental Union, a social and cultural society of Arab Christian immigrants, gave the insignia, carved from mother-of-pearl, as a gift to the Honduran government (figure 5.8).[28]

From the studio setting, to the men with buttoned-up suits, to the seal itself, each element of this photograph is part of a familiar visual language that allows us to make connections across photographs, clearly communicating the status of the subjects that such photos depict. In this picture taken in San Pedro Sula, the subjects are physically connected to the seal of Honduras. The seal, and the nation that it represents, is part of who they are. Or rather, it is part of who they want others to believe they are.

Power and privilege are referents in this image. Who can dress up like this, in suits that fit properly and are not just donned for this occasion? Who can present such a beautiful gift, a symbol of the nation, to the nation? Who would present such a gift to Honduras—who but an outsider, wealthy and working as a guest in a society that sees him as a foreigner? And what might the giver of the gift expect in return?

In any given encounter between an object, a camera, and a photographer, the structures and webs of meaning within which we live are revealed in ways that none of the participants can fully control. This particular image of the gift of the national seal was intended as an allegory of integration. In the photograph, the individuals are identified precisely as citizens. They are represented as one with the nation, offering it an emblem of its own beauty. What they are paying homage to is a discursive formation that we cannot see in the image but that nevertheless has the power to exclude them. Unintentionally encoded in the photograph is the threat of exclusion from the pseudospiritual realm of the nation. It is this realm that structures their

Fig. 5.8. Middle Eastern immigrants donate the national seal to the Republic of Honduras, circa 1928. *From the private collection of Sammie Gabrie.*

day-to-day existence in a foreign land. Their social and economic superiority was in fact precarious. It could not be taken for granted. In other words, this ostentatious display is a dummy phrase, substituting for the real threat of exclusion that Palestinians in Honduras faced in the world outside of the photography studio.

The "gift made to the national representation by the Syrian-Palestinian colony, resident in our country" was reported in the national newspapers:

> September 1923. It was a coat of Honduras, regular sized, carved out of mother of pearl by one of the most famous Oriental artisans. The work— says a newspaper of the North—is a marvel; it was created in Bethlehem, Palestine, by the artist Sogbi Bishara, who has made other similar ones that are in positions of honor in the palaces of London, Moscow and Constantinople.

This account allows us to begin to trace the itineraries of these objects through transnational imagescapes, linking Honduras to palaces in cosmopolitan capitals while also hinting at the ways in which images of the banana republic tended to homogenize local realities that were actually multilayered and, in this case, inflected by Levantine artisanal practices.

But there is a void in the photograph of the members of the Oriental Union giving the carved seal to representatives of the Honduran government. The absence in the photo is that of another image of immigration. The Salvadorans who came in vastly greater numbers to toil in the banana plantations of the United Fruit Company could not have donated such a seal. To find images of these foreign bodies, one has to look in other, less official places, including the Rafael Platero Paz archive.

WITH PRIESTS AND DIPLOMATS IN PALESTINE

Upon their return to Jerusalem in the mid-1920s, the early years of the British Mandate, Guillermo Mahchi's grandparents were met by a welcoming party. The occasion is marked with a medium-long shot that captures the full figures of the guests (figure 5.9). The photograph is not intended to communicate social intimacy between the viewer and subjects, but to document what happened. Much like a photograph of a smiling tourist at the Eiffel Tower that Pierre Bourdieu says creates a pure allegory that then demands a caption to explain who is in it and where he or she is, this image cannot explain itself. Yet this picture serves as a trophy, and similar photographs are on display in the Museum of Anthropology and History of San Pedro Sula, the Museum of National Identity in Tegucigalpa, Mahchi's *Archivo fotográfico del ayer*, and the family photograph collections of other prominent families of Palestinian descent.[29]

The woman in the white hat at the center of the image is Guillermo Mahchi's grandmother, Audelia López Moya. His grandfather, Salomón Mahchi, is the man next to her in the dark suit talking to the taller men, who were certainly British. In the background stands a black servant, probably from North Africa, in a tunic. Two Greek Orthodox priests look on.

So, why was this a photographable moment?

It is because, with the click of a button, the photographer transformed this imperial moment from an ephemeral gathering into an objective image, transforming the intangibility of claims to Old World nobility and New World influence into a monument to both.

At the center of this visual monument are the heroes, whom we cannot recognize without the interpretative assistance of the people who can cash in on the normative generalization presented in this image. In other

Fig. 5.9. With priests and diplomats in the Mandatory State, circa 1920. *From the private collection of Guillermo Mahchi.*

words, we need someone to tell us, "This is my grandfather." Only then can we stand in awe. Otherwise, it is just a picture.

The Mahchis had emigrated, and even other elite Arab Christian immigrants in Honduras did not necessarily recognize the social and cultural capital that the Mahchi family enjoyed in Palestine. This photograph—and many others like it, including studio portraits bearing the stamp of the Armenian photographers working in Jerusalem and ones in which Salomón Mahchi wore his distinctive fez—vouched for the high social standing of the immigrant family. These photographs of home were by no means unique to the Mahchi collection. The Gabrie collection, for example, includes family photos taken at the Jerusalem studio of Garabed Krikorian, an Armenian photographer active from 1870 to 1915. In his studio, Krikorian provided "traditional" clothing and other "Oriental" markers for clients who wanted the cultural space in which the photo was produced to be locatable, even if only by their stereotyped attributes.[30]

The photograph of the Mahchi family with priests and diplomats in Jerusalem tells of the global dispersal of this family and its rearticulation to the homeland and the larger Arab diaspora in the Americas. Similar images appear in Guillermo Mahchi's book, *El archivo fotográfico del ayer.* In the context of Mahchi's visual narrative, photographs of his grandparents returning to Jerusalem for a visit become part of a story of ethnic differentiation and the maintenance of Palestinian identity. Yet the great majority of photographs in Mahchi's story speak of successful integration, not differentiation.[31]

MERCHANTS OF MODERNITY

It was in the network of Palestinian Honduran stores that members of this nationless, civically transnational ethnic minority interacted on a daily basis with Hondurans from all walks of life. In a photograph of Salomón Mahchi's store we see a young member of the Mahchi family attending to West Indian customers (figure 5.10). The store is filled with imported shoes, hats, shirts, belts, and an array of neatly folded textiles. The lines of the shelves, the column, and the goods themselves represent order and an invitation to spend, appealing to the wage earner with some discretionary income. In the center of the frame are the glass display cases, reflecting the intense sunlight streaming in from the street.

When Salomón Mahchi looked at the camera from behind the display case, he was seeking to influence how others would perceive him. For the merchants and their customers, the Mahchis' store was a contact zone, a social space in which people of different cultures met to haggle, negotiate, and insist that promises be kept.

Through publishing photographs of their stores in newspaper advertisements, Arab Christian merchants increased their sales while also creating icons of their important role in bringing modernity to Honduras. Published in 1929, *The Commercial Directory of Honduras* describes Salomón Mahchi's store as a place where English, French, Arabic, and Spanish were spoken.[32] Similarly, a store called the Flower of Palestine enticed customers with these words: "In the last steamship we have just received the following merchandise: special fine hats, clothing made in Palm Beach, fine shirts, embroidered ribbons, lace, fine fantasy genres for ladies, young misses, and gentlemen."[33] Modernity, it seems, was brought to Honduras in a steamship from abroad, and two groups, the US-based fruit companies and the Palestinian immigrants, took the lead in peddling its tokens.

"We are the gypsies who brought the trinkets to Macondo," Guillermo Mahchi notes in a reference to the fictional town in which Gabriel García Márquez's *One Hundred Years of Solitude* takes place.[34] The analogy between Macondo and El Progreso, the gypsies and the Arab Christians, was not unwarranted. Both associations resonated with a biblical plotline in which Edenic innocence was radically disrupted by a traumatic encounter with

Fig. 5.10. "1929—Almacén Salomón Mahchi y Hno," inside Salomón Mahchi's store in El Progreso. *From the private collection of Guillermo Mahchi and published in* Archivo fotográfico del ayer.

modernity. In the novel, the gypsy Melquíades introduces the main character, José Arcadio Buendía, to all sorts of fantastic inventions—from ice to a magnet, from a flying carpet to daguerreotypes and a telescope—inducing him to abandon his pre-Fall Adamic state in which "the world was so recent that many things lacked names, and in order to indicate them it was necessary to point."[35] Having convinced himself that the magnet for which he traded his family's meager means of subsistence—a mule and two goats—could be used "to extract gold from the bowels of the earth," Arcadio Buendía begins to work "with the abnegation of a scientist" to manipulate nature for easy wealth, to invent a new weapon of war, and to discover that "the earth is round, like an orange." But the further he progresses in his headlong quest for instrumental knowledge, the more he loses his sanity. Allegorically colliding in Macondo are the pre-industrial and the industrial, the local and the global, the traditional and the modern. In the beginning, Macondo's only contact with the outside world is through the annual visit of a band of "ragged gypsies" who, to the raucous accompaniment of "pipes and kettledrums," exhibited "new inventions" and other objects of interest in the village.[36] Years later, the arrival of the banana-company train is confused with the return of the gypsies: "During the previous weeks they had seen the gangs who were laying ties and tracks and no one paid attention to them because they thought it was some new trick of the gypsies, coming back with whistles and tambourines and their age-old and discredited song and dance about the qualities of some concoction put together by journeyman geniuses of Jerusalem."[37] The United Fruit Company's seemingly innocent yellow train represents the advent of the disruptive temporality and economic logic of capitalism, bringing joys and calamities to Macondo and ultimately reducing the town to chaos in the climax of the novel, the events of which were based on the massacre of banana workers in Ciénaga, Colombia, in 1928. Beyond rejecting the demands of the US-based fruit company, Macondians rejected the privileging of representations over lived experience, a point that is trenchantly dramatized in the ongoing struggles between José Arcadio Buendía and his wife, Úrsula Iguarán. Fictional Macondo was like the real town of El Progreso in that both were scenes of encounter between some old ways of living and the destabilizing effects of a neocolonial modernity, introduced most dramatically by the gypsies and the United Fruit Company in the novel and the Palestinian merchants and that same company in real life. In comparing his grandfather to the gypsies in Macondo, Guillermo Mahchi identified him as both an agent of modernity hawking international wares and as a perpetual outsider on the existential margins of Honduras.

Arab immigrants quickly became an economic elite upon which members of the aspiring classes across the north coast relied. Perhaps it was the immigrants' rapid ascent and marked otherness that aroused suspicions. In 1928, for example, a large fire destroyed several warehouses in La Lima, another United Fruit Company town less than ten miles from El Progreso. A week after the fire a newspaper reported,

> The fire that occurred last week in Lima Viejo, according to data that we have verified, was not accidental; merchants who were insured there intentionally caused it. We will follow the case to provide comprehensive information in our next issue, stating in advance that we know of some Palestinian elements interested in intervening with large sums so that the criminals go free.[38]

So while they may have trafficked in consumer goods from abroad, that was not enough to insulate Palestinians in Honduras from the coercive and tribal aspects of nationalist sentiment; nor was it enough to integrate them so they could benefit from the cohesion that the nation-state purports to foster among those dwelling within it.

IN-BETWEEN POPULATIONS: PALESTINIAN AND SALVADORAN

The photographs of the Mahchi family are similar to those of other Palestinian Honduran families, and here I would like to offer a thumbnail sketch
of demographic characteristics of their broader community. I will proceed
by contrasting the Arab Christians in Honduras with a different image of
immigration, that of Salvadorans. As an immigrant from El Salvador who
married a Honduran woman, Rafael Platero Paz was somewhat typical. But
as a bilingual artisan and entrepreneur, he enjoyed higher status than most
Salvadoran immigrants, the majority of whom worked as unskilled laborers
on the United Fruit Company's banana plantations. Numerical pictures of
immigration hint at the reasons that Palestinian merchants materially supported the striking banana workers in 1954, going against the wishes of
the United Fruit Company and forging a brief cross-class alliance with their
working-class customers.

Just as in Brazil and Mexico, endogamy helped the Levantine immigrant
community in Honduras to maintain its cultural beliefs and practices.[39] In
1934, the ratio of men to women immigrants was far more balanced among
Palestinians than it was among Salvadorans. Of the 160 Palestinian immigrants to the state of Yoro in Honduras, 65 percent (104 people) were men
and 35 percent (56 people) were women.[40] In contrast, of the 1,840 immigrants from El Salvador, 82 percent (1,505 people) were men and only 18
percent (335 people) were women.

With respect to marital status, a stunning 75 percent (119) of Palestinian immigrants were married, as compared to only 13 percent (234) of
Salvadoran immigrants. Thus most first-generation Palestinians emigrated
with the structures of their nuclear families already in place, and among
those who did not, many traveled back to Palestine to be married and subsequently returned to Honduras to start a family. Cultural continuity was
reinforced by the close proximity within which immigrant families from
the Levant established their businesses and built their houses. The homes
and shops of the most prominent among them—including members of the
Mahchi, Hawit, Gabrie, Solimán, and Bendeck families—surrounded the
Ramón Rosa Plaza and the offices of the municipal government. Although
there were certainly exceptions, as in the Mahchi and Gabrie families,
second-generation immigrants from Palestine most often married within
their ethnic community.

The desire to maintain cultural beliefs and practices was one reason for
intragroup marriage. Another reason was that the largely endogamous
community of Palestinian Hondurans was often rejected by the creole

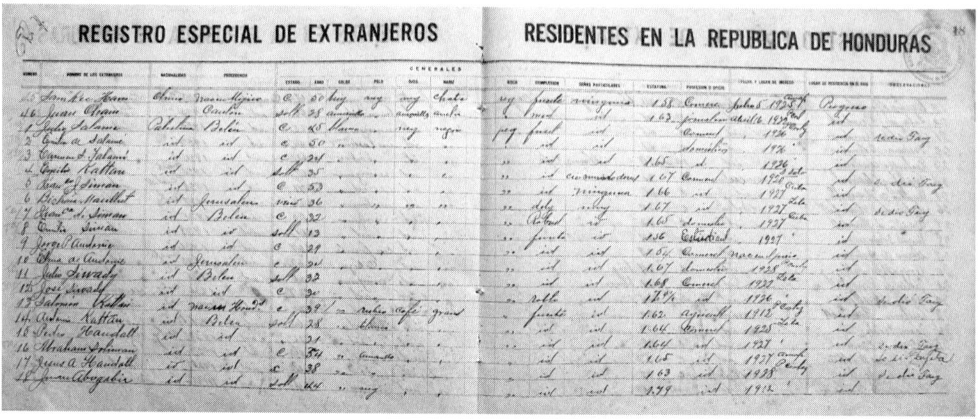

Fig. 5.11. A page from "Registro especial de extranjeros: Residentes en la República de Honduras, 1934." *Archivo de Gobernación, Department of Yoro.*

political elite of Honduras and by the US fruit companies, which, starting in the 1910s, opened their own company stores around their expanding plantations. As historian Darío A. Euraque has noted, Arab Christian merchants complained about the "commercial monopoly" of the United Fruit Company and were then accused by the US consuls of being "non-Honduran agitators." According to Euraque, actions such as these led Palestinian Hondurans to align themselves more with their working-class customers than with the North American fruit companies or the *criollo* political elite that relied upon the economic and industrializing power of the banana companies.[41] Hence Palestinian immigrants had to walk a fine line and were constantly risked betraying their social class.

With respect to race, the low-level Honduran bureaucrats who created the 1934 Registry of Foreigners for the Department of Yoro classified a full 80 percent (115) of Palestinian immigrants as "white"; in contrast, only 9 percent (147) of Salvadoran immigrants were deemed "white."[42]

Fig. 5.12. Although it is listed as 1934, this survey of foreigners living in the Department of Yoro was completed in 1965. Rafael Platero Paz, inscribed here as number 14, was the main photographer for this project of state identification. *Archivo de Gobernación, Department of Yoro.*

Meanwhile, only 18 percent (26) of Palestinian immigrants were marked as brown-skinned (*trigueño*), while 82 percent (1,415) of Salvadoran immigrants were categorized as *trigueño*.[43] This perceived racial difference correlated with sharp differences in occupation for the respective groups. Sixty-two percent (99) of Palestinian immigrants were listed in the registry as merchants, compared with only 1 percent of Salvadoran immigrants. At the same time, 57 percent (1,053) of Salvadorans were listed as day laborers (*jornaleros*). Social class undoubtedly played a role in the "whitening" of Middle Eastern immigrants and the "darkening" of Salvadorans.

With respect to gendered aspects of social mobility, early twentieth-century Palestinian women were slightly freer to work outside of the home than were their Salvadoran counterparts. Perhaps this greater autonomy was due to cultural codes, but it was more likely a by-product of structural forces, including the greater capital reserves that Palestinians could draw upon to open their own businesses. One woman who drew upon these reserves was Emilia Hawit, who founded a bakery in 1948 that is still based in El Progreso and that by 2011 had annual revenue of $5.6 million.[44] Furthermore, Salvadoran women often worked from home, supplementing the incomes of their domestic partners by selling prepared meals or washing clothes. Salvadoran women were more often listed as being dedicated to *oficios domésticos*.[45]

In short, these two immigrant populations—Palestinian and Salvadoran—were very differently constituted. But what they had in common was precisely their status as immigrants, as outsiders. Palestinians in El Progreso stand in for a whole range of in-between populations, all of which were less visible and less able than the Arab Christians to earn public recognition through the legitimate means of donating the seal of the republic or trading in expensive merchandise. Salvadoran artisans and banana workers, Chinese hotel owners, the Garifuna, West Indian laborers, and indigenous Hondurans who strategically claimed descent from ancient Mayan civilizations: each of these groups struggled to be included as equals, as citizens who had the same rights to speak, be seen, and act as the creole elites in Tegucigalpa.

The single example of Salvadorans demonstrates how an even more precarious in-between community negotiated its visual citizenship in Yoro. Between 1946 and 1956, Arab Christian immigrants made up nearly 40 percent of the total number of naturalized Honduran citizens. This is especially striking given the vastly greater number of Salvadorans who were foreigners living in a strange land but did not become naturalized citizens of

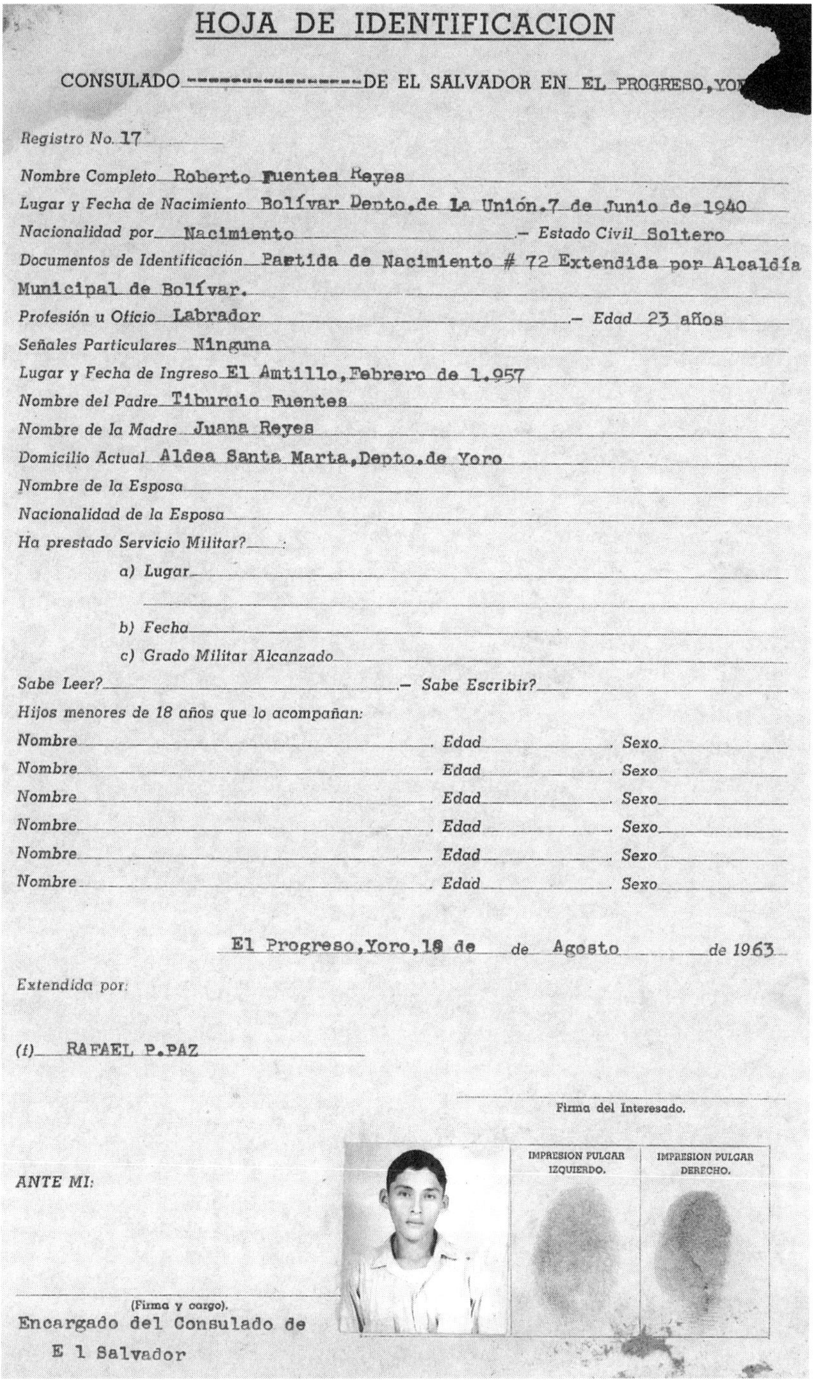

HOJA DE IDENTIFICACION

CONSULADO ~~~~~~~~~~~~~~~DE EL SALVADOR EN EL PROGRESO, YO?

Registro No. 17

Nombre Completo Roberto Fuentes Reyes

Lugar y Fecha de Nacimiento Bolívar Depto.de La Unión.7 de Junio de 1940

Nacionalidad por Nacimiento .— Estado Civil Soltero

Documentos de Identificación Partida de Nacimiento # 72 Extendida por Alcaldía Municipal de Bolívar.

Profesión u Oficio Labrador .— Edad 23 años

Señales Particulares Ninguna

Lugar y Fecha de Ingreso El Amtillo,Febrero de 1.957

Nombre del Padre Tiburcio Fuentes

Nombre de la Madre Juana Reyes

Domicilio Actual Aldea Santa Marta,Depto.de Yoro

Nombre de la Esposa

Nacionalidad de la Esposa

Ha prestado Servicio Militar? :

    a) Lugar

    b) Fecha

    c) Grado Militar Alcanzado

Sabe Leer? .— Sabe Escribir?

Hijos menores de 18 años que lo acompañan:

Nombre _____ Edad _____ Sexo _____

Nombre _____ Edad _____ Sexo _____

Nombre _____ Edad _____ Sexo _____

Nombre _____ Edad _____ Sexo _____

Nombre _____ Edad _____ Sexo _____

Nombre _____ Edad _____ Sexo _____

El Progreso,Yoro,18 de de Agosto de 1963

Extendida por:

(f) RAFAEL P.PAZ

Firma del Interesado.

ANTE MI:

	IMPRESION PULGAR IZQUIERDO.	IMPRESION PULGAR DERECHO.

(Firma y cargo).

Encargado del Consulado de
  E l Salvador

Fig. 5.13. Identification document. *Courtesy of the Rafael Platero Paz Archive.*

Honduras.[46] As we saw in the hunting of Rafael Platero Paz and other Salvadorans during the brief 1969 war with El Salvador, the pressure on the land from the Honduran peasantry was coupled with escalating right-wing rhetoric that increasingly scapegoated the approximately 300,000 undocumented Salvadoran immigrants and the ineffectual first military government of General Oswaldo López Arellano. In 1964, Platero Paz himself had aided the Honduran government in asserting its power to decide who deserved state recognition and protection and who was merely a governed noncitizen. Serving as the Salvadoran consulate's local representative in El Progreso, Platero Paz made hundreds of identity cards for Salvadorans who were compelled by the Honduran government to formally identify themselves as citizens of El Salvador (figure 5.13). Taking each of these ID photos and filling out the *hoja de identificación* for nearly seven hundred Salvadorans living in and around El Progreso certainly increased his income. Little did he realize that, less than five years later, his own work in making visible the boundary between citizen and noncitizen would prove crucial in expelling Salvadorans from Honduran territory. In April 1969, the Honduran government announced that it would expel anyone who was not a Honduran citizen by birth and who had acquired land through the agrarian reform measures that were initiated by President Ramón Villeda Morales in 1958. Between April and July 1969, between 60,000 and 130,000 Salvadorans fled Honduras into an already densely populated El Salvador.

CREATING AN INTERMEDIATE, CREATIVE SPACE

Close readings of the family photographs of Palestinian immigrants reveal how members of this ethnic group appropriated a particular international currency of material and social progress while distancing themselves from those dimensions of Honduran nationalism that posited them as the constitutive other. Even in the case of gifting the national seal to the republic, the outsider status of the givers was revealed by their unfulfilled desire to belong. But while the descendants of Palestinian immigrants have wanted to be considered Honduran in particular contexts, they also sought to maintain their international identity, which often paid greater dividends both at home and abroad.

Being visibly modern has never meant being visibly Honduran. And the past in Honduras is seen as the backwardness (except in the public commemorations that invoke a folkloric past whose signifiers are imported from Mexico) that the country can never quite leave behind. This past was

Rafael Platero Paz created this advertising still and projected it onto the big screen at the local movie theater, Teatro Moderno. *Courtesy of the Rafael Platero Paz Archive.*

Visualizing the landscape. Tela Railroad Company flooding projects on the banana plantations around El Progreso, 1951. *Courtesy of the Rafael Platero Paz Archive.*

Six years after Emanuel Leutze painted his epic *Westward* mural in the US Capitol, Frances Palmer took the same title to make a more explicit picture of western expansionism, *Across the Continent: "Westward the Course of Empire Takes Its Way"* (1868). *Courtesy of the Amon Carter Museum of American Art, Fort Worth, Texas.*

The endpapers of *Conquest of the Tropics*, by Frederick Upham Adams.

"Great White Fleet Cruises from New York to the Caribbean and West Indies, Winter 1939–1940." Equipped with outdoor swimming pools, library, gift shop, lounge, barbershop, hospital, smoking room, and various classes of rooms, the ships carried North American tourists to Guatemala, Havana, Costa Rica, Honduras, Jamaica, Colombia, and the Panama Canal Zone. *United Fruit Passenger Service brochure.*

Carmen Miranda in *The Gang's All Here* (1943).

Consumer culture is often driven by commodity fetishism, a cultural process that effectively erases the labor that goes into making a given product, whether a banana or an iPhone, by transforming it into a fetish object. In a marketing campaign that made working conditions invisible to the consumer, Miss Chiquita invited North Americans to consume the tropics by identifying the image with the product itself, which was emptied of the meaning of its production and the labor that went into growing it. *Chiquita Banana advertisement, circa 1954.*

Poster from the 1971 film.

Postcard by J. A. Doubleday. *Courtesy of the Museo de Antropología e Historia de San Pedro Sula.*

Front and back of a postcard dated August 9, 1911.
Courtesy of Eric Schwimmer.

Front of a postcard dated June 10, 1911.
Courtesy of Eric Schwimmer.

Identification document. *Courtesy of the Rafael Platero Paz Archive.*

HOJA DE IDENTIFICACION

CONSULADO ----------------DE EL SALVADOR EN EL PROGRESO,YO

Registro No. 17

Nombre Completo Roberto Fuentes Reyes
Lugar y Fecha de Nacimiento Bolívar,Depto.de LA Unión.7 de Junio de 1940
Nacionalidad por Nacimiento — Estado Civil Soltero
Documentos de Identificación Partida de Nacimiento # 72 Extendida por Alcaldía
Municipal de Bolívar.
Profesión u Oficio Labrador — Edad 23 años
Señales Particulares Ninguna
Lugar y Fecha de Ingreso El Antillo,Febrero de 1.957
Nombre del Padre Tiburcio Fuentes
Nombre de la Madre Juana Reyes
Domicilio Actual Aldea Santa Marta,Depto.de Yoro
Nombre de la Esposa
Nacionalidad de la Esposa
Ha prestado Servicio Militar?
      a) Lugar
      b) Fecha
      c) Grado Militar Alcanzado
Sabe Leer? — Sabe Escribir?
Hijos menores de 18 años que lo acompañan:
Nombre Edad Sexo
Nombre Edad Sexo
Nombre Edad Sexo
Nombre Edad Sexo
Nombre Edad Sexo
Nombre Edad Sexo

El Progreso,Yoro,18 de de Agosto de 1963

Extendida por:

(f) RAFAEL P.PAZ

ANTE MI:

Encargado del Consulado de
E l Salvador

The gap in Democracy. Or, as Agence France-Presse captioned the image, "One of the lanes of 'La Democracia' bridge over the Ulua river, built by the French in 1963, had its central section collapse due to an earthquake May 28, 2009, in El Progreso, 270 km north of Tegucigalpa." *Courtesy of Orlando Sierra, Agence France-Presse/Getty Images.*

Tegucigalpa, July 2009. With critical media outlets silenced, political activists took to the walls. With several visual slurs, they depicted former President Carlos Roberto Flores Facussé. *Photograph by the author.*

June 29, 2009. This photograph, taken by Esteban Felix for the Associated Press, was published in the *New York Times* and captioned, "The riot police dispersed supporters of the ousted president on Monday near the presidential palace in the capital, Tegucigalpa." *AP Photo/Esteban Felix.*

poignantly represented in the first photograph of Guillermo Mahchi's book, *El archivo fotográfico del ayer*, which depicted "the ancient inhabitants" of El Progreso in front of their straw huts. The construction of the town of El Progreso—by *criollo* elites, the United Fruit Company, and urban notables like the Mahchis—represented a clear break from that past.

The fact that Palestinian immigrants crafted, and were in fact pushed to craft, transnational identities meant that their gaze was cast more toward Jerusalem, Europe, and the United States than it was toward Tegucigalpa. Because of their origins, their occupation, and the communitarian narrowness that they sometimes encountered in Honduras, Arab Christian immigrants often identified more with an imagined community in far-flung capitals than they did with their neighbors in El Progreso. But this means that the unifying power of nationalism, and the sense of mutual responsibility that it inculcates, was less able to work its magic on Palestinian Honduran consciousness. Consequently, the resulting subjective orientation and accompanying sense of moral obligation was largely toward other members of this minority group who found themselves in the sometimes hostile environment of Honduras and toward abstract members of a community of modernity in places farther away.

The Mahchi family photographs exemplify a pattern of representational strategies employed by an ethnic minority that over the course of the twentieth century accumulated deep and diverse capital holdings in Honduras. These photographs helped to produce a new discursive formation, one that was used strategically to supersede a national one that threatened to exclude them. As photographs capture the world, they are simultaneously structuring it. From right within the banana enclave, Palestinian Hondurans asserted a new kind of visual citizenship, one that operated according to a logic of affiliation and belonging within modernity and subtly challenged the extractive, imperial rationality of the banana republic.

Examining the family photographs of Palestinian Hondurans enables us to move beyond contrasting the local to the foreign and to inquire into the intermediate spaces of El Progreso, into the contact zones that Platero Paz's *Garden of Eden* photograph suggests. Palestinian merchants connected ordinary *progreseños* to the outside world through cultural objects of consumption, from Stetson hats to Buicks. Such objects enabled this group of pariah entrepreneurs to overcome their outsider status by presenting themselves as a conduit of transnational artifacts of modernity. While the United Fruit Company brought US science and engineering to the banana plantations, it also brought disciplinary oversight, rigid hierarchies, and constant reminders of exclusion, powerfully condensed in the architecture of the American Zones. The Palestinian merchants likewise brought merchandise from the United States; but unlike the United Fruit Company, they offered these goods to banana workers and their families who came into their stores and interacted with them as potential buyers who incidentally chatted about prices, the weather, and family while choosing whether or not to purchase the goods on offer.

The family photos of Palestinian Hondurans reveal how they laid claim to an intermediate and connective space that was neither wholly Palestinian nor Honduran, but somehow both. These improbably successful merchants and their families produced a transnational imagescape that reflected their somewhat precarious but nevertheless global ties. On the edge of the early twentieth-century US empire, they were local agents of a notion of modernity and group identity that recognized the commodities and symbols of North America and Europe while also preserving cultural and ethnic memories of their homeland. Palestinian Honduran family photographs demonstrate how members of this ethnic group appropriated a particular international currency of material and social progress while distancing themselves from those dimensions of Honduran nationalism that excluded them.

Both Platero Paz's homo-Edenic self-portrait and the family photographs of Palestinians in Honduras suggest that if the banana republic was the cipher of one particular arrangement of what could be seen, said, and done, then that arrangement could be challenged through split-second assertions of subjectivity. That is, in contrast to what Jacques Rancière describes as a politics of disagreement that interrupts how the sensible is distributed, Platero Paz and the Palestinian merchants in Honduras worked a certain redistribution of the sensible through minute acts of self-making, captured and registered by photography. Writing in Arabic, posing naked with another man: these minor feats repartitioned, ever so slightly, the perceptible.

Palestinians and Salvadorans living in the banana-company towns of Honduras could not help but become aware that they were othered and that their ways of doing things were natural to them but not necessarily to Hondurans, West Indians, or US managers living in the American Zone. They, like the workers in the plantations and like the subject before the camera, saw that culture was mutable and that they could, in effect, choose their passions, habits, and ideas. Such self-awareness was part of how Palestinian immigrants managed the impossible, becoming wildly successful economically in the second-poorest country in the Western Hemisphere. Unlike the United Fruit Company officials, Palestinian merchants did not enclose themselves in comparatively luxurious ghettos called American Zones. Salvadorans, for their part, never had the luxury of choosing a self-enclosed existence that was both inside and outside the banana zone.

The nation-state had occasionally attempted to ban Palestinians and physically expel Salvadorans from Honduras. Living in El Progreso, members of each of these groups were pressured at various times throughout the twentieth century to acknowledge that they were not Honduran. In accepting that negative definition, they were simultaneously able to positively define who they were. They could choose to be better than Honduran, which was officially defined more by place of birth than by way of being. Willfully accepting an external compulsion, those who gave the gift of the Honduran seal to the republic demonstrated that they had ascended economically and culturally such that they could recognize and authenticate the nation-state that sometimes sought to exclude them.

SIX

In Visibility in an Exceptional Space

Only by zooming out to see how the Honduran state dealt with the movements for democratic reform prior to the 1954 strike does the incredible visibility of that massive worker-driven declaration of economic, political, and cultural independence begin to make sense. So to get to that event in El Progreso, the moment that redefined modern Honduras, we must first pass through the constitutional dictatorship of Tiburcio Carías Andino, which sought to centralize state power and to produce a population that the state could see, know, and direct. Understanding basic elements of this crucial period will set in firm relief what was at stake when 25,000 workers decided to withhold their labor in 1954.

On the Fourth of July 1944 in the city of San Pedro Sula, a few hundred citizens marked the anniversary of the US Declaration of Independence with a march through the streets. Some demonstrators threatened to go on strike if President Carías, who had been in office since 1932, did not step down within ten days. The Carías regime responded by arresting the demonstrators. A prominent group of *sampedranos*—including Rodolfo

Pastor Zelaya and Graciela Bográn—immediately formed a strike committee to protest the arrests. Two days later, with the explicit authorization of the minister of war, Juan Manuel Gálvez, a peaceful and silent group of urban middle- and working-class citizens began to process silently through the streets of San Pedro Sula. Suddenly, with no warning or provocation, a soldier shot one of the prodemocracy demonstrators, Alejandro Irías. The army then opened fire on the crowd. The US vice consul later confirmed that the military had gunned down at least twenty-two people and wounded many men, women, and children.[1]

This was a turning point. The indiscriminate murder of democratic reformists in San Pedro Sula laid bare the regime's two-pronged approach to governing: clientelistic privileges for its supporters, the most stalwart of which were the large landholders, and brute force against those who questioned the legitimacy of Carías's continued rule.[2] As Julio César Rivera, a schoolteacher and labor leader from El Progreso, later recalled, "The massacre that occurred in San Pedro Sula in 1944 shocked the Honduran people and dramatically impressed me. It crossed all barriers of inhumanity. Days later, I began to ponder the injustice, and ultimately, that led me to fight to change the political situation."[3] The killing of innocent people for publicly expressing their political views congealed into a sort of mental picture that Liberal Party activists and the Honduran Left carried with them as a reminder of what they wanted to change. It facilitated their further separation from the regime, giving them reasons for de-identifying with the Carías government and new ideas around which to nurture an alternative vision for their country. The dictatorship rightly detected that in publicly demonstrating, an influential sector of the Honduran middle class had subjectively aligned itself with north coast labor to produce new truths. As they performed their disagreement with the regime and dared to make democratic demands, workers and Liberals began to reintroduce politics back into the public sphere, challenging the pact between Carías's National Party and the United Fruit Company to produce a properly Honduran political discourse. But given that the government had banned public assembly, such marches were considered criminal acts, and combating threats to the public order provided the justification for Carías to remain in power. "I prefer to assume all of the resulting historical responsibilities," Carías declared years earlier, "rather than see my Country serving again as a pasture for criminal guerrilla groups and irresponsible agitators."[4]

Under Carías, the country was materially, and not merely rhetorically, a banana republic, with a dictator who owed much of his power to the US fruit companies. If the banana enclaves were spatial exceptions, then the banana republic was the nationalization of this legal black hole. In declaring and maintaining an *estado de sitio*, or martial law, for seven years, the Carías regime and its congressional enablers decoupled the entirety of Honduran territory from its own constitutional framework and subjected the population to the whims of a personalist authoritarian leader who was propped up by US companies.

STATE OF SIEGE

The 1898 constitution was by any measure a triumph of liberal thought, as it created a legal framework for the development of a free and representative government. But even this constitution spelled out that when a state of siege (*estado de sitio*) was declared, "any or all of the following guarantees are suspended:

> Free immigration and emigration.
> Movement.
> Assembly, except for scientific and industrial objectives or for diversions.
> Due process for the crimes referred to in Article 5 [treason, rebellion, and sedition, and against the peace, independence, and sovereignty of the Republic].
> Inviolability of the home.
> Freedom of the press.
> Inviolability of correspondence by letter or telegraph, and
> Trial by jury for crimes within the jurisdiction of military authorities.[5]

Subsequent Honduran constitutions would widen the scope of the state of siege law, and nearly every president between 1890 and 1956 would exercise the emergency measures that it legally permitted. During this period, an *estado de sitio* was declared or extended on at least seventy-four occasions. In addition, freedoms of speech, the press, assembly, and private property were suspended at least twenty-nine times, and five constitutions were signed.[6]

Honduran legal documents denote the state of siege as *estado de sitio*.[7] Both terms precisely denote a case in which the sovereign suspends the guarantees of the law to preserve the legal order. Who the "sovereign" is changes from one context to another—it can be a popular collective agent embodied in a supreme court or the president of a country. The key, though, is that the declaration of a state of siege exposes some portion of the population to the violence that the sovereign, with the repressive apparatus at his disposal, wishes to inflict to purportedly hold off anarchy. In suspending the writ of habeas corpus, for example, the president and Congress simultaneously suspend judicial oversight of police and military detentions, no longer requiring that jailers bring their prisoners before judges to state the crimes of which they are accused. So in suspending the judicial review of detentions that was guaranteed by Article 27 of the Honduran Constitution of 1906, the executive and legislative branches prevented judges from fulfilling one of their most important duties.[8] The suspension clause undoes judicial oversight and holds in abeyance the authority of judges to inspect what the administrative and repressive arms of the state are doing to the

Fig. 6.1. The surveillance photos created by Carías's National Police reveal the tight connection between the suspension of the law and rendering the citizenry visible to the sovereign. Historian Jesús Evelio Inestroza unearthed a trove of secret documents on political dissidents, including photographs of their intercepted correspondence and sketches of their residences. From the documents, it is clear that the secret police closely tracked the communications and movement of hundreds, perhaps thousands, of people that it considered its opponents. Photographs became photocopies for sharing information within the police state. *From the private collection of Jesús Evelio Inestroza M.*

governed. Furthermore, the state of siege does not simply apply to one individual (such as a convicted criminal); it extends to "the Republic, or part of it." To suspend the entitlements of a people to move, speak, and live freely is to take freedom and power away from ordinary citizens so that it can be concentrated in the hands of the head of state.

Examining the Honduran state's use of the legal mechanism of suspending the law thus enables a reconsideration of the lives of those set outside the law, people whom the sovereign decided could be legally killed. These two poles—authoritarian power and the power of the dispossessed working together—form one axis of inquiry. A second axis, intersecting with the first, is visibility, with the seen on one side and the unseen on the other. One way of understanding the struggles of workers on the banana plantations is as an ongoing struggle to make their plight visible to power. But with such vast inequalities and differential access to instruments of violence, creating conditions of visibility often entailed clandestinity. In the state of exception, the sovereign commanded but never fully achieved that those deemed "rebels" remain either silent and invisible or in exile. And even then, they could still find themselves vulnerable to the authorized violence of the state.

FORCE OF LAW, 1933-1948

The most important issue in the elections of October 1932 was the position of candidates vis-à-vis the United States. The candidate from the Liberal Party was an urban intellectual named Ángel Zúñiga Huete; he stood to the left of the relatively moderate Liberal president he wished to succeed. The candidate from the National Party, Tiburcio Carías Andino, was a caudillo who built a disciplined political organization and cultivated the moral and material support of the United Fruit Company. After Carías won in a landslide, disaffected military officers revolted on November 12, 1932. Sitting President Vicente Mejía Colindres immediately declared a state of exception and renewed it in December.[9] Then Mejía Colindres—who had been continually dogged by the uprisings of campesinos and workers led by populists like Gregorio Ferrera from within his own Liberal Party—turned to Carías for help. Seeking to secure his succession to the presidency, Carías shrewdly agreed and began coopting dissidents from the Liberal Party and establishing bases of local support in each of the country's departments. As the Honduran state faced the threat of another civil war and found itself without cash to pay its fighting force, it turned to the United Fruit Company, which loaned the government $25,000 to continue paying loyal troops to put down the rebellion. The only condition on the loan was that the new government adopt measures beneficial to the company on pending issues.[10] There would be no more official protests that the company was building illegal and clandestine railway lines while failing to build the interoceanic railroad that it had promised.

It worked. Carías was sworn in as president on February 1, 1933. Exactly two weeks later, he issued Decree Number 123, indefinitely extending the state of siege issued by Mejía Colindres a couple of months earlier.[11] Liberals and Nationals thus cited prior decrees of an *estado de sitio* as a way to render their own suspension of constitutional guarantees legitimate. This topology of citation and decision—of the extension of a state of exception already in effect and the declaration that civil laws were indefinitely suspended—is the defining feature of Carías's rule. Early twentieth-century Honduran legal history thus illustrates the facticity of the sovereign's decision. As the threshold for what counted as a necessary reason for suspending the law was successively lowered, the suspension of legal guarantees came to rest less on the decision and more on the momentum of precedent. Once in a state of exception, the point of decision often came about on a case-by-case basis as the sovereign and his deputies decided who counted as a "rebel," a "terrorist," or a "traitor."

After taking office, Carías continued to enjoy the financial support of the United Fruit Company. Renewing and indefinitely extending the state of siege not only allowed him to act with impunity to quell dissent in the countryside but also enabled him to keep frequent injections of fruit-company money off the official books and to arm his newly salaried recruits to clear his political opponents from the countryside.[12] Carías's regional military commanders enjoyed good, regular salaries as well as funds to build schools, roads, and bridges and the authorization to use force at their discretion. These commanders were the ones who meted out especially violent and capricious punishments for criticizing the government. For example, the *comandante de armas* of Atlántida, Carlos Sanabria, ordered the assassination of Arturo Martínez Galindo, a journalist, literary critic, and outspoken dissident.[13] Beyond the regional military commanders, who earned a quite respectable salary of between 8,000 and 10,000 lempiras a month, Carías created a special forces unit that the US banana and mining companies supported with housing, transportation, food, and weapons.[14] To further exert control over the countryside, he created a mounted police unit and an air force. Through intimidation and patronage, the Cariato built a centralized state capable of projecting its power and propaganda throughout Honduran territory.

From before the postelection uprisings that Carías helped to put down and throughout his nearly sixteen years in office, lawmaking and law-preserving violence formed the bedrock of the *cariísta* state.[15] The indefinite state of exception continued in effect into 1934, and then the Congress renewed it again, this time setting it to expire at the end of July 1934.[16]

Fig. 6.2. In this photo from 1933, President Carías, Lowell Yerex, and various functionaries pose in front of the new Stinson monoplanes purchased for the Honduran air force. As early as 1931, well before he even took office, Carías ordered the bombing of positions held by dissident liberals. In 1934 he founded the Escuela de Aviación Militar, and throughout nearly the entire *cariísta* dictatorship it was run by US Army Colonel William Brooks, who also helped out by flying reconnaissance and military resupply missions. By 1942 the air force had twenty-two planes and an arsenal of new machine guns, rifles, bombs, and other equipment, much of it purchased from the United States at less than 10 percent of the cost of the material delivered. The regime also regularly outsourced the shipment of arms, supplies, and troops to various companies, including Empresa Dean, TACA, and the United and Standard Fruit Companies. For the first time, as soon as resistance erupted, the Honduran state was able to snuff it out before it spread. *Courtesy of Eric Schwimmer.*

Fig. 6.3. The countenance of Carías. *From the Colección Guilbert of the Instituto Hondureño de Antropología e Historia.*

WE ARE REVEALED BEFORE HIM

In government offices throughout the country, imposing portraits of Carías hung on the walls. Below each portrait of the president was the following: "Honduras acclaims that General Carías, the voice of the people, is the voice of God."[17] In the enormous portraits of the leader with his furrowed brow, thick mustache, direct gaze, and presidential sash across his chest, Carías made himself present to the people. The regime—through embedding visual images in a reliogio-political narrative disseminated through its own newspapers and in radio broadcasts—managed to endow its leader with sacred qualities. From the Reforma Liberal of the 1880s up until the reign of Carías, Honduran leaders had invoked God and nation, but without forging a way for the people to experience their citizenship as sacred.[18] Carías brought "Peace and Order." In the foyer of the Palace of the Central District in Tegucigalpa, a plaque gushingly expressed the theological drive behind *cariísta* politics:

Facing the Portrait of General Carías
By Alejandro Alfaro Arraga

We are revealed before him, his name inspires
This moral strength that carries the symbol
And the glory has encircled his head like a halo.
[. . .]
Revering the sounds of his name
And leaning, looking at his portrait.[19]

In coming to power through bloodshed, Carías sought to reestablish the Honduran state. In maintaining his power through an ongoing state of siege and an unstinting use of law-preserving violence, the Carías regime decided who could be set outside the political community and who belonged within it. Through a vast apparatus of surveillance, the governed were quite literally revealed before him. And in photographs of the head of state and his loyalists, the *cariístas* made their leader present, at least through simulacra, to the governed. He could see them and they could see him. But the governed were imperfect images of General Carías. While identifying with his rural-urban masculine persona—as a rustic general with a bushy mustache and as a three-piece-suit-wearing executive in Tegucigalpa—they also feared that he might, at any moment, cast them out of the Garden.

The main innovation of the Constitution of 1936 was that it extended the presidential term limits from four to six years, enabling Carías to continue in office without facing elections until 1943.[20] Given that the authoritarian populist was indeed elected in 1932, the Constitution of 1936 marks the official beginning of the Carías dictatorship, shrouded in the transcendental rhetoric of the nation. With this, the sovereign reenacted his lawmaking power: the constitutional convention "worked patriotically to give the nation a new constitution more in line with current trends toward the greater good and the highest culture."[21] Such patriotic work was helped along with $200,000 from the United Fruit Company for the "political expenses" of engineering *continuismo*.[22] In 1936, Congress also elaborated a new law for the state of siege and the Ley de Amparo (a legal protection that is broader than habeas corpus in that it enables a failure to properly implement a law to be transformed into a violation of the Constitution).[23] While the Constitution of 1924 emphasized relations between labor and capital, the Constitution of 1936 shifted the focus to work and the family.[24]

"Dios también es continuista" were the words of Plutarco Muñoz, president of the National Congress and a Carías loyalist. In December 1940, the Congress decreed that Carías would govern until 1949 and bestowed a new title upon him: "Founder and Defender of the Peace of Honduras and Benefactor of the Patria."[25] A year later, the executive branch solicited "the suspension of constitutional guarantees as a consequence of the declaration of war made by Honduras against the Japanese empire, motivated by the illegitimate aggression of this country against the United States of America, with whom Honduras maintains friendly relations and agreements of solidarity and mutual cooperation." On these grounds, the law was set aside in Honduras for five more years, from 1941 to 1946.[26]

To drive home the point, Congress also signed off on a bill that required government censorship of the mail, emphasizing that Honduras was now in a state of war with Japan and that all individual civil liberties had been suspended.[27] In 1943, Congress decreed a strict new censorship law that not only monitored what private citizens and the press said and published but also required that companies get government approval prior to publishing works on the politics, economy, and social life of the nation.[28]

THE GALLERY OF DELINQUENTS

The monthly government magazine *La Revista de Policía* began publication in 1932 and continued throughout the Carías dictatorship. Each issue featured prominent advertisements from the most important brands: TACA airlines, Pepsi, Goodyear, Seagram's, Cerveza Imperial, Victoria soaps and candles, Esso, King Bee cigarettes and local vendors Casa Rossner, Bon Marché owned by Salomón Barjun, La Palestina de Julio Mourra, La Selecta owned by Carmen Matamoros, Santos Soto Sucursales, and La Moda de París owned by Hasbum and Brothers. Cultural critic Héctor M. Leyva has argued that this large-circulation magazine was crucial to the Cariato's construction and policing of public morality. Comprised of several sections— literature, history, identification of delinquents, updates on police training and scientific discoveries that could be used in policing—the magazine was produced to persuade, shame, and publicly demonstrate the severity and righteousness of the Carías regime's pursuit of order and progress. Each month, between 1,000 and 1,500 copies were printed and distributed throughout Honduras, including to subscribers in El Progreso and abroad.[29]

The magazine was part of the regime's focus on showing the public the wide support it enjoyed through parades in honor of Carías and letters he received from across the country and by the way he humbly declined to have a statue erected in his honor. The magazine performed the seeing and showing characteristic of the Cariato. On the one hand, the *Revista de Policía* offered a monthly reminder that the regime could prevent, find, and punish wrongs committed anywhere in Honduran territory. On the other, it was a place for citizens to regularly broadcast their joy at "being identified with the constructive politics of our Chief of State."[30] But just as the regime displayed the dangerous unseen threats to the body politic, it may also have revealed that such perceived threats were not so scary and that the punishments meted out were heavy-handed.

In the "Galería de Deliquentes," readers found photographs of children and poor people publicly shamed for such minor crimes as pilfering a steel brush from a carpenter's shop, snatching hens from a neighbor's yard, nabbing a fountain pen, and making off with small quantities of money and a bracelet (figure 6.4). Twelve-year-old boys and eight-year-old girls were regularly subjected to the violence of an encounter with a camera and a public that the regime sought to construct and mobilize. The making of the photographs enacted each subject's induction under the law. These subjects—young María Eva Amador Medina and Leonor Mendieta Yanes, for example—were made to appear before the law and before the camera and were subsequently displayed as being outside the social order. In the *Revista de Policía*, the Carías regime repeatedly performed its construction of three kinds of visual citizens: those who showed their loyalty to the caudillo, those who embodied the force of law, and those who tried and failed to act beyond the reach of the law. As the state directed its subject-making pedagogy almost entirely at the poor and children who had allegedly committed minor acts of thievery, the privileged subjects against which it was not bringing the forces of law and photography to bear were exempted from the menacing scrutiny of the Carías regime. The US-owned fruit companies and the excessively brutal *comandantes de armas* continued to act without public scrutiny or the oversight of the judicial system.

During the very years in which the protections of the law were suspended by statutory means, the Carías regime waxed eloquent about the ethics of the police and the need for citizens to lawfully conduct themselves. "Public order and social norms consist of respecting the laws of the country," the *Revista de Policía* editorialized on a page advertising Zeizz-Ikon cameras and film and Leonar photographic paper that could be purchased at the stores of Werner Rischbieth and Company in Tegucigalpa.[31] In the Cariato, the languages of law and photography were simultaneously called

Fig. 6.4. An eighteen-year-old girl is arrested for stealing a wristwatch and a sixteen-year-old girl for stealing a small amount of money. *Revista de Policía*, April 1941.

upon to construct a new Honduras. The Carías government's "doctrine of peace should enter into the flesh and marrow of the Honduran people, along with sovereignty and national dignity."[32] But even as law was invoked, only the suspension clause was in effect. Meanwhile, photographic realism often rendered the very people whom the regime sought to brand as criminals and delinquents as nonthreatening children and destitute people who might have even been worthy of sympathy for having been unfairly made into public spectacles.

In early twentieth-century Brazil and Argentina, nationalist imaginaries were produced and made manifest in museums, monuments, and maps, as Jens Andermann has demonstrated. Applying Andermann's insight to the Honduran context enables us to understand how the Carías dictatorship created representations that trained a new way of seeing.[33] In the state of siege, the "Gallery of Delinquents," and the orchestrated mass support for the Carías government, we note the asymmetrical presence of a regime that sought to consolidate the institutions and ideology of the Honduran nation-state while also attempting to suppress the possibility of popular citizenship.

PUBLIC RALLIES

In early July 1944, just four days after the demonstrations against Carías that ended with state forces killing at least twenty-two people in San Pedro Sula, the pro-government newspapers began reporting on massive rallies in support of "our supreme leader, General Tiburcio Carías Andino."[34] The purpose of the rallies was to show the public, the opposition, and the United States that the dictatorship enjoyed broad popular backing. At each of the rallies, citizens were asked to publicly ally themselves with the regime by signing petitions. Newspapers featured testimonials from loyal supporters and photographs of throngs of adherents. The scenes were organized for the camera. In two front-page pictures, the masses in Tela face the photographer and, presumably, the speaker on the stage (figure 6.5). Flags wave prominently. These pictures were supplemented with numerous textual accounts of such demonstrations of support throughout the country. These were the first photographs ever published of the country's masses; it is no accident that they purported to show the massive support behind the Carías regime. Yet the march in San Pedro Sula and the violence directed against its participants were not seen in photographs. Instead, dissidence remained officially suppressed and persistently present in disturbing, unsanctioned mental images of what the public was not supposed to see.

But by late 1944, the United Fruit Company was looking for a way to transition, as Thomas J. Dodd has put it, "to a strongman who had popular support."[35] By 1946, Carías had decided to gradually turn power over to his handpicked successor, Juan Manuel Gálvez. That year, Carías lifted the state of siege, released many political prisoners, and allowed three opposition newspapers to open. In most of Central America, the period from 1944 to 1948 was generally one of reforms, democratization, and labor militancy; in contrast, Honduras experienced this era as one in which the guarantees of the constitution had only begun to be restored.[36] Such reforms were not,

Fig. 6.5. Pro-Carías masses in Tela. *La Época*, July 8, 1944, 4.

however, inconsequential. The relative opening and loosening of controls permitted long-repressed elements of civil society to begin reconstituting themselves. Still, reformism had its limits. In 1946, Congress decreed another law threatening foreigners with imprisonment or exile if they participated in "totalitarian activities" such as communist propagandizing.[37] The Carías dictatorship reversed the small gains made by workers during the 1920s and 1930s. It had imprisoned, exiled, and killed organizers of the labor movement while doing nothing to address the underlying grievances and the frustrations of workers.

A HONDURAN SPRING, 1946–1954

From January 1946 until December 1954, Hondurans generally enjoyed the guarantees of their constitution. Since 1890, this was the longest uninterrupted period in which constitutional protections of speech and movement and against unlawful search and seizure had been operative. Up until 1946, one law, the Ley de Estado de Sitio, had been consistently invoked, while nearly all the others, especially those that protected the rights of citizens, were suspended.

In contrast, during the reformist regime of President Juan Manuel Gálvez (1949–1954), the state of siege provision sat inoperative while nearly all of the other laws, including due process, freedom of speech and circulation, and habeas corpus, were in effect. During this crucial period, Hondurans could begin to publicly discuss their political differences and material grievances. Allowing exiled members of the Liberal Party to return home, Gálvez encouraged the gradual opening of the political sphere that had begun under Carías in 1946. The Gálvez administration initiated new efforts to modernize the state, enacting the country's first income tax law and creating the Banco Central and the Banco Nacional de Desarrollo, which provided credit for cotton growers, sugar cultivators, cattle ranchers, and small farmers.[38] The Gálvez administration also invested more in education and granted autonomy to the National University, a sharp departure from the politics of his mentor. In addition, Gálvez spent much of his time supervising public works projects and meeting with people in the villages.[39] In 1952, his administration signed a new law protecting working women and minors.[40]

But perhaps the most difficult and substantive demonstration of Gálvez's commitment to democracy and constitutional rule was his position toward labor. Five years after the massacre in San Pedro Sula and just eight months after Carías finally stepped down from seventeen years as president, a group of students decided to test how President Gálvez would respond to demands from the public. In August 1949, the Federación de Estudiantes

Fig. 6.6. Student demonstration in Tegucigalpa against the Tela Railroad Company, August 28, 1949. *Courtesy of Eric Schwimmer.*

Universitarios took to the streets of Tegucigalpa to protest the possibility that the government would sign a contract with the Tela Railroad Company to renew and expand all of its previous concessions for an additional twenty-five years.[41] The students carried signs reading, "We tell the people, Careful with the Company!" "Mothers tell their children: Avoid bad company!" "Not all people are students, but all students are people." "[United Fruit's] Virgil E. Scott believes that we are asleep. We will demonstrate to him that we are awake."

Another sign made a distinction that the United Fruit Company was unwilling to make—"With the Yankee people, yes! With Wall Street, no!" That is, it was not the people of the United States the students were protesting, it was the policies of US corporations. On a couple of banners, the students had painted an octopus, an iconic caricature of the United Fruit Company, with its eight arms wrapped around the entire territory of Honduras. A few students carried signs that paid homage to Padre José Trinidad Reyes, the founder of the Autonomous National University of Honduras: "Long live my students, Fr. Trino" and "Through my race, my spirit will speak." As the university students made their position known, onlookers gathered to watch the procession.

Joined by other *tegucigalpeños*, the students marched past a photography studio named Yo ("I") (figure 6.7). The plural *nosotros* ("we") was photographed as it passed the singular "Yo." The photographic capture of the crowd as it passed the studio suggests that perhaps the photographer selected a vantage point from which his own storefront could be inserted into the scene of a historic public action. This collective street show was itself designed for a spectator who saw with a camera eye. The photograph doubles the first mise-en-scène, in which the students staged a public dispute with the company to make a claim for Honduran sovereignty. The photographer then captured the crowd in front of a photo studio rather than in the Parque Central or in front of the offices of the municipal government or the national cathedral. Thus the image enacts a threefold visual interpellation: first, the active citizenry hails the photographer to recognize and re-present it as a group of political subjects marching collectively; second, in the very act of regarding itself being photographed, the active citizenry recognizes itself as such; and third, the photographer and the photograph hail the spectator who is removed from the immediate spatiotemporality of the public demonstration to recognize the active citizenry depicted.[42] Meanwhile, the studio whose sign announces its presence speaks of a more private and individualized mode of visual citizenship, one that is staged

Fig. 6.7. Student demonstration in Tegucigalpa against the Tela
Railroad Company, August 28, 1949. *Courtesy of Eric Schwimmer.*

within the confines of a room secluded from public view, a room with props that accepts one customer or a small group of customers at a time.

While none of the daily newspapers published photographs of the student demonstration, all of them offered what Marianne Hirsch might have called "prose pictures" of the event.[43] *Prensa Libre* noted, "It was an eminently civic demonstration." The article continued: "On Sunday it was confirmed once again that we are living through a democratic rebirth. . . . It was also confirmed, and the people applaud this, that with sober reasoning the current government is disposed to respect the rights of the citizenry." The article underscored the self-conscious, deliberate staging of the demonstration as a spectacle whose meanings the students sought to make palatable for a conservative society. "Along the entire route of the protest rally, only university students spoke so as to avoid misinterpretations," the paper reported, listing the names of eight student orators. "In the most important moment of the day, the students became solemn as they placed a laurel wreath over the bust of Fr. Reyes and sang, even more fervently than they had through the entire march, our National Anthem."[44] At least three daily newspapers—*Prensa Libre*, *El Día*, and *Vanguardia Revolucionaria*—explicitly discussed the negotiation of a new contract in terms of national sovereignty and the economic and legal control that the United Fruit Company stood to further consolidate if the contract were to be approved.[45] In a story on the company's treatment of its railroad workers, *Vanguardia Revolucionaria* also noted that in forcing its machinists and operators to work sixty-hour shifts, United Fruit was in violation of Article 191 of the Honduran Constitution: "But in Honduras . . . everything is permitted for the blond bosses and everything is denied to the workers."[46]

As the students enjoined their representatives in Congress to be "loyal servants of Honduras, a shoeless, sickly nation weakened in a thousand ways," they publicly dramatized a renewed and precarious quest for national sovereignty.[47] The cautious reaction of the main newspapers, pleasantly surprised that the Gálvez administration permitted the public to demonstrate against a policy that the traditional political class supported, points to why this mass demonstration was an extraordinary moment.

UNDERGROUND VERBAL PICTURES

The *Revista de Policía*, with its "Gallery of Delinquents," and *La Época*, with its photographs of massive rallies in support of the dictator, epitomize two different modes through which the Carías regime visually mediated the political. First, it exposed those it decided were outside the social order. Second, it delivered images of the people enthusiastically supporting their leader.

In historicizing the use of the suspension clause by the Carías dictatorship, I have attempted to offer a contingent reading of the *estado de sitio* that contrasts with the primitive law that philosopher Giorgio Agamben, in *Homo Sacer*, deduces from philological examples.[48] Contrary to what we might expect by applying Agamben's rather ahistorical notion of *homo sacer* to this Central American context, the suspension of the law in Honduras was based neither on a "first foundation of political life" nor on a metaphysical law of power.[49] Rather, the Carías regime declared a state of siege under specific neocolonial circumstances. My historical materialist reading of the suspension of the law privileged the state-making and economic development goals of early twentieth-century Honduran liberals and caudillos, the strategic interventions of US-based capital, and the instrumental uses of photography, newspapers, and airplanes, as well as the construction of public discourses of morality that were deployed to enlist the governed in a national project.

The Carías regime's visual mediation of the political also contrasts with the ways that the intended elimination of political dissent under a prolonged and repeated state of siege entailed the near-invisibility of opposition to the regime. We do not have photographs of protest during the most intense years of the Cariato. But as with the memories of the 1944 massacre in San Pedro Sula, the visual was verbally represented in what might be termed an underground movement of textual pictures that was paradoxically powerful for the absence of images of lives taken.[50] For such photographic images might have particularized that which language and memory had generalized. The San Pedro Sula massacre was not simply about the killing of Alejandro Irías and at least twenty-one other people; it was also about the government's willingness to physically eliminate any hint of opposition that might question or attempt to limit Carías's power. It was, most especially, about the dictatorship's unaccountable violence. The excessive indexicality of photographs may have singularized and localized what exiled Honduran intellectuals and local democratic activists took to be a metaphor for the broader conduct of the seventeen-year-old regime. And just as the Cariato banned visible opposition, the actual images of its peace and order could not but disappoint. The children, impoverished peasants, and urban squatters who were routinely featured in the "Gallery of Delinquents" looked a lot like the majority of Hondurans at the time.

Even in a situation of enforced invisibility, oppositional politics will not entirely disappear. Rather, through the most repressive period of the constitutional dictatorship of Tiburcio Carías Andino, complaints, outrage, and a sense that things could be otherwise were, for the most part, verbally mediated. As the historical possibility of openly making democratic demands was gradually created, the grievances and the rebellious spirit of an oppressed people would again become manifest. When Liberal Party activists, workers, and intellectuals took to the streets of San Pedro Sula in 1944, they prompted the regime to show that its continued rule was based primarily on force. By juridically and physically setting the governed outside the law, the Carías regime manufactured a presumed people out of a collection of individuals spread throughout the territory of Honduras. The emergence of a more cohesive and self-determined public would come later, in the collective political subjectivization of the 1954 strike.

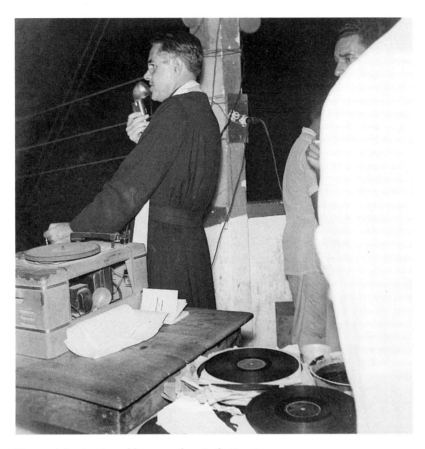

Fig. 7.1. A Jesuit priest addresses strikers in the Ramón
Rosa Plaza, 1954. *Courtesy of the Rafael Platero Paz Archive.*

SEVEN

Photographs of a Prayer

Sometime in May 1954, Joseph D. Wade, a Jesuit priest from the United States who served in El Progreso, addressed the striking banana workers who had gathered in the Ramón Rosa Plaza, a small urban park with a giant German-made clock atop an elevated gazebo. The rotunda from which he spoke was the architectural focal point of the offices of the municipal government on one side of the plaza and the stores of various Palestinian merchants that lined its other sides. As Fr. Wade addressed the workers, Rafael Platero Paz took a picture of him. The priest's clerical garb, age, nationality, and assumed learnedness conveyed authority. Unlike the studio portraits for which he was paid, Platero Paz most likely made this photograph without hope of remuneration, and more to document one moment in an important historical event (figure 7.1).

As a Jesuit trained in theology, philosophy, and Latin, Fr. Wade had made a series of decisions to separate himself from the day-to-day worries of secular and married life so that he could channel his energy into being a Catholic missionary in Honduras. His years of pastoral work with the banana-company laborers gave him a privileged vantage point for observing the strike. The attention that he had long paid to his own interior movements meant that he was especially attuned to observing how others experienced their own subjective transformations. When Platero Paz's photographs of the strike are contextualized with official sources as well as the testimonial literature created by the leaders of the strike and Fr. Wade's memoir of the event, it becomes clear that withholding one's labor in a situation of exploitation and humiliation has a purpose not unlike that of the Ignatian Spiritual Exercises, for both a work stoppage and a daily examination of conscience aim at conquering the self and regulating one's life free from inordinate attachments.[1] A priest, a photographer, and the testimonies of the workers themselves chart, from different vantage points, the workers' realization of their own political capacities as they dared to step away from their daily routines to demand higher wages and better treatment from the United Fruit Company. This stepping away from the established system of low but reliable wages to insist on a better arrangement hinged on an ethical operation. In agreeing to temporarily leave their quotidian world, the workers took a crucial step in cultivating their own ways of being, and in the process, they set about realizing their vision for a more equal relationship between Honduras and the United Fruit Company.

As a document, this picture is evidence of Fr. Wade's presence during the strike. His memoirs supplement this image, retrospectively describing his experience of the sixty-nine days when the banana workers withheld their labor. Platero Paz's social documentary photograph also hints at the theatrical and public nature of the strike. This priest was not in a church addressing parishioners from the altar. He was in the civic space of the Ramón Rosa Plaza.

Part of the event character of the strike was that it was staged as a spectacle, as a series of acts that were meant to be seen locally, nationally, and internationally. The 1954 strike was a declaration of independence performed by and for the workers. The force of that declaration was multiplied when a dispersed community of spectators could see the plight of those who labored in the plantations and hear their demands. Likewise, it was blunted by the workers' lack of exposure, by the fact that they toiled anonymously. Hence the strike was also staged for the camera, which duplicated the workers' acts of collective self-rule and made their demands visible to others beyond the immediate scene.

With the scene set for the 1954 strike, it is now time to examine photographs from El Progreso that called forth a new reality. They did so by denouncing an unjust situation in the workers' present and by enacting and demanding, in the photographic now and for the future, an alternative set of economic and social relations. It is the perhaps, the yet-to-come, that can be seen in the images that Platero Paz made of workers during the strike against the Boston-based company. But I will also suggest that these photographs reveal something more than the yet-to-come. These strike photos emphatically announce the here-already of new political subjects creating a view into their own situation and a differently arranged space in which to live and work together. Platero Paz's photographs of the 1954 strike are thus image objects that have encoded, in addition to the that-has-been, two additional temporalities: the here-already and the yet-to-come. Both of these effect a break, rejecting the order of the past in which workers simply accepted their lot as the time of yesterday, the time that fruit-company managers sought to bring back. Thus the uncertainty about whether or not the workers would be able to maintain their heterotopic space of collective self-governance also permeates these photographs, especially a photo of the workers praying reverently at an outdoor Mass in the Ramón Rosa Plaza.

A NEW SPIRIT AMONG THE MEN

Fr. Wade recalls that early in 1954, he "continued to hear rumors of discontent, and of the possibility of a strike and the anti-religious tone of the movement." Worried, he went to confer with the archbishop in Tegucigalpa: "I told him that I had good evidence that the organizers of the strike were having secret meetings everywhere in the Camps of the Ulúa Valley and of the Valley of the Aguán, and that the whole affair seemed ominous." The archbishop granted the Jesuit permission to meet with the potential strikers to try to convince them that "the Church would not condemn them . . . provided they agree not to attack or condemn the Church, or the Hierarchy." Wade writes that he then went to meet with the US ambassador, who agreed to Fr. Wade's proposition but added that the potential strikers should "not condemn the American Government."[2]

Thinking about ways that he could make contact with the strike leaders, Fr. Wade returned to El Progreso. A couple of weeks later, he found an opportunity:

> One evening, well after the dark of the night, a certain man, about middle age, tall, slender and intelligent looking came to my office and said he wanted to speak to me in absolute secrecy. . . . He leaned close to me, and spoke to me in a whisper. "Father, I have committed a great sin. I

have joined the Communist Party and I see my error, and want out, but I do not know how to get out safely." We talked a long time and finally I advised him to remain with them exteriorly but to come to me occasionally to report on their activities.[3]

Fr. Wade, known to *progreseños* as Padre José, instructed the man to keep up appearances but to put his mind and body toward infiltration. Beyond counseling tactical insincerity, it is also clear that Fr. Wade had been dedicated to his pastoral outreach in the banana camps and that he had inspired the confidence of a worker who disagreed with the strike and the "foreign" doctrines that he felt the labor leaders were introducing.

Fr. Wade's informant told him that in a couple of days the leaders would have a meeting. When the priest showed up at the appointed time at a farm just outside of El Progreso, about twenty men were seated around tables that had been lined up in a large cleared space near a house. Wade recounts, "One after another stood up and gave a report on what he and his friends were doing and where they lived. . . . It was a rather repetitious account of men spreading the word of discontent and rebellion against the Company and the Government. No mention of the Church."[4] Finally, Fr. Wade was asked what he had to say. "I tried to speak calmly, and told them of my great sympathy for the workers in their hardships, but that I came seeking a peaceful solution to their problems. Then I told them that the Church and the American Government could take a neutral stand with regard to the strike," provided the strikers not denounce the Catholic Church or the US government. The leader of the group dismissed Fr. Wade without comment.

From distinct ideological positions, the gamut of sources—official, testimonial, and photographic—bears witness to a new way of thinking that the banana workers were creating. Some feared it. Others embraced it. Among the former, Fr. Wade reflected on how, "about six months before the strike, a new spirit began to appear among the men. They were meeting in small groups, planning secretly, complaining, conceiving new ideas of better conditions of work, of hours, of wages, prices of clothes and food."[5] Among the latter, labor leader Julio César Rivera recalls that workers were already predisposed to fight for their rights before leftist organizers arrived in the banana camps: "When we went to the banana plantations to talk with the workers, there was already a fighting spirit within the laborer and a desire to organize."[6] Newspapers reported that Central America was "convulsing."[7] The United Fruit Company and the US government went on red alert.

Photographers grabbed their cameras and ran to the scenes of the strike.

Each of these sources also reports on the workers' encampments in front of United Fruit's offices in the American Zone and at the Ramón Rosa Plaza, in front of the town hall. Fr. Wade recalls the massive gatherings:

> The strike continued during all the month of May. Every day the lead-ers ordered a mass meeting at the raised platform which was in front of the main office of the Company, in the south part of town, and near the railroad bridge across the Río Pelo. There would gather some eight or nine thousand men and women, not counting hundreds of children scattered all about. The management of the strike had set up a public address sys-tem run by an electric motor placed not far away. These sessions would go on from about nine thirty to noon time, always giving instructions to the people, and explaining the reason for the strike, and voicing the great injustices the people were suffering at the hands of the Company.[8]

While Fr. Wade had long enjoyed addressing his congregations from the altar, here he listened to a new popular and secular authority. He had to ask others "to allow me to speak by the P.A. system to the people." In this small space outside the local headquarters of a transnational corporation, the workers had become sovereign, if only for a moment.

The workers maintained their minipolity, their community under con-struction, with some of the same tools that the company and the state used to maintain their fiefdoms, including a bit of surveillance and some strate-gic public relations. Fr. Wade's experience of the shift in local relations of authority is indicative of the development of a new and, however brief, pop-ular sovereignty. Antonio Handal, a Palestinian Christian merchant whose store looked out onto the Ramón Rosa Plaza, warned the priest:

> "It is said that they have put you at the top of the list of men who must be eliminated when they take the power of the government into their hands. You are a marked man." Then I went out into the Plaza, moving about, speaking to those who came near me. After a few moments, a man came up to me and said in a whisper, "Father, a man is following you with a camera trying to get a face view and picture of you. Don't look directly in his direction." I looked around and saw the camera, but continued, not turning towards him. After maybe half an hour, I suddenly found myself surrounded by about fifty people, with a few shouting at me, accusing me of being in favor of the Company, and against the rights of the workman.[9]

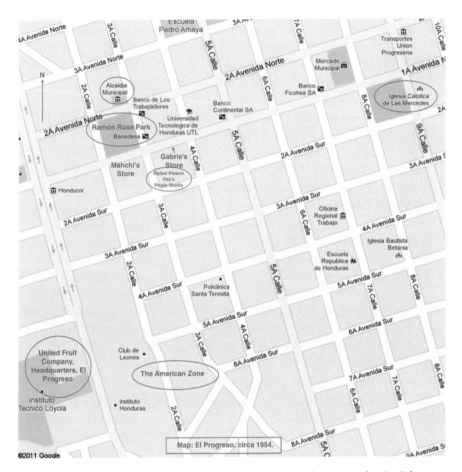

Map 7.1. El Progreso, with circles indicating significant places in the 1954 strike. The Tela Railroad Company's trains ran right in front of its local headquarters on what is now a major thoroughfare, designated by arrows on the map as a two-way street. Strikers set up camps in front of the company's offices and in the Ramón Rosa Park. Map data © 2011 Google.

Intimated in this story is the idea that the workers wanted a frontal picture of Fr. Wade to identify and repress him. This wariness, whether rooted in actual events or the product of an overactive memory, indexes the disjunction between the priest and his flock, between his unchanged mode of being and the workers' new subjectivity, between the social relations obtained before the strike and those that were being produced as the workers inserted themselves into history as active subjects.

TESTIMONY, PHOTOGRAPHS, AND PLACE

On May Day 1954, the procession of workers arrived in the American Zone at around 11:30 a.m. Those whose shifts had just ended immediately joined the demonstration. As the mass of men proceeded down Primera Avenida toward the cemetery and then doubled back toward the Ramón Rosa Plaza, women and children closed the doors to their houses to join the procession in solidarity. According to Agapito Robleda, a United Fruit Company construction worker, the group of laborers and their families returned from the American Zone to the plaza at around 2 p.m. with eight thousand people.[10] The mood was festive, and from the open pavilion in the center of the plaza, various speakers addressed the group. From the elevated platform, Miguel Toro read the workers' declaration of a general strike.[11] At this point, the declaration was more like a secular prayer than a social fact. No one knew whether a couple of relatively small strikes by longshoremen and mechanics in Puerto Cortés and engineering and construction workers in El Progreso would develop into a strike by workers in all industries.

Meanwhile, that same day the US Central Intelligence Agency (CIA) launched *La Voz de Liberación*, a propagandistic radio program meant to disorient Guatemalans and to aid the United States in overthrowing their president, Jacobo Árbenz Guzmán. The Honduran Left denounced the effort to destabilize Guatemala as a threat to that country's sovereignty and the freedom of its people.[12] On May 2, the strikers in El Progreso sent emissaries out into the surrounding plantations to propose that field hands join in withholding their labor. The same day, US and Honduran officials alleged that a military airplane from Guatemala landed without permission in Puerto Cortés, which, according to them, suggested that the banana workers' strike was really orchestrated from Guatemala City. The Árbenz government responded that it had sent the plane to investigate the possibility of an invasion by Carlos Castillo Armas, the Guatemalan military officer who was the public face of the CIA's clandestine operation to end democratic governance in Guatemala.[13]

In each of the photographs of the 1954 strike, the workers demonstrate their awareness that they are the subjects of this historic event, that they have seized a degree of power, and that it is they who are being photographically documented, acting as if the strike itself was intended as much for the management of the United Fruit Company as it was for the distant spectators that the camera implied. In the photograph of the strikers

Fig. 7.2. Marching strikers, El Progreso, 1954. As the workers point at the camera, they demonstrate that they are aware they are becoming the subjects of their own history. With their presence and their banners, the workers boldly declare, "El pulpo dominado por la masa obrera y campesina." *Courtesy of the Rafael Platero Paz Archive.*

demonstrating in the streets of El Progreso, the viewer sees that the workers demonstrate significant control over the message they are sending. They know they are making history, and they acknowledge the role of the camera in documenting their moment as active political subjects (figure 7.2).

Three components of this photo overdetermine the resulting message. First, the workers were communicating, through their sheer mass, the strength of a group agent. Second, with explicit text etched on signs that they carried above the crowd, the workers were declaring solidarity with one another and their joint purpose. Finally, the workers had drawn images of themselves as typical *campeños*—with rolled-up sleeves, strong arms, and sombreros—cutting an arm off of the octopus, an international icon of imperialism. Thus, while Platero Paz created this picture, the workers themselves left nothing to chance and worked to ensure that others knew what they were fighting for. To the extent they could, these *campeños*, which is Honduran slang for someone who works for the banana companies, made clear and consistent representations of their purposes.

As the workers watch themselves being photographed as a collective subject, they are clearly aware of their own power in reclaiming this public space, of converting it, in this moment, from a space for commerce to one for civic debate. They cannot yet know that massive floods are coming, that 40 percent of them will be fired just three months later, that the company will increasingly rely on chemicals and less on unskilled workers, and, finally, that the company will begin to pull back from the risks of production, shifting those risks onto locals while continuing to reap enormous profits from the sale of the fruit, literally, of their labor. In the moment when they looked into the lens of the camera and the photographer clicked the button, the "posing" subjects and the photographer must have had several potential spectators in mind: fellow workers, neighbors and friends in El Progreso, newspaper readers, the company and its management, and, perhaps, posterity.

This last issue, of the photograph as a document for future generations, raises questions about the historian's interpretive approach to visual material. Outside the photographic event, the spectator can imagine what it would be like to be a subject of this particular image. Such a viewer can attempt to imaginatively transpose herself into that subject's horizon. This reflective act does not cancel out the viewer's own horizon (I'm still here in the comfort of my North American home looking at this decades-old picture). And in transposing herself into the horizon of the photographed striker, the viewer cannot collapse the horizon of the other. The two horizons—that of the spectator and that of the photographed subject—coexist in tension with one another. But it is precisely this aspect of viewing a photograph that can upset present-mindedness.

Photographs of a particular event can enable the historicizing of that event. In looking at a photographic image, the spectator is invited into what Alan Trachtenberg has called the "narrative time" of the photographer and her subjects.[14] The retrospective uses of the image are brought to it but do not necessarily inhere in it. Inherent in the image is only the record of an event, a moment when the shutter opened to let the light that was reflected off an object be captured on film. From this physical process, photographs get their denotative force and testimonial authority. That testimonial authority is what draws us into old photos. This is the new kind of consciousness that the photograph provokes; it was what Barthes called an awareness of "having-been-there." The photograph, in a word, lends itself to historicism.

In this photograph of the mass of striking workers, the content of the placards refers concretely to the moment that these working people were bringing about and the new political space that they were constructing. A giant poster carried through the streets of El Progreso depicts a life-sized *campeño*. Shirtless and with sturdy legs firmly supporting him, he has just swung an ax down into a writhing octopus. The caption reads, "THESTRIKE [sic], GIVING IT GOOD to the OCTOPUS of the Tela RRCo." Thus when this sign was created, the strike had already begun. Furthermore, the sign refers not to the transnational enterprise, but to its local subsidiary, the Tela Railroad Company. This degree of specificity at a time when workers in different regions of the north coast were protesting United Fruit's other local subsidiary, the Truxillo Railroad Company, and its main competitor, the Standard Fruit Company, indicates that workers in El Progreso made the octopus sign themselves. The other posters are also replete with local references and orthographic innocence—"Long live the Cectional [sic] syndicalist committee of the electrical department, in solidareity [sic] with the other departments, Honduras live free." "Long live the Union Committee of the Workshop for Tractors and motorcars, Union, Liberty, Justice, Labor." "Long live the Department of Agriculture." "Syndicalist Committee of the Engineering Department." Such local color was not fabricated from afar but produced on the ground in El Progreso. Thus the surface meanings of photos are the meanings of real surfaces and actual moments, giving viewers a sense for the odd but meaningful specificities of particular places and times as living people—workers, merchants, managers, priests, and photographers—inscribed their wills upon those surfaces and in those moments.

In the striking workers caricaturing themselves as *campeños*, this photograph also discloses their direct engagement with the issue of reproducibility. If, as Benjamin says, photography is the pivotal technology in the era of mechanical reproducibility, then these laborers make legible both their consciousness of having been made into a hardened sociological type and that they can actively resignify the category on their own terms. These placards show, moreover, the ways in which this agential act is not simply oppositional. Implicitly juxtaposed with the image of the bedraggled peasant or worker is the modern, cultured type produced through photographs of elite Honduran men and women. But as the workers marched through the streets with a self-caricature, they reproduced and enlarged the *campeño* as a static species to reclaim it through the labor of self-narrativization that is the very labor of self-poiesis. This is the logic of repetition with a difference, one that evinces an understanding of the reproducibility of imagery and the creation of selfhood as part of the same production process. This process of producing social types often leads to exploitation and consumption of the other through cultural cannibalism. Yet as this photograph manifests, the deliberate reworking of a socially assigned type may also lead to participation.[15]

LABOR LEADERS AND *COMPORTAMIENTO*

"All day instructions were given to workers through the loudspeakers: on their conduct [*comportamiento*], on the necessity of organizing, and that they register themselves as members of a future union," recalls Julio César Rivera.[16] In his testimony, Rivera confirms what is abundantly clear from the photographs: the workers and the strike leaders were aware of their own historicity. They knew that they were risking their lives and livelihoods in withholding their labor from the company. But they did so with particular goals in mind—the right to join a labor union, the right to be fairly

Fig. 7.3. A labor leader addresses workers from the open pavilion in the center of the Ramón Rosa Plaza, 1954. *Courtesy of the Rafael Platero Paz Archive.*

compensated for services rendered, and the right to be treated as dignified human beings. Yet the strikers' attention to their own *comportamiento*
was perhaps their greatest political demand. They made the demand by performing it. Through the strike, the workers became aware of the mutability
of their own behavior. That is, the strike allowed them to denaturalize the
social and cultural codes that they had taken for granted in their everyday lives. Through the strike, they realized that they could write new codes
for how to govern themselves. The strike enabled them to practice living
according to their own rules. They performed it through a sort of self-help
guide in which the organizing Comité Central de Huelga issued directives
about behavior: do not drink, line up at the collective kitchens, participate
in the worker-run field hospitals and security forces, and divvy up the tasks
among different committees. Thus they were being encouraged to realize
themselves and their goals immediately in their own conduct, in their own
miniature political community.

The strike leaders understood their role as agents who could deliberately
work to dehabituate the laboring masses and to rehabituate them to self-
respect (figure 7.3). Perhaps this was the most significant threat to the company and the Honduran state, for even as both continued to report that
the strike was completely nonviolent and that the workers were conducting
themselves with notable self-discipline, they continually sought to discredit
the movement. The recognition among the workers and the representatives
from among their ranks that they could reprogram themselves posed a radical challenge to the established order. The strike movement had already
changed the behavior of tens of thousands of workers and was enabling new
subjectivities. This was self-help with the potential to cultivate a new collective self.[17]

The strike leader set against the backdrop of the Honduran flag indicates that the workers put forward their demands and made their claims to
dignity as Hondurans. The content of this self-presentation bespeaks the
possibility of a new Honduran citizen and of a future Honduras that might
respond to demands from below. The workers are enacting the phrase "we
the people." Captured here as a project under construction, the photograph
helps to habituate workers into what they might become, into who they
might make of themselves, as workers and as people newly awakened to
their own potential.

Note that as the speaker addresses the mass of workers, his colleague
watches the photographer. The gaze of this worker demonstrates two
important facts. First, he is aware that he is being photographed, and he

does not feign to be caught in a candid moment. Second, he communicates to the photographer that he too is being watched. He directly addresses the photographer and the spectator with this visual *énoncé*: "I am watching you." This "I" stands with rolled-up shirtsleeves in front of his country's flag, defying his employer and demanding respect. He is clearly aware of his presence before spectators. In looking directly into the camera, he notifies potential viewers that they are also present before him. Viewers of this image cannot look on with detachment, as if they were omniscient beings observing others unbeknownst to them. In the 1954 strike, workers demonstrated that while they knew that they were being subjected to company and government surveillance, they would also monitor their new and fragile space of social autonomy.

Why did this worker look into the camera as Rafael Platero Paz was taking the picture? Quite apart from the strike as a mass spectacle, this was a momentous occasion. He stood to lose his job if they failed. Hundreds, perhaps thousands, of his coworkers had gathered to hear from members of the strike committee. The police and soldiers could turn against the unarmed workers at any moment. As this worker watches Platero Paz, he is allowing the strike to be documented. It is as if the speaker addressing the workers is unaware of the camera and as if viewers of the image could silently witness these events as observers but not participants. But the worker who looks into the camera reminds viewers, and especially the photographer himself, that they are participant observers and that they too have some role in determining how these events unfold. In this way, the worker's direct gaze into the camera has multiple effects. He asserts his own dignity. He seeks to interpellate spectators into this historic project. With the power of his gaze, he converts Platero Paz (and the viewers of the photographer's images) into subjects for him. And short of these effects, he firmly and nonviolently warns reactionaries that he too is watching. He is a brave man, and he does not reject the camera and the power it implies.

In photographs like this one, Platero Paz captured the knot of sovereignty at the heart of El Progreso. His photos document exercises in individual and collective self-forging in a neocolonial space, reflecting how people practiced becoming independent in the banana republic.

When Platero Paz took these pictures, the outcome of this leap into the unknown against known power structures was still highly uncertain. When the camera shutter opened, the workers were still in the moment of decision. They knew what they were trying to change—the hunger, the misery of being disrespected by their employer—they knew what they wanted, and they were embodying it as organized men and women working together in common cause. What they could not know was how the strike would turn out.

Thus these are photographs of the perhaps, the maybe-it-will-turn-out. They are pictures of self-governance. These workers are more materially poor than ever before. Yet they have become spiritually rich in their moment of decision and in their ongoing commitment to reaffirm their decision to strike for better treatment. As this image of a worker looking directly into the lens of the camera reminds us, the striking workers recognized that photography was not a passive, objective apparatus of documentation; it was, instead, integral to setting up this new space in which laborers practiced a different mode of being, one that responded to their needs and their will.

COLLECTIVE KITCHENS AND ORDERLY LINES

By May 3, United Fruit's entire Tela Division was on strike. The workers had paralyzed the movement of trains and were marching on the railroad tracks to El Progreso from the plantations.[18] Women began to throw together collective kitchens to feed the thousands of striking workers who had converged upon El Progreso. Three times a day, the workers queued up for

Fig. 7.4. A woman praying while others prepare food for strikers. *Courtesy of the Rafael Platero Paz Archive.*

guineo verde, boiled green bananas typically accompanied by a small side of sliced onion, jalapeño peppers, carrots, and bay leaves pickled in white vinegar. When a rancher slaughtered a cow, they each got a small piece of meat. When a merchant or a peasant donated beans, corn, eggs, or chickens, they rounded out their meals. "The *negra* Mélida López," Agapito Robleda recalls, "commanded a squad of women to ensure order and discipline in the kitchen."[19]

Platero Paz's photograph of an outdoor collective kitchen captures another way that women participated in the strike movement. Two women face the camera, grinding *masa* for the tortillas. Other women stand near black cast-iron cauldrons, smoke rising from beneath them. Closest to the photographer, a humble middle-aged woman prays with great devotion (figure 7.4).

Platero Paz took several pictures of queues of striking workers. The distinct line of people is a theme that recurs in his photos of the strike, from those of the masses who meticulously stayed within the boundaries of the Ramón Rosa Plaza, leaving the street completely unobstructed, to those of workers assembled on the railroad tracks in front of United Fruit's offices in the American Zone. Julio César Rivera comments on the community kitchens of El Progreso and the orderly lines that workers formed:

> The strike was supported by almost all of the people [*pueblo*]. A great number of families, peasants, in the area of El Progreso gave almost everything they had so that the strike would not fail. It was common to see in the homes of El Progreso workers lined up to get something to eat. . . . In any street, wherever you went, you could see the workers waiting for their food.[20]

To form a line is to engage in a social practice with deep institutional roots. This form of conduct is learned in schools, on the job, in the military, and at Mass, in the queue to receive Holy Communion. As workers lined up to get a meal from a community kitchen, they were citing a kind of modern institutional order. Forming lines was yet another way that they participated in a modernizing project on the north coast of Honduras.

The pictures of men lining up reflect the workers' self-policing during the strike, while also displaying the community rules that the laborers enacted to instantiate the social relations they were demanding. The immanence of this new political order posed a powerful challenge to the fruit companies' claims that it was they who were bringing progress, rationalization, and order to the unproductive spaces of the Honduran north coast. Likewise,

Figs. 7.5 and 7.6. Rafael Platero Paz made many photographs of the striking workers standing in orderly lines. *Courtesy of the Rafael Platero Paz Archive*. Diagram of the composition of this photograph. I thank Jens Andermann for alerting me to this aspect of the picture.

the Honduran political class had long assumed that it was responsible for disciplining what it regarded as the notoriously rowdy, rebellious, and uncultured hordes. But for sixty-nine heady days, an ethnically and socially diverse group of more than 25,000 workers maintained strict order while demanding that their dignity and rights be respected. While they withheld their labor, the workers did so without infringing upon the parallel rights of others. That spirit of self-government was embodied in the lines that workers formed to receive their daily meals from the collective kitchens.

Beyond the historical moment it documents, the very composition of Platero Paz's photograph of the workers lined up waiting for a meal creates an image of solidarity (figures 7.5 and 7.6). Those closest to the camera's vantage point are singularized, rendered knowable by their faces. As I see the Other, who is there, right in front of me, I am challenged by his very presence to think about where I am in relation to him. This photograph positions the viewer directly at eye level and in close proximity to a few striking workers, enabling the distance between the beholder and the beheld to be overcome. As the line continues, the distance between the viewer and the workers increases. The men I see up close are individuals, while those who are farther away appear as a collective. Platero Paz's visual eloquence thus captures both the fundamental ethical question that underlies our encounters with others and the solidarity created by individuals, each of whom decides to make a difference for a common goal. Before the strike, their United Fruit Company overseers had lined these workers up, and they had also been lined up at church and at school. But now they lined themselves up. In doing so, they exposed, while also inverting, the previously reigning order. From an order that had positioned them as objects that could be acted upon, as people who worked and even thought using a script that was not their own, they moved to create a different social order, one that began by instituting local sovereignty and soon expanded beyond El Progreso in an assertion of national sovereignty that the United Fruit Company and the US government found themselves obligated to recognize.

In lining themselves up, the workers were becoming active human subjects, people who were writing their own rules for interacting with each other. Platero Paz captured this individual and collective act of practicing self-governance, creating the possibility that spectators in other places might someday look into the faces of these workers, consider their countenances of stoic resolve, and wonder whether they too might break time into a before and after the event of their decision, writing new rules for themselves and their community and enacting a new way of being workers and being citizens.

THE MIRACULOUS VIRGIN ON STRIKE

Surrounded by a crowd of newly sovereign subjects in the Ramón Rosa Plaza, Fr. Wade feared for his life. Somebody wielded a camera and maneuvered to get a frontal image of the priest. The resulting photo could be used to identify him. It could be shown to workers and others. They were spectators. He was the unwilling object of their gaze. His authority was being displaced. They had authorized themselves to look at him in new ways.

Fr. Wade's account of being an unwilling subject in a photographic encounter highlights the political logic that motivated the workers. The striking workers had drawn an internal frontier between themselves (as a laboring class and as Hondurans) and the United Fruit Company and its allies. In the 1954 strike, field and factory workers successfully aligned with key sectors of the middle class against a common enemy. This is the logic of populism. The "empty signifiers," to invoke Ernesto Laclau, that linked the demands of workers were the idea of the ordinary Honduran, the dignity of the *obrero*, and the inherent but long-denied worth of "Juan Pueblo."[21] In light of the strike, it is easy to see that in his presidential campaign of 1954, Ramón Villeda Morales was not so much the author of a populist discourse as the beneficiary of one that had already burst forth from below. Fr. Wade's account also highlights how the workers drew a frontier between themselves and the official position of the Catholic Church in Honduras, without giving up their deeply felt religiosity.

Collective kitchens and community policing are just two of the ways in which the striking workers pursued a common agenda and asserted a degree of control over how they were represented. In establishing their own working groups, security units, and health clinics, the banana workers temporarily enacted a more egalitarian political community. The striking workers in El Progreso banned the consumption of alcohol, enforcing a standard of public order that was far more severe than the one that typically reigned in the town. They were sober and in control of themselves. In their practices of self-care, in their clear demands, in their modes of organization, and in their steady, intent looks into the camera, the striking workers demonstrated themselves to be anything but a violent and unruly mob.

But that is not what Fr. Wade saw. He shuddered: "They were not sincere friends discussing this with me, wild, and violent, with what I could not interpret other than hatred. Not a single one of them in the group near me was a man whom I had ever seen before on any trip to the Camps. They were all strangers."[22]

Padre José, notwithstanding his adopted name, was an outsider. He knew it. And that knowledge was important. Even though he met with the archbishop and the US ambassador, he still felt that he had sufficiently integrated into the local community that he could consider himself to be a friend, even a shepherd, of the workers. But now, with an unknown person pointing the camera at him, he was being watched. He was identified as the other, as the enemy. He was presumed guilty. His cleric's collar was only a fig leaf to cover his intimate relationship with the local fruit-company executives from the United States. Those were his friends. They were the ones with whom he shared meals, a glass of wine, and a laugh.

Surrounded by dozens of workers in the Ramón Rosa Plaza, Fr. Wade felt that he was among strangers. Here again the strike produced a radical antagonism—between the company and its workers—that was simultaneously a new condition of visibility. Before the strike, it was difficult to determine who the friend and enemy were. How could one know? What if that person really was a friend? But during the strike, friends and enemies suddenly became identifiable. Not only could a worker now identify the other, even if it was his own parish priest; he could also identify himself and where he stood in relation to the other. But this heightened visibility brought with it greater vulnerability. The company could now see exactly who had struck and who the troublemakers were. Once the company regained control of the situation, it would separate its friends from its enemies.

But with Fr. Wade still in the crowd, pursued by a camera-wielding worker, the laboring classes performed their own sovereignty:

> Fear grabbed me, as they were growing louder and more excited. Suddenly the little monarch, dived into the center of them, and spoke with intense and absolute authority, and shouted "Leave this man alone, if you do anything to him now, it will hurt our movement." Then he turned to me, and ordered me out of the circle. I was shaken, and left them, and the Plaza also. I realized that I was marked for elimination.[23]

In Fr. Wade's account, the local leader was a "little monarch." The workers had successfully, even if temporarily, instituted a new law.

But the strikers' distrust of their priests and perceptions of them as allies of the United Fruit Company does not mean that the workers were atheists or even agnostics. Instead, it highlights a gulf between the aspirations and popular religious practices of the laborers and the quite accurately perceived sympathies of their clergymen. Fr. Wade himself reports on the

fervent religiosity of the striking workers. After two of their representatives returned from negotiations in Tegucigalpa, "the first thing they [the
workers waiting in El Progreso] did was all go to the Church of Mercedes
and light a few candles and Thank God for their safe return."[24]

Beyond the demands that workers were making—for the right to join labor
unions, higher wages, and better treatment from their bosses—they were
also enacting a new social and juridical order. Again, one of the foundations
of that new order was the establishment of a worker-directed disciplinary
apparatus. Fr. John Murphy, SJ, commented to Fr. Wade on the strikers'
local security brigade:

> The leaders had the town blockaded. Every road going out of town had a
> few men with rifles forbidding everyone to leave. None could enter either.
> . . . I was called to visit a dying man in Santa Rita and I got in my jeep
> and went to Santa Rita road. At the point leaving town I was stopped and
> asked why I wanted to leave town. I said for a sick call. They said, "No." So
> I had to return.[25]

According to this unsympathetic observer, the workers physically controlled
the space, and they did so, in part, with the threat of violence. As the official Catholic Church aligned itself with the United Fruit Company and the
United States in continuing to deny workers their basic rights, the workers
also ended up challenging the tradition of deferring to clerical authority. By
the same token, if Fr. Murphy's account is true, then it suggests that even
as the workers went about founding a new order of equality, they did so by
adopting a means of separating and disciplining people that was integral to
the old order of the state and the corporation.

The skepticism with which the striking workers regarded men of the
cloth is further revealed in Fr. Murphy's being blamed for bringing in the
Honduran military: "I was accused of sending a message so that the army
would send soldiers to free the town from the communists, but I had nothing to do with it." Nevertheless, the soldiers came. Their effect on the strike
movement was immediate, as Fr. Murphy reports to Fr. Wade:

> After this plane came four more, five in all parked with soldiers in full
> battle gear. About three hundred men with rifles and bayonets, hand
> grenades, pistols, tear gas canisters, and submachine guns and gas masks,
> were in town. They immediately formed into a front of twenty men in
> line, one after the other, and marched into town. . . . With this sudden

show of military force, like ghosts from a distant planet, the people in awe and fear gathered before the platform near the Company offices, maybe ten thousand of them. The Army did not waste time. They formed their front about fifteen abreast, and marched toward the center of town . . . . When the Captain at their front got within speaking distance by using his "bull-horn" he shouted "all disperse and leave this area. I will come toward you walking, but after a certain distance I will give the order of double time." Their rifles worn their bayonets, glistening in the sun, and the men with full battle gear. . . . The people scrambled to escape, and to run away, down the street, toward the river. . . . In a few hours half of the men had returned to their Camps, happy to get out of Progreso.[26]

At the behest of the United Fruit Company, the government quickly reestablished control over the town of El Progreso.

Upon arriving, the soldiers' first order of business was to force the workers to leave the American Zone.[27] For about ten days, the factory and field workers had succeeded in greatly increasing what could be seen and said in this neocolonial locality. But being driven from the American Zone only strengthened their identification with the whole of Honduran society. Even though most of the strikers worked for the United Fruit Company, they were at the bottom of the hierarchy, a status conspicuously underscored by the architecture of the American Zone itself. Likewise, though most of the strikers were Honduran, they enjoyed few of the rights and protections of citizenship and were clearly not members of the political elite. On May 18, the strike committee demanded, to no avail, that the soldiers be withdrawn.[28]

The military had been used to eliminate the strikers' presence in the American Zone and to restore the previous distribution of what could be said and seen. The earlier forms of exclusion would be strictly enforced, especially in this important region of the city. Certain bodies and particular modes of being were allowed in this space and others were not. The first repressive step that the state and the company took toward restoring the old order involved physically and symbolically driving the workers from the heart of El Progreso. Cast out from the American Zone, the workers were the embodiment of the Honduran people. This is perhaps one reason, three weeks into the strike, that the CIA reported that the majority of Hondurans sympathized with the strikers and that the company had "practically no friends."[29] Here, in the Ramón Rosa Plaza, banana workers, a group that hitherto had no securely defined place in the Honduran imaginary, could stand in for the whole of Honduran society.[30]

Fig. 7.7. Open-air Mass in the Ramón Rosa Plaza during
the 1954 strike. *Courtesy of the Rafael Platero Paz Archive.*

The extreme Right sought to brand the strike leaders as communists
manipulating the working masses. Such views were aggressively put forward by people like presidential candidate Abraham Williams Calderón of
the National Reformist Movement, an offshoot of former dictator Tiburcio Carías Andino's National Party. For the National Reformist Movement,
the popular religiosity of the workers, their self-imposed ban on alcohol,
and their claims to patriotism were simply Soviet camouflage or further evidence of their naïveté, which it mocked: "There's even Mass in the blessed
strike."[31] At the same time, Ambassador Whiting Willauer reported that
the archbishop of San Pedro Sula, Monsignor Antonio Capdevilla, was
"very useful in dividing the strike leaders from the extremist strike leaders,
supporting the former with a considerable campaign through the priests
accompanying the workers."[32]

But in contrast to the claims of the hard Right and the official position of
the Catholic Church in Honduras is Rafael Platero Paz's photograph of the
striking workers participating in an open-air Mass in the Ramón Rosa Plaza
(figure 7.7). In the image, dozens of people can be seen facing an improvised
altar. Wearing white vestments, the Jesuit priest has his back turned to
the congregation. Many of the women have covered their heads; men have
removed their hats. Looking closely, one can see the deep stains on their
work shirts. Most everyone within earshot of the priest appears to be reverently praying or paying attention.

The evidentiary function of the photo testifies to an authentically religious crowd. The group of people depicted subordinates itself to the authority of the priest. While respecting the priest and appealing to the divine, the workers had also succeeded in bringing the priest and the sacrament out of the church and into the autonomous space that they had created. The workers made the space holy. Work and civic life, religion and demands to be treated with dignity: the striking workers brought them all together in the Ramón Rosa Plaza. Far from the priests converting the workers, the 1954 strike may have begun the process of conversion for the Jesuits working in Honduras.

Such a reading of this image would help to square the private disdain that these priests showed for the strike movement with the way that they publicly tended to the spiritual needs of the workers. For instance, a newspaper correspondent from El Progreso reported with admiration:

> The miraculous Virgin of Suyapa is on strike. The workers carried Her image to the Ramón Rosa Plaza, headquarters of the strike, and erected a beautiful altar, which they keep illuminated with a profusion of candles. They sang the Rosary to Her and held an Outdoor Mass, which the priests of our sacred parish church celebrated.[33]

In the 1954 strike, workers not only asserted their dignity vis-à-vis the United Fruit Company and the Honduran state, they also refashioned their relation to the Catholic Church. The workers and their families remained fervently Catholic even as they enacted a popular religiosity that reflected their specific worldly needs.

And just as the workers and the fruit company were mobile, so too was the Virgin of Suyapa. In 1747, so the story goes, a laborer who was clearing cornfields near Tegucigalpa discovered the Virgin of Suyapa. She came in the form of a 2.3-inch statuette. He threw her away, but somehow she just kept coming back. She was an itinerant, reappearing virgin with miraculous powers. While she may have been safe in the interior of the country, through her image, she virtually accompanied the workers on the north coast. While the Church may have abandoned the workers in their time of need, the patroness of Honduras had not.

As the striking workers carried a likeness of the Virgin of Suyapa through the streets of El Progreso to the Ramón Rosa Plaza, they reminded themselves, the Honduran state, the United Fruit Company, and the Catholic Church that there was a force mightier than each of them. The most powerful virgin in Honduras was on the side of the workers. In this outdoor

setting—abandoned but pleading for protection from the state, the company, and the church—the workers transformed themselves from a heterogeneous group of isolated individuals into a collective agent with specific
purposes and distinctive ways of representing itself. In doing so, they reori-
ented the existing normative order in the three most fundamental realms
of power: political, economic, and religious. First, the workers reminded the
Honduran government that it had a duty to care for those it governed, especially the factory and field laborers of the north coast. Second, the workers
insisted that the United Fruit Company had a duty to respect the rights of
its employees, skilled and unskilled, women and men. Third, by forcefully
asserting their inherent dignity, the workers and their families reminded
the Catholic Church that it had a duty to care for the poor and for working
people. But in constructing this new social reality in which dominant enti-
ties could be compelled to take up their duties toward their less powerful
constituents, the workers needed more than a list of demands. As a newspaper in El Progreso reported, they summoned the *milagrosa*: "The mothers,
the wives, the daughters, the sisters of the workers on strike, every night
they pray to the Virgin and they ask her to help them through this painful
and delicate trance."[34]

Rafael Platero Paz was there to convert their prayers to the Virgin into
allegorical still images of and for *progreseños*. This open-air Mass could thus
be interpreted as a rebellion against the local Father in both his avatars, as
the United Fruit Company and as Fr. Joseph Wade. Thus, within a Christian model of subjectivity, the striking workers de-reified the corporate
neoimperial structure of domination and the religious support that under-
girded those dependent relations of production. The event of the strike thus
sought to uproot the structures that had been built into the core of the
workers' psyches and to rework those basic materials. This was achieved
through the invention of an emancipatory politics that retrieved and reac-
tivated a popular Catholicism that could serve at once as a source of inner
strength while also offering the possibility of transcendental standards of
love and justice against which the company, the state, the Church, and peasants would have to measure themselves.[35]

But allow me now to propose a literal interpretation of the Honduran
newspaper report on the Virgin of Suyapa. "The miraculous Virgin of Suyapa is on strike" would mean that she was not willing to intercede on behalf
of the workers. There was no need to. They were already changing their lives
on their own. In other words, the 1954 strike also reveals the secularization
of self-sculpting. The banana workers in Honduras demonstrated that the

strike is labor's despiritualized High Mass: a set of ascetic practices self-imposed and publicly staged to activate an ethical response from spectators in the company, in the state, and in a transnational community of those who might see these pictures.

In each Catholic Mass, the transubstantiation of bread and wine is dramatized, a ritual that encourages the faithful to contemplate their own lives in the context of a story that takes the universal, makes it human and tragic, only to pass again into the eternal and redemptive. The Mass escorts the believer through interior exercises in which the devotee adopts a transcendent, God's-eye view of herself and considers what it might take to pass from this life into eternal life.[36] This is a mental doubling not unlike the material doubling that photography enables between one's real self and one's ideal self. On strike and praying in the Ramón Rosa Plaza, the workers were coaching themselves, shoring up a frame of mind that would give them confidence in the inner acts and private decisions that were the true source of power in the 1954 strike, an outer collective act by which they attempted to secure a better place for themselves in this world.

EIGHT

Possibility Eruption Exists

Beyond attempting to publicly ignore the strike in Honduras while quietly seeking to crush it beneath a narrative of a communist Guatemala, the United States took concrete steps to interrupt the banana workers as they made their democratic demands. On May 21, 1954, Carlos Castillo Armas sent some of his men to provide additional force to the company.[1] Then, less than four weeks into the strike, the United States signed a bilateral military agreement with Honduras. High-level Honduran military officers were given custody of new weapons, transferred under the US-Honduran military agreement.[2] So just as the United States was violently overthrowing the constitutional government of Guatemala to install a military dictatorship, it also finalized an agreement to give Honduran political elites new tools of repression to use against their own people.

In the middle of the strike and on the advice of his military attaché, Ambassador Whiting Willauer recommended US intervention:

If the United States Government will promptly act there is an excellent chance that the Combat Battalion Team provided for under the Military Assistance Treaty can be made reasonably ready prior to the October 10 presidential elections when there is every expectation of internal disorder. Although this team is primarily designed for *hemisphere defense* and the *ordinary internal security* of the country should be handled by existing forces, the new situation created by present Communist infiltration of the Honduran labor movement may require extraordinary internal security measures at any time between now and the forthcoming elections.[3]

It was the striking workers who in his view had created a "new situation" that might "require extraordinary internal security measures." In other words, the alliance between the US and Honduran governments and the United Fruit Company could answer the demands of the workers by declaring a state of exception and enforcing it with a US-trained combat battalion team. The US ambassador continued: "With eight weeks of training the men should have fairly good discipline, and would know enough about shooting, etc., to give a good account of themselves against any local opposition. Because of the strike airlift will be required for items needed to get started."[4] In spinning a tale of pervasive communist infiltration, the US government and its local allies created a parallel story that never intersected with what actually drove tens of thousands of banana workers to go on strike. But the net of that imagined reality was cast widely enough to eventually trap the workers within it. Even as the United States critically gazed upon the strike, that gaze itself contained a prescriptive possibility that at once invented the object to be feared and the necessity of destroying it.

Aside from the legalization of labor unions, the US-Honduran bilateral military agreement was the most important and lasting structural change to emerge from the 1954 strike. Thirty years later, as the United States sought to roll back alleged communism in Nicaragua, El Salvador, and Guatemala, this military pact served as the cornerstone of US covert operations in the region, leading one observer to dub it "the USS Honduras."[5]

The strike thus exposed two different visions for the relationship between the state, capital, and labor. Against the interests of the banana workers, the US government sought to keep the Honduran government in alignment with monopoly capitalism. Meanwhile, to the distress of foreign capital, the workers sought to bring the Honduran state into alignment with their class and national interests.

From the perspective of US government and corporate expansionists, there were two targets: local and transnational class solidarity had to be undermined and so too did the possibility that the Honduran government might defend its citizens against the interests of the company. When Honduras's laboring people suddenly appeared as worker-citizens making demands, the company, with the support of the US government and much of the international press, committed itself to bringing about their unappearance.

LIFE MAGAZINE PHOTOS OF STRIKING BANANA WORKERS

In June 1954, *Life* ran a photoessay entitled "Guatemalan Reds Worry Neighbors—Honduras and Nicaragua Fuss over Arms."[6] The first picture was of rifles, "marked with the Russian hammer and sickle (figure 8.1)." The last was of the masses of unarmed workers, withholding their labor in Honduras (figure 8.2).

These were the halcyon days of photojournalism and, indeed, much of this story was communicated visually. The first and most prominent photograph shows a man and four children peering through a glass display at several symmetrically aligned rifles. A photo in the middle of the page depicts a resolute man with arms crossed, a truncated mustache, and a handgun tucked into his pants. Hanging on the wall is a pennant for Tegucigalpa's short-lived basketball team. Placed atop a wooden case holding radio equipment stands the flag of Guatemala. The accompanying caption orients the viewer to see Colonel Carlos Castillo Armas, a Guatemalan exile working in Honduras "to foment revolt in his native land."

At the bottom of the page, a large photo provides a visible response to the other images. The reader of the magazine is positioned such that she shares the perspective of a hefty, close-cropped man in uniform. The man is teaching a group of younger, darker-skinned men who are also wearing uniforms. They look on attentively. They are the students, with two men crammed awkwardly into each small desk. The teacher stands behind a machine gun that rests on a wooden surface with its barrel pointed toward the students. The caption escorts readers through the image: "Honduran Training Class hears Colonel Milton Shattuck, commanding the US military mission, explain the workings of a machine gun to the officers and noncoms selected to organize a projected US-equipped battalion."

Following the page on which Castillo Armas is sandwiched between communist guns marked with the hammer and sickle and capitalist guns wielded by US Army Colonel Shattuck, the story continues with a dramatic 14" × 13"

Figs. 8.1 and 8.2. Original captions: "Guatemalan Reds Worry Neighbors" and "A Communist Objective." *Life*, June 14, 1954.

photograph of a man with dark aviator sunglasses addressing a vast group of humble men wearing simple hats. The viewer of this image is positioned beside and somewhat behind the speaker and thus able to witness the presence of a densely packed crowd that extended from the foreground to the horizon. From the vantage point of the strike leader, the viewer of this photograph gets an up-close view of the grave countenances of the workers. There are no fists raised. No signs. Not a single smile. Some of the workers appear to be adolescents, while others are middle-aged. Most of the individual workers stand pensively, looking at their labor leader. A few do not avoid the gaze of their white photographer from the United States. Captured while reading "an anti-Communist resolution," the caption informs us, Manuel Jesus Valencia is "a moderate with a good deal of official support" who "was strengthened recently when the government arrested a group of Communists who were attempting to disrupt settlement negotiations." The motives of the striking workers are explained as "a squabble over double pay for Sunday work." While *Life* photographer Ralph Morse took other powerful pictures of the 1954 banana workers' strike, this is the only one that made it into print.

In this photoessay, *Life* presented its readers with a visual asyndeton that released a logic that they were left to piece together. Communists supplying guns to Guatemala. A Guatemalan ready to invade his own country. The US military training Honduran soldiers. Twenty-five thousand banana workers against the United Fruit Company in Honduras.

Directly opposite the full-page photograph of the striking workers in Honduras is an advertisement for Union Oil Company (figure 8.3). In the ad, a young boy sits with his feet up on a crate as he reclines while eating a gigantic slice of watermelon. The caption asks, "What's wrong with this picture?" The juxtaposition of the weathered workers and the boy gorging himself most likely went unnoticed by most of *Life*'s readers; but for that reason, it may have been all the more persuasive. The advertisement seeks to directly interpellate the viewer-reader: "You probably have a snapshot like it in your own photograph album." This could be your child—identify with him, the ad emphatically directs. Beyond the verbal hailing, the everydayness of the image is induced through the framing of the picture on the page with corner stickers and by the boy's raggedy tennis shoes and rolled-up jeans. The advertisement concludes, "Union Oil, like so many so-called 'big' companies, is really getting smaller all the time!"

Against the implied US suburban averageness of the boy eating watermelon, the opposite page depicts a dense mass of brown-skinned male workers with a bold caption that begins, "A COMMUNIST OBJECTIVE." The strike and its workers, the caption notes, were the objective that communists were pursuing. The textual accompaniment to the photo intimates that the workers could easily be manipulated while it trivializes their reasons for striking. But the caption also shows some restraint. It does not accuse the workers of being communists; it only suggests that they were vulnerable to "Communist penetration." And the photograph itself exceeds its caption. The workers who look past their labor leader and at the photographer, and therefore their imagined viewer, establish a moment of virtual direct address between themselves and their viewers in the United States. As they look past the microphone-holding, sunglasses-wearing speaker, the striking workers also signal that they are not entirely in the thrall of their leader.

While relatively few photographs were printed of the striking banana workers, dozens of daily newspapers reported their actions. From May through December 1954, the *New York Times* alone ran 51 news articles and editorials that made note of the strike. In just May and June 1954, a total of

What's wrong with this picture?

You probably have a snapshot like it in your own photograph album.

It happens when you get too close to your subject, and the camera can't handle the perspective.

In another sense, you can get an equally distorted picture of the modern corporation. For viewed too close-up, it frequently looks bigger than it is.

Take Union Oil. In 1910 — when we did but a $12,000,000 volume — we seemed much smaller. *Yet at the time this was 23% of the total petroleum business in the western states.*

In 1953 we looked much bigger because we did a whopping $325,000,000 volume. *But this was only 13% of the petroleum business in the West.*

Certainly we've grown. We've *had* to grow to serve a bigger market, to meet increased competition and to satisfy more consumer needs. *But in proportion to the total business, we aren't as big as we were 44 years ago.*

Seen in perspective, the picture is clear: Union Oil, like so many so-called "big" companies, is really getting smaller all the time!

UNION OIL 76 COMPANY

OF CALIFORNIA

Buy American and protect your standard of living

Fig. 8.3. Original caption: "What's wrong with this picture?" *Life*, June 14, 1954.

147 news stories in key English-language periodicals either were dedicated exclusively to the strike in Honduras or mentioned the strike in connection with the events surrounding the US-led overthrow of Jacobo Árbenz Guzmán in Guatemala. In addition to the *New York Times*, stories on the strike appeared in the *Chicago Daily Tribune*, the *Atlanta Daily World*, the *Washington Post and Times-Herald*, the *Los Angeles Times*, *Barron's National Business and Financial Weekly*, the *Times of India*, and the *Courier* of Pittsburgh. Most of these news stories were not written to capture the poverty and day-to-day concerns of the workers; instead they portrayed the strikers as unduly influenced by Guatemalan communists, providing an interpretive frame consistent with how the fruit companies and the US and Honduran governments represented the labor-led events on the north coast.

Fig. 8.4. Original caption: "Students crowded on the balconies of a Medical school holding banners, Carlos Castillo Armas being kicked out of Honduras into Guatemala, during time of the Guatemalan Revolt." *Life*, July 5, 1954. *George Silk/ The LIFE Picture Collection/Getty Images.*

Fig. 8.5. Unpublished photograph by Ralph Morse. Caption from *Life*'s online archives: "United Fruit Co. workers & families in workers compound on plantation during strike." June 1, 1954. *Ralph Morse/The LIFE Picture Collection/Getty Images.*

The magazine had the personnel in Honduras to report on the strike. In addition to Morse, *Life*'s Leonard McCombe and George Silk took pictures in Tegucigalpa and La Lima and near the border with Guatemala. Generally ignoring the strike, *Life* instead guided its readers through another set of images from Central America. One picture of men with bloodied backs was captioned "Freed Anti-Communists in Guatemala City Show Scars from Prison Beatings to Crowds in the Streets." A photojournalistic essay entitled "Reds' Priority: Pin War on Us" noted, "In Honduras, where Castillo organized his invasion, a Red-tinted student group called for 'public solidarity with the Guatemalan people' and resurrected the ghost of Augusto Sandino, who battled U.S. Marines in Nicaragua in the '20s."[7] In total, *Life* ran five photoessays on Guatemala over a two-month period in 1954. While extensively documenting Castillo Armas's overthrow of "the Reds" in Guatemala, the magazine published only one photograph of the massive strike that was unfolding simultaneously in Honduras.

HUNGER AND DIGNITY MADE VISIBLE

In June 1954, the Cuban magazine *Bohemia* published twenty-four photos of the banana workers' strike in Honduras.[8] The images and text countered the dominant narrative of the strike. Spread over six pages and accompanied by an article by a North American journalist and peace activist named Henry Wallace, these photographs elicited the solidarity of the magazine's readership, dispersed throughout the major cities of early Cold War Latin America; founded in Havana in 1908, by 1953 *Bohemia* had an international weekly circulation of 260,000 copies. In contrast to the photoessay in *Life*, the imagetext in *Bohemia* made it clear that poverty and hunger were what motivated the strikers, not foreign ideologies. In *Bohemia*, women and children were represented as crucial to a struggle for a measure of economic justice in the banana plantations. While the strike was under way, the magazine documented and thus reinforced the appearance of a new kind of being, a new subject in Honduras: workers and their families aware of their own political capacities.

Figs. 8.6 and 8.7. First and last pages of a photojournalistic essay by Henry Wallace in *Bohemia* on the 1954 strike. *Courtesy of the Archivo Nacional de Honduras.*

The first photo in this article is of a naked little boy holding an empty bowl in his hand (figure 8.6). He is crying and looking straight at the viewer. With this opening image of vulnerability, the photographer and the editors of the magazine sought to create an imaginary relation between the represented boy and their transnational readership. By positioning the reader as a person addressed by a hungry toddler in need, the image producers constructed a vantage point from which one was prompted to feel concern for the boy.

As the spectator-reader continues across and between the photographs, she joins them together, constructing personal meaning out of the pictive and scriptive elements.Across a photojournalistic essay, it is in the gaps between the photos, as well as between the images and the text, that the viewer-reader constructs her own sense of continuity while also being challenged to problematize her own position in relation to the depicted subjects.[9] Throughout the *Bohemia* piece, the image of the young boy may nag at the reader's conscience. The series of images unfolds cinematically, in shot-reverse-shot sequences. Just as the toddler is looked upon, so too is he looking imploringly at potential viewers. The final photo is of a banana worker walking away as he holds his young son's hand: their backs are to the spectator, and they walk on their own (figure 8.7). The reader-viewer is left to imagine what kind of future they are walking into and whether they will be accompanied.

The social relations encoded in the *Bohemia* photographs are of poor but self-reliant workers who are directing their own lives. Absent are the managers of the United Fruit Company. Nor are the Honduran military or police to be seen. Instead, several photos show the workers policing themselves, maintaining the nonviolent and disciplined struggle for recognition of their right to be treated with dignity, to govern themselves, and to care for each other. The children naked and hungry testify to the United Fruit Company's exploitation of its workers. In this way, the new social relations that the workers are creating directly challenge the silent but known superordinate element: the company itself. These workers are treating each other in their own health clinics, preparing their own food, policing each other, and electing leaders from within their own ranks. The physical absence of the plantation overseer, the military, and the US boss is substituted with the presence of organized workers, giving the viewer a glimpse of the kinds of social relations that might be formed in the space in which labor has suspended outside authority.

The striking workers, the photographers, and the publishers of *Bohemia* worked together to portray the plight and self-reliance of the laborers and their families. Together, they labored to forge a new Honduran. They had spent enough time producing bananas. Now was their time to produce themselves. As they were photographed, the striking workers became increasingly aware of themselves as the subjects of this visually mediated event. They were being photographed in new structures and group relations that they themselves were creating. Not only were they demanding respect from their employer, they were also boldly demanding it from a diverse and dispersed global spectatorship. These are organized, organizing people, the phototext affirms, who need neither the help of the United Fruit Company nor that of the United States. What they did need, and what *Bohemia*'s story in images sought to cultivate, was solidarity—a sense among people who shared neither family nor national ties, neither occupation nor this specific plight, that they had interests in common.

Multiple photos emphasize the workers' awareness of themselves as the authors of this moment in history. As a woman looks squarely into the camera while nursing her baby, she becomes a symbol of life and maternal nurturing that all viewers can understand. The bold type above the photo puts the visual message into words: "The Strike of the Honduran Banana Workers: A Shout That Has Resonated throughout the World." As the photographer attempted to document the strike, the way workers peered into the camera undid many of the candid shots. In their direct gazes, these industrial farmhands revealed that they knew they were objects of international interest precisely because they were challenging a powerful transnational corporation. This point was put succinctly in the caption accompanying a photo of an enthusiastic crowd of workers in La Lima, a neighboring town just across the Ulúa River: "When BOHEMIA arrived with a magnificent article on the situation on the north coast, the workers cheered this great magazine and the people of Cuba. Here you see the edition from May 6th lifted over the heads of hundreds of workers by Mario S. Tamayo, general secretary in the La Lima camp."[10]

The women and girls portrayed in *Bohemia*'s photos of the 1954 strike are mothers, caregivers, and nurses. They are also citizens, occupying a public space to make economic and political demands. The photograph of the striking women of El Progreso, for example, shows their entire bodies (figure 8.8). They have taken to the streets in their long dresses and with their purses. But they also carry batons, simple pieces of wood that they have transformed into symbols of their local self-governing authority. In a line that stretches from the immediate foreground into the horizon of the compositional space, some look into the camera, connecting with the

Las mujeres protestan en Progreso, otro de los centros de la huelga. Dicen que si la compañia no accede a sus demandas de mejores sueldos y viviendas y reconocimiento del sindicato, ellas morirán luchando.

Los trabajadores bananeros viven en condiciones bastante primitivas, que la huelga hace peores aun. El calor, las moscas (aquí se les ve molestando a una niña) y el hambre hacen de sus campos un verdadero infierno. A pesar de eso, la moral de los obreros se mantiene muy alta.

Este huelguista cuida de sus hijos mientras su mujer cocina para los millares de hombres, mujeres y niños que comen diariamente en los campos huelguísticos. El hondureño se destaca por su paciencia y su pasividad.

El enemigo más encarnizado del huelguista es el hambre. Pero ella no es nada nuevo para él. La ha conocido durante toda su vida y sabe ofrecerle fuerte resistencia. Los vientres de los niños se hinchan y las madres enflaquecen, pero no pierden la fe en su movimiento.

Los huelguistas construyen sus propios refugios en el campo de deportes de La Lima. El campo se llama "Chula Vista", pero los huelguistas le han puesto "Campo de Liberación".

Fig. 8.8. *Bohemia*, June 1954. *Courtesy of the Archivo Nacional de Honduras.*

viewer from a distance that reinforces their stature as political subjects. In fact, only one of the twenty-four photos could be interpreted as situating a woman in a domestic setting. The other eight photos in which women are key participants portray them in public or communal settings. Aside from the photo of the nurse, the article includes a picture in which a group of women, joined by a man and a young boy, are separating a large quantity of kidney beans to cook for the strikers and their families. The worker and his domestic partner come together in solidarity as the group suffers and struggles as one—this is, at least, the ideal represented in these images of the strike.

The bookends of this photographic essay are characterized by radically different focal distances. From the tight shot of the hungry and naked boy to the long shot of the worker holding his son's hand as they walk away from the camera through a banana plantation, the struggle continues. The suffering may not end. These are pictures of faith in humanity. But they are likewise, and most essentially, pictures of politics. These images capture what Jacques Rancière might call the moment of "torsion" in which workers assert their equality in denouncing a wrong.[11] It was precisely in making demands that the workers presupposed a fundamental relation of equality between themselves, as speakers, and their employers, as listeners. The strike gained momentum from the presupposed equality among those who participated in the photographic events of this moment of disagreement: any of the scattered spectators who might encounter these images could, potentially, understand the reasoning and urgency behind the workers' demands.

The captions of these photos function like arrows in diagrams, pointing out what the illustrator wants the viewer to notice. The argument is made in both documentary and mythological registers. The images, like the text, document the 1954 strike. But the photographs go further than the text, lending it an affective quality that is altogether absent from the text itself.

Like Platero Paz's photographs of the strike, the *Bohemia* photos capture the moment of the workers' decision, their leap into the *quizás*, the perhaps. Beyond the decision as such, the photographs as indexical image objects always point to the historical subject of that decision. As the *Bohemia* photos make clear, it was the workers who brought themselves into existence as self-aware laborers and citizens. It was they who supported their own appearance on the international stage. The strike was an evanescent event of workers discovering and asserting their own capacity as political subjects.[12] Platero Paz intuitively understood that the character of the strike was mediated and extended photographically. So in the face of a massive demonstration of workers' ability to speak publicly about their own needs and interests, the company and influential media outlets sought to reestablish the subjective incapacity of labor.

Meanwhile, *Bohemia* had the means, as the event was unfolding, to disseminate images of capable workers who were reorganizing their own subjectivities, expelling their old submissive selves and assembling new, more assertive self-respecting selves, to effect an outward rearrangement of the relations and institutions that constrained their ability to decide on the economic, social, and political matters that impinged most on their daily lives. Photography and the (non)circulation of images of the strike were thus bound up with the workers' interior exercises in their liberation and their more outwardly visible, methodical, and concerted attempt to expand their civil and economic liberties.

Bohemia was specific in its captions; it drew attention to the actions of the workers, referring to them as *los huelgistas, el huelgista,* and *este huelgista*—the strikers, the striker, this striker. That is, they are subjects defined in terms of what they are doing, not who they are—workers, men, women. In presenting them as subjects of a particular kind of act and not by their socially ascribed identities, *Bohemia* communicated that it was through withholding their labor that they ceased to be who they were and began to become the subjects of dignity that they wished to be seen as. Another caption refers to "el campo huelgístico" (the field of the strike); *el campo* denotes "a field," as in a piece of land used for a particular purpose, but also an area on which a battle is fought, or a space in which a subject of scientific study or artistic representation can be observed in its natural location, as well as, finally, a sphere of activity or interest. In highlighting the space that the workers had created through their actions, the magazine consistently represented the capacity of the workers to organize themselves and to struggle publicly for their rights. Put differently, the creators of this photojournalistic essay highlighted the particular mode of subjectification rather than the name of the subject. And insofar as *huelgista* is a name for a subject, it is the name of a subject in transition; as soon as the strikers' demands are met or as soon as they give up, they cease to be *huelgistas*. At that moment, their identities are again served up with a more stable designation, such as "workers." *Bohemia* described a process of subjectification that was under way. In doing so, the magazine, like Platero Paz, captured and extended the banana workers' quicksilver leap into the perhaps.

Bohemia published powerful photos of women's participation in the strike. The caption for a picture of children gathered around a big cast-iron cauldron reads, "What's for dinner? Green plantains. The preparation of corn is a task taken on by men, women, and children. This latter group will eat it raw if their elders are not looking."[13] Not only does this photograph, and the text that accompanies it, remind viewers of the new politics being enacted through the collective preparation of meals, it also underscores what the strike is about: the children and the possibility that they might inherit a better future. In this way, these carefully selected photographs accomplished what newspaper articles, memoirs, statistical data on wages and prices, and official government documents could not.

The image of barefoot children huddled around a community cauldron figures them as vulnerable, as deserving protection. An image of hungry children permits spectators to see in a new way what is at stake in the strike. It facilitates the uptake of the strikers' message and allows spectators to identify with their cause. While neither the company nor the state sees these children as full citizens, as creatures who ought to enjoy some minimal entitlements and freedoms, the photograph creates an affective pathway for spectators to reach this conclusion. The viewer of the image surely intuits that children have rights as human beings—especially the right to food—and that they need special care and protection. In light of this photograph, even hard-core anticommunists would have had a difficult time obfuscating what motivated the striking workers and their families to risk so much.

More problematic for those who feared a communist takeover of Central America were images of stick-wielding workers (figure 8.4). The caption to one of *Bohemia*'s photographs of a worker as security guard alludes to this fear: "The strikers maintain order with their own police. They do not allow alcoholic beverages in the camps, nor do they allow any kind of weapon. The batons that they carry were referred to derogatorily as 'dreadful billy clubs.'" This textual chaperon seeks to neutralize one of the anxieties that the alliance between the United Fruit Company, the US and Honduran governments, and the conservative press outlets in both countries were creating about the striking workers armed with "dreadful billy clubs." Yet this mode of self-policing is not unambiguously liberatory. Workers maintaining order by suspending the presence of external governing powers, both corporate and state, enriched their experience of functioning as a collective agent. This order was guaranteed by the possibility of a repressive force that was certainly less powerful than those of the police and military. Nevertheless,

LA HUELGA DE LOS BANANEROS HONDUREÑOS: UN GRITO QUE HA RESONADO EN TODO EL MUNDO.

carece de legislación obrera, de tradición de lucha proletaria, de sindicatos. Era considerada el único país donde los obreros eran suficientemente dóciles como para aceptar lo que se les daba sin pedir nada.

Pero en estas últimas seis semanas los trabajadores bananeros de Honduras han demostrado cuán equivocados estaban los funcionarios de la compañía y los demás al

creer que ellos no sabían que el mundo estaba cambiando, que ignoraban que los obreros también son un factor en la industria del banano que debe ser tomado en cuenta.

Buscando desatinadamente una explicación de por qué esos pacíficos trabajadores se han levantado en protesta por los salarios y los procedimientos de la compañía, los defensores de ésta han tratado de

Este es uno de los lugares más populares en el campo huelguístico de La Lima, centro del imperio bananero. Aquí los niños —y los mayores también— pueden refrescarse un poco, huyendo del feroz sol tropical. Pero hay 25,000 y pocos sitios como éste.

AL fin la Historia ha llegado a las plantaciones bananeras de la United Fruit Company en la costa norte de Honduras.

Después de cincuenta años de dominación de esa área —y a veces del país entero también— los prósperos pioneros del negocio del banano se han enfrentado con un problema que no podrán resolver comprando la protección de los jefes militares locales ni derrocando un presidente en Tegucigalpa.

Los "buenos tiempos viejos" de dominio feudal han terminado y una nueva época está en camino.

Los humildes obreros de la "Frutera" al fin han levantado su voz, y su grito ha sido oído en todo el mundo.

El fin de la era de la United Fruit Company como único árbitro de los destinos de más de 100,000 personas en Honduras comenzó en los alrededores del primero de mayo, cuando 25,000 trabajadores abandonaron las plantaciones y los talleres en un movimiento unido que dejó boquiabiertos a los funcionarios de la compañía.

Pero la huelga también asombró al resto de las Américas. Honduras

Entre los que más sufren después de varias semanas de huelga están las mujeres que tienen hijos pequeños. Aquí esperan en una larga cola para recibir su ración diaria. Muchos niños han muerto a consecuencia de la mala nutrición.

Los huelguistas mantienen sus propios centros de primeros auxilios, donde hay enfermeras que atienden a centenares de personas diariamente. El hospital ya tiene más de 600 enfermos. El gobierno hondureño mantiene brigadas sanitarias en la región, pero hay peligro de epidemia.

Los huelguistas mantienen el orden con sus propios policías. No permiten que se introduzcan bebidas alcohílas en los campamentos, ni armas de ninguna clase. Los bastones que llevan fueron calificados por la Frutera de "pavorosos toletes".

Fig. 8.9. *Bohemia*, June 1954. *Courtesy of* Bohemia.

it rested upon a potential threat of violence, indicating that workers could not completely set themselves apart from entrenched methods for organizing a social order.

Rather than directly counter a scary image conjured up by the dominant narrative of the strike, the photograph of workers carrying batons instead problematizes the strike as a visually constituted event. The composition of the image encourages the viewer to adopt multiple perspectives. It is a *contre-plongée* medium shot, and the viewer might first consider the scene as a whole. The security guard takes up nearly the entire frame and commands the attention of those around him. The camera offers a view of the worker who has ceased to be externally disciplined. He has appropriated a symbol of physical force and casually holds it across his broad shoulders. His shirt is threadbare, and he wears an armband. The viewer might then shift her gaze to that of a few workers who are looking at their companion, a designated enforcer of their collective will. From there, the spectator's attention might slip, as she suddenly notices a couple of children who are observing the photographer taking the picture and reflects on the fact that this event is being photographed. The photographer is being watched and cannot see without being seen. Constructing a new reality and making demands to be paid enough to feed one's family is, the photo reminds us, fundamentally about showing and seeing.[14] The viewer might also imaginatively move into the position of the baton-carrying worker, standing confidently looking out at the spectators gathered around him. Taken together, the intersecting gazes within this single image and the depicted subjects watching the photographer create a metapicture of the event that produces, by staging, the coming into being of the workers as a self-disciplinary collective agent.

Abstaining from violence but carrying sticks, impoverished laboring peoples created a scene in which they could be captured using their faculties of self-government. As illustrated by the single photograph of the striking workers published by *Life*, such visuals of plebeians organizing themselves in large groups were difficult to contain. The semiotic openness of the images meant that even the communist/anticommunist logic of the Cold War could not render the strikers unambiguously. A caption could be used to label them as "communists," but viewers might still see ordinary people who were worthy of respect and support. This is likely the reason that only the one image was used. It was not the only photograph that *Life* took of the striking workers, but none of the others were ever published; they remain buried in the *Time Life* archives. The same was true locally: in 1944, Honduran newspapers had carried multiple images of the masses "spontaneously" supporting dictator Tiburcio Carías Andino, but ten years later, none decided to print photographs of the striking banana workers. Textual accounts of the strike were simply easier to control. The photos capture women forging themselves as political subjects. The images capture but do not contain the supposed sociocultural type of the *campeño*. Relaying the spirit of collective action of the unwashed, who are seen densely packed together listening to their representatives or building refuges from the scorching sun, these televisual objects help the workers to make civil claims at a distance, harnessing the sympathy, or at least the dim awareness, of spectators located far from the plantations. The text provides the narrative infrastructure for understanding the strike, but the photos provide the sensuous, embodied moment of decision, as subaltern subjects leap into the perhaps.

Yet as fragmentary artifacts of civil claims-making, the series of images in *Bohemia* goes further still. These pictures highlight the ways that photojournalism is itself, as Robert Hariman and John Louis Lucaites put it, "an important technology of liberal-democratic citizenship."[15] It bears repeating that photographers of different nationalities independently made dozens of photographs of the strike, but somehow those images remained largely absent from the public sphere. Taking the existence of such images together with their limited circulation suggests that the editors at prominent news outlets in the United States and Honduras were well aware that such photos had a unique power to equip viewers to act as citizens. In viewing a tightly framed scene of a banana worker and his family or, alternatively, a group of workers visually articulating democratic demands in front of United Fruit's divisional offices, the spectator in Tegucigalpa or Boston might seek to understand the story and experiences of the depicted subjects. This is not to say that photojournalistic images are ideologically neutral or that the wide circulation of such images leads inexorably to liberal-democratic politics. Rather, I am content to make the obvious point that publicly circulating photographic images facilitate certain kinds of identification and affiliation. In the case of the 1954 strike, *Life* had an abundance of beautiful photographs of the sixty-nine-day event, but it only published one. *Life* could have provided its audience with the visual means for establishing emotional connections to civic actors in Honduras; but it hid those images away and instead published pictures of military personnel and a US-funded mercenary. In contrast, *Bohemia* published twenty-four images of the striking workers, using the photographic image to document and extend the workers' performance of their embodied citizenship.

DANGEROUS POSSIBILITY OF A WORKER-CITIZEN

The strike, the financial losses to the US-owned fruit companies, and the clandestine operation to overthrow Árbenz by way of Honduras: each was a source of great concern to officials in the United States. So the US ambassador conducted "an aerial survey of the area to determine whether there is any actual infiltration into Honduras from Guatemala which would add to the unsettled labor and political conditions in Honduras." Given that "the United States might wish to provide direct military assistance to Honduras," this was an act with secretly declared military ends that was reminiscent of the Cariato's use of US pilots and US-supplied airplanes to subdue rival strongmen and uppity banana workers. In contemplating "urgent and forceful action by the United States" to deal with the "unsettled labor conditions on the north coast," US officials were considering, once again, the possibility of placing workers into a state of exception.[16] As workers stood up, cable traffic between Tegucigalpa and Washington intensified. Each piece of official correspondence scrutinized how to put the workers back down: through military force? by dividing the movement? by giving in to some of their demands? The US and Honduran response to the strike turned out to be a combination of those approaches.

While the United States was prepared from the outset to use force, the striking workers did not give the state a pretext for violently cracking down on them. In Honduras and abroad, observers noted that the workers consistently conducted themselves nonviolently and in accordance with the law, as the US State Department reported early in the strike:

> 9 May 1954: Strike on north coast is going on, but everything is orderly. The leaders of the Government believe they can maintain peace in the area (and Ambassador Willauer agrees with them) for two reasons: (1) the Government has shown strength; and (2) the leaders of the strikers have shown a remarkable control over the strikers.[17]

The Honduran government had already sent troops to occupy El Progreso, Lima, Tela, Ceiba, and Puerto Cortés. Local, national, and international hardliners had already denounced the strikers as "communists," funded or at least spurred on by Guatemalan radicals. The United States, in particular, showed its commitment to fueling the conspiracy that Guatemala was involved in the strike. But even the United Fruit Company acknowledged that "not a single act of violence has been recorded in the two divisions of the Tela Railroad Company."[18]

The United States sent military personnel to small United Fruit Company towns to assess the situation. In a memo copied to the US Army, Air Force, and Navy, the US embassy's military attaché reported that two of his representatives "visited La Lima and La Ceiba, afternoon May 9, purpose on spot observation. Present situation static and non-violent." That is, the workers had already created an event. The US military was monitoring the situation closely, in the very sites that workers had created and which had now become objects of a disciplinary US gaze. The US military attaché continued: United Fruit Company "compounds sealed off by pickets and American residents requested keep to homes. Arrangements made both places for emergency radio communications via Tropical Radio and Attaché aircraft." Labor was asserting a claim to sovereignty, and US citizens had to prepare to make a hasty retreat. What remained unfathomable was that the workers themselves might be capable of making demands: "Responsible opinion Tegucigalpa and north coast indicates strike undoubtedly Communist inspired and directed." The best way to combat the workers' ability to govern themselves was to deny that they were even capable of self-government, obliterating their acts of self-sculpting by rendering them incomprehensible. But neither the Honduran nor the US government had any proof of communist intervention, despite the "Embassy making every effort obtain concrete evidence this point." The military attaché concluded his missive: "Though situation presently non-violent; possibility eruption exists and must be borne in mind."

"Possibility eruption exists." The workers had suddenly appeared. They were an unexpected and unforeseen political force. The US government continued to provide real-time monitoring of the event. Its officials were watching the sites of an unintelligible, because it escaped regulation, appearance of labor's power to govern itself. Visiting the key sites of the strike, embassy officials captured the workers as they were creating a historical rupture. The terse, ungrammatical secret cables sutured the visual and the verbal, conveying time-lapse images of an eruption of a worker-being. The US military official continued, "Assistant Alusna and Embassy representative visiting Puerto Cortes, La Lima, and San Pedro Sula afternoon May 10 for further information. List of names alleged strike leaders being forwarded separate dispatch for checking by all agencies. Tegucigalpa quiet."[19] Workers who, nine days before, had not existed as political subjects were now deemed leaders to be identified and separated from the others. Meanwhile, the site of worker-being had not yet imposed itself on Tegucigalpa.

The memo reveals how the United States sought to lend its mobile apparatus of violence to exert control over bodies and minds to which it had no claim. The impulse to answer the strike with brute force was not just felt by US officials; the embassy reported that General J. Antonio Inestroza of the Gálvez administration was also "recommending martial law."[20] A week later, Secretary of State John Foster Dulles examined possible scenarios in which the United States could intervene militarily to "give immediate assistance" to Honduras. He made clear that the United States would not publicly declare its intention to provide military assistance in the event of an attack. But Dulles invoked the Rio Treaty of 1947, also known as the Hemispheric Defense Doctrine, to warn that if Guatemala attacked Honduras, "the signatory states have in principle approved action in advance." Dulles then quietly conflated the banana workers' strike with an armed attack by Guatemala, suggesting that "the developments in Honduras" might be reason enough to provide military assistance.[21]

THE COMPREHENSIBLE INCOMPREHENSIBLE

By the early 1950s, workers, peasants, and the north coast industrialists whose business interests had been adversely affected by the Carías–United Fruit alliance suddenly found a range of political alternatives, from the newly moderate National Party to the long-exiled Liberal Party and even the less visible Honduran Democratic Revolutionary Party. In addition, members of the Honduran middle classes, student activists, labor leaders, and intellectuals found inspiration in the Guatemalan example of labor and land reform. Besides, as the United States began to back away from Carías, President Gálvez's relative openness and moderate respect for human rights gave labor activists a bit more room to maneuver. By 1954, many Hondurans, and especially wage laborers on the north coast, were conscious of the ways that they were politically, socially, and economically excluded. They were also well aware that their situation could be improved upon. Even the US Embassy in Tegucigalpa stated that the workers were justified in demanding a pay increase and that 99 percent of them were legitimate workers who genuinely believed in the cause of fighting for labor protections.[22] In other words, what had been taken to be incomprehensible, unless the presumed role of nefarious communist agitators was posited, was really quite easy to understand by simply looking at local conditions and proximate causes.

By May 1954, the cost of living in Honduras had risen dramatically without any corresponding increase in wages.[23] In April 1953, a day laborer earned the equivalent of US$0.21 per hour. After an eight-hour workday, he would have $1.68. If he went to the United Fruit Company's commissaries, where plantation workers were often obligated to shop, he would pay $0.55

a pound for rice, $0.60 a pound for kidney beans, $0.55 a pound for sugar, and $2.00 a pound for cheese. (Most towns had locally owned shops that offered lower prices and domestically produced staples.) After a full day of work, he would have earned enough money to buy just six ounces of Kellogg's Corn Flakes. The milk to go with his cereal—as well as other essentials like cooking oil, clothing, shoes, kerosene, soap, and coffee—would have to wait for another day's wages.[24] But for people who had never participated in a wage economy, having money of one's own was quite a thrill: "It was only then that I was able to see money in my hands," recalled Gabriel David Galeano. "I began to buy clothes, shoes, and other necessary things."[25] High prices did not decrease the desire to consume; they only frustrated it.

A glut in the labor market exacerbated problems. By March 1954, United Fruit was looking for ways to reduce the size of its Honduran workforce. In an internal memorandum, one manager in Boston proposed the following to the Bocas del Toro Division in Panama:

> Such labor is available in Honduras and if we select and transfer to you laborers presently working for the Company in Honduras, it would be possible for you to dispense with some of the Indians that you are using who are doubtless inefficient and cannot be considered permanent employees. We consider that the Company has a surplus of laborers on its payroll in Honduras and what we have in mind would accomplish the double purpose of relieving Honduras of excess workers and providing you with a supply of dependable, experienced workers.[26]

The manager emphasized that the workers would be carefully screened: "no barbers, banjo players or members of similar professions" would be sent. In other words, prior to the strike, the company planned to reduce its workforce in Honduras. The company's practice of moving "excess" Honduran workers to its Panama Division reveals another key factor in the strike: the mobility and transnational experiences of the banana workers.[27]

The company showed great alacrity in moving its Honduran workers from one country to another. In 1945, for example, United Fruit accused twelve Hondurans of leading a strike on its abaca plantations in Panama. The company enlisted the police to jail the labor leaders and then repatriated all twelve back to Honduras.[28] While workers often migrated from their places and countries of origin to provide better opportunities for their families, this incident illustrates that some Honduran workers were restive and that the company often initiated the movement of labor between Central American countries. Later, in 1951, the company spent $27,880 to send 400 men, 90 women, and 166 children from the plantations in Honduras to work in Bocas del Toro.[29] A banana blight had wiped out the plantations in Honduras, prompting one company manager to argue in 1951 that "these families are barely subsisting. They want work."[30] Honduran Vice President Julio Lozano Díaz was actively involved in facilitating the movement of labor. The company transported the Honduran workers on one of its own ships, the *Omoa*. About a year later, managers were unhappy with the arrangement and found that "439 laborers, women and children were imported from Honduras during the year, but that a total of 204, or 46 percent, had to be repatriated presumably because they were, for one reason or another, unsuited for work in Almirante."[31]

In addition to the direct costs, United Fruit recognized that by relocating its laborers, it was facilitating the circulation among workers in its various divisions of ideas about their rights. In July 1953, for instance, the company identified forty-eight men who had allegedly organized an "illegal strike" and sabotaged Farm 31 of the Changuinola District of the Bocas del Toro Division, chopping down banana plants. Thirty-two of those forty-eight men were Hondurans, whom the company promptly repatriated.[32] The role of Honduran workers in the strike in Panama prompted a manager with the Tela Railroad Company to observe that some of the repatriated workers "were not hesitant to complain bitterly about the company." Aware that ideas about workers' rights were circulating between Panama and Honduras, the manager worried that some of the laborers "have interested themselves considerably in the privileges and legal rights of workers in Panama." He concluded, "Some of our labor going to Panama may be getting a sort of indoctrination which they feel inclined to want to exercise when they return to Honduras."[33] Beyond ideas and the experience of working in countries that guaranteed better conditions for their workers, Honduran laborers in Panama found concrete models for organizing to protect their own interests. The president of the Labor Union of the Chiriqui Land Company, a United Fruit subsidiary, compiled a nine-page list of about 450 workers who were union members.[34] On the list were 78 Hondurans. As members of trade unions in Panama or Costa Rica, a significant number of Honduran workers gained experiences that informed the claims to dignity that they then made back in their own country. In short, the composition of the banana-company workforce was international and multiethnic; moreover, the ideas and organizational models that circulated at the time were generated in diverse sites and forged in a variety of local struggles, from Panama to Honduras and beyond.

The United Fruit Company's internal memos reveal that it only reluctantly recognized the rights of its workers. Rather than implementing a companywide labor policy, the corporation sought to exploit workers in each country to the extent that the host country's laws would allow. Hence the fear that Hondurans who had worked in countries—such as Panama, Costa Rica, and Guatemala—that afforded them more protections, including the right to join a union, might return to Honduras and infect a workforce that was still forbidden from unionizing. Drawing on their experiences of working under better conditions in other parts of Central America, some of the banana workers in Honduras may have come to see a confrontation with the United Fruit Company as not only a possibility but a necessity.

While a significant number of laborers learned from their experiences of working in other countries under more humane labor regimes, the 1954 strike was nevertheless a singular event produced under the specific conditions of the Honduran north coast. As we have seen, the strike movement was not merely the result of political agitation and a coherent agenda. A number of social and economic factors contributed to the workers' frustration, most particularly the rising cost of living and the poor treatment they received from their employers.[35] Ezequiel Escoto, a resident of El Progreso, describes this constellation of grievances that workers suddenly expressed in the strike:

> Outbreak of protests, contagion of popular indignation, trail of rebellion. It seems nothing more than the explosion of so many repressed feelings, so many frustrated aspirations, and so many thwarted longings. Neither the Government of the Republic nor the Companies that operate on the north coast have paid attention to the living conditions of this suffering but not resigned people.[36]

This *progreseño* aptly describes the movement of consciousness initiated within workers who had long been affronted by their employer and by their national government. The company had itself produced this sense of indignation and shame within its labor force. Unable to openly lobby for gradual change and modest protections, workers had little option but to turn the daily indignities that they suffered in the workplace inward. Such humiliation and "thwarted longings" congealed into anger and rage, the subjective wellsprings of the event that became the 1954 strike.

"Shame is already revolution of a kind," Karl Marx wrote in 1843 to his friend Arnold Ruge. "Shame is a kind of anger which is turned inward. And if a whole nation really experienced a sense of shame, it would be like a lion, crouching ready to spring."[37] Shame transformed into anger creates the subjective potential for a militant leap. But as we saw in Rafael Platero Paz's joyful *Garden of Eden*, this process of subjectivization is realized only when an externally imposed shame—in that particular case, a neocolonial and heteronormative structuring of his social world—is rejected in an act of exteriorization. Platero Paz took society's shame outside of himself; he momentarily expelled the superego that agro-export capitalism had installed in him, and in a fragmentary, yet vividly truthful gesture, he depicted himself as nakedly equal to an agent of US capital. The *Garden of Eden* photo thus suggests that the refusal to own and accept shame is predicated on a performance of equality—in this case, homoerotic and enacted equality between self and one's object of desire. As the one who might be expected to feel ashamed rejects the emotion assigned to her, she rehumanizes herself as a self-confident thinking subject, equal in kind to the one who has attempted to make her feel she was less. In describing a "contagion of popular indignation," Ezequiel Escoto identifies the collective potential for rebellion that a shared experience of shame produces. Hence "this suffering but not resigned people" was like Marx's crouching lion, ready to make a leap. The suffering was something they shared in common, as was the desire for a "wage that supports a decent life." The refusal to resign themselves to a future of suffering at the hands of the company and the state meant that the shame had not turned into melancholy, that the anger had not been converted into self-destructive bile. As a collective agent created itself as a sovereign subject that could make demands as an equal to the company and the Honduran state, shared suffering and the lack of resignation combined in "the explosion of so many repressed sentiments."

THE IMAGES THAT WE GET TO SEE

In 1914, Frederick Upham Adams's *Conquest of the Tropics* denigrated the agricultural and political capacities of the peoples of Latin America and the Caribbean who had cultivated bananas for hundreds of years. Forty years later, *Life* sought to do the same, revealing a continuity between the World War I–era imagescape of *Conquest* and the magazine's own in the early Cold War years.

We might conclude our discussion of the battle of photojournalistic images by examining a privately held picture from the United Fruit Company Photograph Collection at Harvard University. This photo exemplifies the making invisible of popular governmental power in an exceptional space. The image is significant for what it does not show, but what its caption suggests. Captions typically narrow the range of possible interpretations of a picture, remote-controlling the viewer toward a particular reading of the depicted scene or subject; but rather than anchoring meaning, this caption leads the viewer out of the photograph and into the strike that is taking place outside the frame.

The photo itself, capturing soldiers with guns and two bulldozers, provides the consummate metaphor for the company's methods (figure 8.11). The image is composed of three planes, with a backdrop of heavy machinery and a reworked landscape, a middle plane of what the linguistic

Mezapa project, showing deliberate levee break made on May 8th to relieve impounded flood waters from farm. This action was necessary as strikers closed down project drainage pumps which later were serviced and put back into operation and operated by foreign personnel. Before levee was cut the farms were flooded and by making this deliberate break many acres of cultivations were saved. Break was later repaired by dragline working under military guard. Picture taken after release of water from farms to the floodway area.
TELA, HONDURAS   June 15, 1954

Fig. 8.10. Original caption: "Mezapa project, showing deliberate levee break made on May 8th to relieve impounded flood waters from farm. This action was necessary as strikers closed down project drainage pumps which later were serviced and put back into operation and operated by foreign personnel. TELA, HONDURAS. June 15, 1954." *Courtesy of the United Fruit Company Photograph Collection, Baker Library Historical Collections, Harvard Business School.*

Fig. 8.11. Original caption: "Part of foreign personnel crew which made emergency repairs under military guard. Foreigners shown in picture, left to right, are Wiedeman, Troop, Wrenn and Hartness and government military personnel. At times our emergency crew was split and worked on two jobs in different sectors simultaneously, which was the case on this particular day. TELA, HONDURAS. June 15, 1954." *Courtesy of the United Fruit Company Photograph Collection, Baker Library Historical Collections, Harvard Business School.*

accompaniment describes as "foreign personnel" (identified by last names), and in front, nearest the camera, soldiers holding their rifles. The striking workers are erased from the scene and rendered unseen as the archive repeats the violence of pretending to grow bananas without the agency of local labor. The company accused the strikers of being duped by outside agitators even as it brought in, by its own acknowledgment, foreign workers to keep its essential operations on track. Meanwhile, Honduran soldiers, authorized to shoot, are put in a position in which they must regard the striking workers as domestic enemies, an internal threat that the company must be defended against.

The middle-aged white men smile for the camera, while the younger, brown-skinned soldiers maintain their serious demeanor. The respective positions of their lips and cheeks have much to do with different cultural conventions of portraiture. In the United States, the advertising industry had already trained a habitual reflex that caused a subject to tighten exactly the right muscles as soon as he posed for a snapshot with friends or family, conveying a sense of perpetual happiness and satisfaction. In Honduras, particularly among poor and rural people whose young men joined the military, such cultural programming had not yet taken place, leaving the subject to respond through other gestures, including those that were generally understood to indicate seriousness and dignity.

But this disjuncture of culturally synchronized smiling may also signal emotions that each party felt at the time. Beyond certain conventions of portraiture that dictated a given repertoire of behaviors and poses before the camera, the white United Fruit Company engineers and heavy-equipment operators may have felt genuinely satisfied at repairing a levee and partially subverting the will of the striking workers. The smiles, in this case, would be the outward display of a will that was claiming a victory, reshaping a landscape when the local workers had said, "No, no work until our needs are addressed." Likewise, if we take the straight faces of the Honduran soldiers at face value, their serious demeanor might reveal the discomfort they felt at having to obey orders to contradict the will of the tens of thousands of men who looked like them and who came from similar backgrounds. If this feeling is what lies behind the straight faces, then the uniforms and proximity to bulldozers and US supervisors could not fully override their own misgivings about their part in threatening to execute brute force to contervene the actions of their counterparts who toiled on the company's plantations. But the photo will not yield the sentiments that motivated the outward expressions it captured. So while the Honduran soldiers working on behalf of the company may have felt ashamed at betraying their laboring countrymen, it is entirely possible that they felt quite satisfied in having separated themselves from those who looked like them to work on behalf of the company.

Figs. 9.1 and 9.2. Strikers on top of train when President Juan Manuel Gálvez came to town. These are two of Rafael Platero Paz's photographs on display in the offices of the local TV station TeleProgreso and in El Progreso's Casa de la Cultura. *Courtesy of the Rafael Platero Paz Archive.*

NINE

Between Is and Ought

Aída López de Castillo wrote a subdued caption for one of her father's most dramatic photographs: "With Engine 155 pulling a long line of cars, thousands of workers came from the banana fields to this city for an important meeting related to their labor interests." The photo is now a local favorite, hanging in El Progreso's Casa de la Cultura and reproduced in televisual montages.

Since the dawn of the Reforma Liberal of the 1880s, Honduran political elites had sought to build a national railroad. By the 1920s, through a series of concessions and land transfers, the country had a partial railroad that snaked through the banana plantations, serving only the US-based companies while leaving Honduras deep in debt for rail lines that it neither owned nor controlled. Now, as a result of the strike and for the first time ever, Hondurans controlled the railroads in their country. Platero Paz's photographs of workers riding on top of the train make manifest this historic reversal.

A couple of weeks into the 1954 strike, the Honduran state repossessed the north coast railroads, which had been in the hands of the United Fruit Company. The reason was simple:

In light of developments that have emerged on the north coast, the Ministry of Development and Labor takes over the administration of the National Railroad, of which the Tela RR Co. was previously in charge. The public is hereby warned that given that the National Railroad is property of the State, the Government will not permit its interests to be harmed.[1]

The railroad, for which Hondurans had traded away their most fertile land and accrued debts that would take nearly a century to pay off, was legally back in the hands of Hondurans. The workers had scared the company into giving this symbolically charged infrastructure to the dependable governing class, which showed itself, once again, to be a tool of the multinational banana conglomerates and not genuine representatives of "the public." By claiming the railroad as state property, the Honduran government took away one of the workers' key rallying points while also intimating that the workers might commit acts of sabotage. Would the workers both rally in the name of Honduras and damage state property? By publishing this notice, the companies and the government warned the workers of the consequences of damaging their property. They also revealed what the workers had long known: the fruit companies controlled the most valuable means of production and distribution—the land, the railroads, and the ports—on the north coast. Finally, they recognized that the workers' demands were, at the most fundamental level, about sovereignty. Honduras was an independent state that rarely behaved like one. The workers sought to change that. Just as Latin America was entering the dark tunnel of US-sponsored Cold War terrorism, and just as the CIA was putting the final pieces in place to overthrow President Jacobo Guzmán Árbenz in Guatemala, the United Fruit Company openly gave the Honduran state possession of the railroad that it had controlled for more than forty years.[2]

To translate these events into historiographical terms, we would do well to recall historian Arturo Taracena Arriola's riff on "Order and Progress," the motto of Latin American liberals: "While the modernity that liberals called for asked much of the toiling masses in the name of progress, order gave them little in exchange."[3] By the end of the strike, the workers had taken over the symbol of economic progress and completely disrupted the disciplinary order that had kept them in their place for so many decades.

The mode of economic development pursued by Central American liberals between 1870 and 1929 was one of progress built on the backs of workers, subsistence farmers, the indigenous, and women, all of whom, until around 1945, remained effectively sidelined from the political game.

Experiences within Central America varied enormously, from the singularity of Costa Rica's reformist movement under Rafael Ángel Calderón Guardia to the Carías dictatorship in Honduras. But by the end of World War II, as historian Víctor Hugo Acuña Ortega argues, the general trend was to abandon, under pressure from the popular classes, the model of the liberal oligarchic state of "progress" and "order." In its place, the reformist development state began to emerge.[4]

With respect to Honduras, I would argue that the transfer of responsibility for the railroad from the United Fruit Company to the Honduran state was the emblematic moment in the transition from the era of the liberal oligarchic state, and the attendant politics and aesthetics of the banana republic that it facilitated, to the era of the reformist development state. This transition, furthermore, is one that we can see figuratively enacted in and by these photographs. This post-1954 configuration of the Honduran state was characterized by a central government that took more of an interventionist approach to promoting economic development and to addressing the demands of the popular classes.[5] At the height of the strike, the company and the state publicly acknowledged that the workers were a real social and political force. The concession-granting and subservient liberal oligarchic state was, albeit briefly, a railroad-controlling mediator between its worker-citizens and the powerful fruit company interests. Platero Paz's photo captures the exact moment when Honduras pivoted from one era to another.

Directly engaging in the politics of representation, Platero Paz created a pictorial story that resonated in its own time and continues to resonate in ours. His photos bring drama and affect to the newspaper notice that documents the legal transfer of responsibility for the railroad. This particular image is an objective document of the workers' conquest. It renders the social fact of the strike. Within the discursive framework of the "banana republic," it condenses and makes visible a crucial moment of contestation and redefinition. "Whose railroads?" "Our railroads!" As the workers reinvented themselves and their nation, they simultaneously changed how others perceived them and how they perceived themselves. They dented, ever so slightly, the regime of visibility that positioned them as neocolonial dependents of a powerful multinational corporation backed by the Marine Corps and diplomats of the US government.

The photo is also a subjective record of how the strike was seen. It registers the embodied dimension of individual and collective sight. In this image and others, we have Platero Paz's distinct gaze. It was one that valued the workers as historical agents and facilitated their claims to social rights and political recognition. With his photographs, Platero Paz helped to translate the demands of workers into claims made by citizens. We have seen that through images, workers addressed themselves to multiple audiences: the managers of the United Fruit Company, officials in the Honduran government, their fellow Hondurans, and a dispersed community of spectators in places like the United States, Cuba, and Mexico. Through images, the workers became fuller citizens within the boundaries of the nation-state. At the same time, they became citizens in a broader, less bounded civil space that theorist Ariella Azoulay might describe as "the citizenry of photography." The claims that workers made reverberated in each of these civil spheres. The images that circulated within and beyond Honduras put pressure on the fruit companies, as well as the Honduran and US governments, to quickly resolve the strike.

As a local photographer in a transnational and transcultural site, Rafael Platero Paz played a crucial role in producing modern subjects in El Progreso. By placing the Platero Paz and United Fruit Company photo archives in tension with each other, we have uncovered battles over the very meaning of representation as well as the specific locations and historical conditions in which certain acts could be made visible. The qualitative difference between the two archives reveals two different visualities, two different collective projects, neither of which was monolithic and both of which contained images that lead us outside of the frame and into the worlds in which the photographic subjects were acting. Created through a steady accretion of images produced by agents of sight who acted according to distinct logics and desires, each archive contained a different way, indeed multiple ways, of being-unto-a-goal.[6]

Platero Paz's photographs—the entire body of images that he created over the course of five decades of living and working in El Progreso— enabled workers to forge a visual subculture that could compete, at least locally, with the scopic regimes of the United Fruit Company, the Honduran government, and the Honduran press.[7] Recalling the decades of repression that workers faced under the Carías dictatorship, we have seen how the workers' demands only gained real force once they physically occupied the public spaces of the United Fruit Company town: by camping out in front of the company's local headquarters, by standing on the railroad tracks outside the gates of the American Zone, and by taking over the Ramón Rosa Plaza in front of the offices of the local municipal government. By staging this encounter between themselves, their bosses, and their government, the workers simultaneously staged an encounter with a dispersed spectatorship. For ordinary Hondurans, this was a David and Goliath story, as the narrative of an unequal fight triggered nationalist pride and fostered a spectatorship of solidarity. Suddenly, the workers were everyman, and their fight became the fight of all Hondurans.

Images of the United Fruit Company as an octopus sucking the life out of Latin America had long circulated in leftist newspapers. The strike, however, accelerated and intensified the circulation of such images and grounded them in an opportunity for Hondurans, and viewers beyond Honduras, to witness the struggle of tens of thousands of humble workers against a powerful corporation. Their political claims thus passed through visuality, and visuality itself passed through a narrative of an unfair fight. The workers' assertion of dignity and their performative enactment of a new micropolity changed the unspoken rules about what could be represented, produced, and circulated. These workers and their photographer were helped along by the anti-imperialist literary realism of writers like Ramón Amaya Amador, who narrativized the struggle in advance. Meanwhile, Rafael Platero Paz, an unsung hero, helped to ease the passage of workers from mere marginalized and disposable bodies into active political subjects. In this neocolonial space, for the workers to become political subjects, they first had to become visual subjects.

In the United Fruit Company Photograph Collection at the Harvard Business School, there are 1,426 photographs of the company's operations in Honduras between 1891 and 1962. The United Fruit photo archive contains dozens of images of banana plants, healthy and diseased, of the flooding of plantations, and of microscopes and other scientific paraphernalia in the company's plant physiology laboratory in Lancetilla, Honduras. In the seventy-year period that this archive covers, the 1954 strike was the most consequential event to take place in the company's Honduran plantations, and yet there are only two photos that, with the decisive assistance of their captions, document it. The sixty-nine-day strike was an event driven by the willful actions of workers rather than the determinism of fungi or hurricanes, but somehow it barely registered in the massive and otherwise systematic United Fruit archive. Evidently, the company did not consider its politically engaged workers as legitimate objects of sight, except for purposes of surveillance and repression.[8] Instead, the United Fruit Company's instrumental use of photography fit within the broader approach to the North American "science of work," epitomized by Taylorism and Fordism, that held sway in the early decades of the twentieth century. As historian

Elspeth H. Brown has shown, US corporations used photography both to standardize mass production and to rationalize mass consumption.[9] Striking workers were unrepresentable within this visual regime. Competent scientists handling snakes in the company's serpentarium and time-lapse photos of ripening bananas: these were recognizable subjects. The plethora of images from the company's operations in Honduras coupled with only the faintest trace of the 1954 strike bring to mind Michel-Rolph Trouillot's pointed observation: "One 'silences' a fact or an individual as a silencer silences a gun."[10] The official archive muffles the violence that brought it into being.

In contrast, Platero Paz's images, found in boxes piled high in the shower stall of a nonoperational bathroom in Profesora Aída's house in El Progreso, offer the incarnate gaze of the workers' lensman. They offered the laborers a new way to see themselves, as individuals, as families, and as a collective agent that had taken over the railroad. In occupying the train, the striking workers converted the nominal transfer of responsibility for the railroad—from the company to the Honduran state—into a substantive fact. But with a twist, for now "the public" had wildly taken control over what had been entrusted to the calm and reasonable governing class.

This chaotic symbolic conquest resulted from the workers' decision to withhold their labor. The photographs of men swarming the trains document and reinforce the role of workers in Honduran civil society. They were the ones who insisted upon and created the political conditions for enacting the Labor Code of 1959 (Código de Trabajo), which essentially enshrined a product of their will into law. They were the nation builders who not only changed the legal structures of their society but also created new institutions of political affiliation, which began as underground workers' committees and were eventually converted into aboveground labor unions. In these new intermediate associations, the workers created organizations that both the company and the state were obligated, by the new situation on the ground, to recognize as legitimate representatives of the workers. Their leaders, representing the different departments within the United Fruit Company, served as the mediators between the Honduran state, the company, the regular workers, and the local population. The workers and campesinos of the north coast were, in turn, the base for the Liberal Party as well as the Honduran Democratic Revolutionary Party and even the small Communist Party of Honduras. This was one other way that the working men and women of El Progreso articulated themselves and their concerns to the nation-state. In doing so, they made their concerns—about dignified work, sovereignty, and their rights as laborers and citizens—heard in the United States, Guatemala, Mexico, and Cuba.

The photographs of workers atop the train capture and extend the exultant moment when they reclaimed the fruits of their labor and the symbol of Honduras's dependent development. From the stories of the glory days of the *poquiteros* of the 1890s–1910s through the monopoly landownership and political repression of the United Fruit Company's imperial heyday from the 1920s to 1954, these photographs are a testament to the risen worker, awake to his potential when acting in concert with his fellow workers. Meanwhile, we had a silent witness in Rafael Platero Paz, who, like a midwife, coaxed and soothed this new cultural formation into being. Through his photographs, he delivered this collective action back to the workers, to his society, and, inadvertently, to us.

These pasts—of land, tools, surplus labor, scattered photographs, and a general strike—were part of capitalist accumulation on the north coast of Honduras. They were part of an aesthetics of empire and plantation agriculture. But, to follow Dipesh Chakrabarty's reading of Marx, such elements of capital do not always aid in its reproduction. Instead, occasionally, they "interrupt and punctuate the run of capital's own logic."[11] El Progreso was a small town with a remarkably diverse citizenry, comprised of Honduran mestizos and creoles, Salvadoran fieldworkers and entrepreneurs, North American managers and engineers, Palestinian and Chinese merchants, West Indian blacks, and Garifuna. Out of that heterogeneity, which was, in early twentieth-century El Progreso, intertwined with the production interests of the United Fruit Company, multiple possibilities emerged. A Salvadoran photographer and a North American employee of the United Fruit Company posed together unclothed: for a moment, the two lived in "intimate and plural relationships to capital."[12] The gay *Garden of Eden* perfectly allegorizes an unexpected past, alluding to a pre-fallen paradise when nature herself was divinity and humans were demiurgic artists.

Yet another past interrupting the logic of capital was that of the Palestinian merchants in El Progreso. When the Arab Christian migrants gave the carved tortoiseshell seal of the republic to the Honduran state in 1928, they performed a divided visuality, one that appealed to Honduran nationalism by way of their homeland in Palestine. They belonged in both of these communities, and yet they didn't. Or, more dramatically, the workers who briefly colonized the company's trains represented themselves as the interruption, as that which briefly halted the totalizing march of progress, as those who insisted: We belong. We are progress. We are the new.

Rafael Platero Paz was there to translate all of this from the four dimensions of space and time into the two dimensions of photographs.[13] He did so from his particular position in the world. In leaving us another visuality, he left us the possibility of a different narrative of US–Latin American encounters. I have sought to contextualize his photos and to offer an analytical history of the connections between North American capital, visual images, and political claims-making on the north coast of Honduras. Yet Platero Paz's photographs offer something more.

Platero Paz's images invited me into the affective worlds of *progreseños*, into worlds of difference and particularity. This was where I found thousands of photographed individuals—most of whom, at least for me, will always remain unnamed—reaching out to one another, occasionally denouncing an injustice, but mostly just trying to represent themselves in the best possible light. Encoded in each of these images are glimpses of the worlds that individual visual subjects had and toward which each strived. Thus, in picturing *progreseños*, Platero Paz inscribed onto photographic paper what was and what people hoped was to come.

Photography thus takes place at the intersection of is and ought. Someone beat a Chinese merchant in early twentieth-century El Progreso. He should not have been beaten. The photographer and his subject collaborated to document what happened and, by visually denouncing it, to construct a claim for more humane treatment in the future. Photographs document facts and realize norms. Photographers make still images. The photographer and his subject, the image and the viewer of that image: each acts on and in the world. Photographs thus provide us with traces of pasts that we would not otherwise have access to. Is and ought, was and could have been. The fact and the norm were both captured and made manifest through images.

I understand this relationship between the factual and the normative in photography through the image of the elderly woman fervently praying near a smoky cauldron in the depths of the 1954 strike. Like all photographs, this one contains the that-has-been that Roland Barthes called the *noeme*, or essence, of photography.[14] This image is quite obviously evidence of the fact that at some point this woman and the cauldron were in front of Platero Paz's camera lens. In a different essay, Barthes refers to this as the "denotative" aspect of photography.[15] It is this feature of photography that has enabled the present study. Under a very different visual regime, it is this same epistemological realism that governed the United Fruit Company's use of photography. And it is the reason that photos are used in courtrooms as transparent documents of "truth." But photographs contain more than dead referents signaling what was.

The photographs that I have been most interested in are the ones that called forth a new reality. These were images that sought to change the world. Some of them did so by denouncing a situation in their present and by positing, for the future, an alternative set of circumstances and social relations. Other photos, even in and through their very mundaneness, sought to change the world ever so slightly. Posing for a portrait is always, and essentially, an act of self-representation. It was this representational act, and its accompanying representational space on photographic paper, that Platero Paz made available to the laboring masses of the north coast. The thousands upon thousands of negatives of studio portraits that he left behind reveal traces of who people were and who they wanted others to believe they were. When they borrowed one of the ties and the suit jacket that he kept on hand as props, the subjects also indicated something about who they wanted to become.

This future-perfect tense of photographs is quite different from the that-has-been. It is the prayer of the woman next to the community cauldron. It is the yet-to-come of which Jacques Derrida spoke in another context. Derrida gives us two versions of the yet-to-come. He concludes *The Politics of Friendship* by saying, "For democracy remains to come; this is its essence in so far as it remains: not only will it remain indefinitely perfectible, hence always insufficient and future, but, belonging to the time of the promise, it will always remain, in each of its future times, to come."[16] Here he is speaking of willing into being a new reality, one that always slips from our grasp. This to-come is justice, but not law; democracy, but not our corruption-ridden electoral approximation of it. It is friendship beyond family, gender, nation, or species. It is the political community of freedom and equality that we strive for even as it escapes us. It is, for me, Platero Paz's *Garden of Eden*. It is the workers on top of the train in the final days of the 1954 strike. It is the Chinese merchant exposing his wounds for the camera. It is, most especially, the prayer of the old woman in the outdoor community kitchen. This spirit of photography, this visuality that escaped the logic of the banana republic even as it was inscribed within it, is the perhaps, the yet-to-come. It is the democratic impulse, revealed in strategic acts of self-forging, of a people who had been excluded.

In contrast to this future-oriented moment of decision that comes as subjects attempt, in their present, to alter their circumstances, in *Specters of Marx* Derrida attempts to theorize a "hauntological temporality." He does so in the context of reflecting upon our inheritance from Marx: "There are several times of the specter. It is a proper characteristic of the specter, if there is any, that no one can be sure if by returning it testifies to a living past or to a living future, for the *revenant* may already mark the promised return of the specter of living being."[17] Which ghosts of the banana plantations have disappeared only to unexpectedly reappear? Manuel Cálix Herrera and Juan Pablo Wainwright, communist organizers in the second decade of the twentieth century, returned in spirit in 1954. The massacre of Liberal Party activists in 1944 came back to haunt Gálvez in 1954. The anticommunist priest Joseph Wade was succeeded by Fr. James "Guadalupe" Carney, who, from his thatch hut in El Progreso, accompanied the campesino movement of the 1960s and 1970s in its relatively successful push for agrarian reform. In 2009, Roberto Micheletti Bain, grandson of Guillermo Bain, the first mayor of El Progreso, led the overthrow of President Manuel Zelaya. Meanwhile, those working to restore constitutional rule in Honduras summoned the fortitude of a previous generation of democratic activists, the striking workers of 1954.

As the young woman in her starched white dress stood on Rafael Platero Paz's front porch, what dreams were going through her head? What hopes for the future did she hold? What prayers would she offer? I don't know. What I do know is that she sought to represent herself with dignity. That alone says something about her past, her present, and the future she hoped for. In claiming this moment of dignity in a staged photographic event, she sought to bring about other such moments. In doing so, she asserted what Nicholas Mirzoeff might call her "right to look." Power claims for itself the right to classify, to separate, and to make its order feel natural. The right to look counters that power. This right, as Mirzoeff theorizes it, is not messianic or to come, but is grounded in "the right to existence."[18] So, even within the visual complex of a United Fruit Company town in a country that had not yet granted women the right to vote, as a subject in an assemblage that assigned her a proper place—economically and socially, sexually and geographically—she could still assert her right to look. While men may have looked at her, in at least one photograph she looked back, proudly and forcefully.

In the strike, the workers drew upon the rhetoric of anti-imperialist Honduran intellectuals and political parties that offered visions of reform and popular participation. But in asserting not only their right to look but a demand that they, and their legitimate claims, be recognized, laboring people constructed the most powerful countervisuality in the history of modern Honduras. Applying Mirzoeff's notion of countervisuality to this case entails considering how the workers created a new regime of classification, separation, and aestheticization.[19] The workers contested the iconic complex that rendered them docile and replaceable. By refusing to work, the laborers changed how the company was seen at home and abroad. No longer could it be represented as the epitome of progress and the key to Honduran prosperity. En masse, the workers rejected the old account, shattered the graven images, and replaced them with an icon of exploitation: the octopus. They not only asserted their right to look, they also demanded recognition, higher wages, and institutions that represented them and their interests.

Through the strike and in place of the image of the benevolent North American corporation, the workers gave others a way to envision who they, as United Fruit employees, were, where they belonged, and what might constitute normal treatment. In and through the strike, the workers fought for economic rights and, in the process, changed the parceling out of places and forms of participation in Honduran society. In a single stroke, the producers transformed the material system that subjected them to the nearly unchecked authority of the company's executives and managers, while also altering the mental means through which that authority usually worked. With the labor union, the workers created a structure for collectively negotiating with the company. With the strike itself, they denaturalized the order that had kept them in compliance for so long. They called into question who the company deemed them to be, how it separated them from each other, and how it allowed and disallowed certain modes of association.

The workers had suddenly delegitimized the aesthetics of progress and US ingenuity that had once played such a powerful role in authorizing the conquest of the tropics. In its place, they built an aesthetic with a populist wedge, separating the worker-citizens from the US-based multinational fruit company. On the side of the people, it was institutions and relationships premised upon the collective well-being of the workers and their families that now seemed right. We have examined the aesthetics and politics of the collective kitchens, the outdoor masses, and the strike leaders addressing hundreds of workers. This countervisuality turned the figure of the banana republic on its head. In the strike, the workers succeeded in unstitching the United Fruit Company's authority from its power. The company was still formidable. But it was suddenly unable to get its workers to comply with, much less consent to, its demands. Oversight had been undermined. The workers suddenly became an authorizing force in north coast politics. Nineteen fifty-four produced the Honduran popular hero: the banana worker. It created a new imaginary of the people and offered a powerful aesthetic of transformation.

A POST-1954 VISUAL COMPLEX

A few months after the 1954 strike was settled, voters went to the polls. The social democratic candidate of the Liberal Party, Ramón Villeda Morales, was favored to win by a wide margin in a contest against a divided National Party. But in the face of the broad and enthusiastic support that the rejuvenated Liberal Party enjoyed, the National Party, and its disaffected contingent in the National Reformist Movement, turned to repression to hold onto power. The US Embassy in Tegucigalpa reported that it had "received a deputation of Liberal feminine leaders who escorted to the Embassy a group of Liberals who showed the marks of severe floggings which they said

Figs. 9.3 and 9.4. Photojournalistic denunciations of abuse Liberals suffered at the hands of supporters of the National Party. Captioned "The Aggression of a Cariísta," one photograph depicts what is purported to be a supporter of Tiburcio Carías wielding a huge machete against a group of Liberals (*El Pueblo*, July 1, 1954). In "El 'Terror Negro' en Honduras," a supporter of the Liberal Party in 1948 exposes the way he was beaten by Carías's police force (*El Pueblo*, July 27, 1954).

they had received in El Progreso, Yoro, at the orders of Reformist Commandant General Matías Arriaga on and just before Election Day October 10,
1954." The embassy continued:

> The ladies desired an Embassy officer personally to witness the evidence
> of these floggings. The evidence was clearly authentic. Most of the men's
> backs were heavily discolored and the skin was broken in raw welts. One
> of the victims was Dr. Alfonso BENNATON, a Liberal delegate to the local
> Electoral Board ("Mesa") no. 30 in El Progreso. . . . All said that they had
> been picked up, at different times, by a carload of civilian "pistoleros" and
> delivered to soldiers of General Arriaga's command who beat them with
> an oxhide whip and then forced them to walk about 8 to 10 hours from El
> Progreso to San Pedro Sula. They of course missed all participation in the
> election of October 10. . . . These victims were obviously brought to Tegu-
> cigalpa by the Liberal Party for propaganda purposes. Their photographs
> appeared in EL CRONISTA and EL PUEBLO, and they were also seen by
> TIMES correspondent Henry WALLACE.[20]

Demonstrating an understanding of the power of the official US witness
who was made to see the wounds of *progreseños*, women made visible the
violence and political intimidation directed at Liberal candidates, peasants,
and workers. Clearly these women political activists also understood the
value of a newspaper photograph documenting the violence and bringing
it before the eyes of the reading publics in Honduras and the United States.

The embassy concluded its report to Washington by noting that were
it not for the violence exercised by the ruling National Party, "the Liberals
would have won a clear popular majority in Yoro, which would in turn have
put them that much closer to the countrywide popular majority and to the
two-thirds congressional quorum necessary to elect a Liberal president."
Violence worked "to whittle down the effect of the Liberals' undoubted
popular strength."[21] Liberal Party candidate Ramón Villeda Morales fell just
short of winning the absolute majority needed to secure the presidency.

The Constitution of 1936 stipulated that in the event that no presidential
candidate obtained an absolute majority, the National Congress had twenty
days to certify that the first- and second-place finishers were, respectively,
the newly elected president and vice president. While the National Party
had physically intimidated supporters of Villeda Morales and the Liberal
Party, the official results still gave the liberals a plurality of the electorate.[22]
Tiburcio Carías, now an aging caudillo, promptly ordered the congressional

representatives from his party not to attend the legislative session that would certify Ramón Villeda Morales as the duly elected president. By refusing to assemble, the National Party and the National Reformist Movement effected a rupture in constitutional rule.

On November 15, 1954, in the midst of the unresolved electoral crisis, President Gálvez abruptly transferred power, purportedly because of ill health, to Julio Lozano Díaz. Less than a month later, Lozano Díaz decreed that he was assuming all powers of the state and would convoke a constitutional convention when the opportunity presented itself. Beyond ascending from vice president to president and then engineering his continuation in power, Lozano Díaz also suspended the rule of law:

> From this date, and for a period of thirty days that may be extended if the Head of State deems it necessary, all meetings, assemblies, and political demonstrations are prohibited, just as is any oral or written publication that directly or indirectly tends to disturb the public tranquility. The Government reserves full freedom of action in this regard.[23]

By setting the guarantees of freedom of speech and assembly aside and by reserving for himself the right to act with impunity against those who he determined had violated this new law, Lozano Díaz and the conservative landowning class created the conditions to reverse the incredible gains that workers and social democrats had made since May.

In the face of the emerging democratic politics that the workers' movement had brought into being, Lozano placed the entire country into a state of exception. Under the banner of an anticommunist struggle, his regime jailed and exiled a number of the most important activists from Honduras's democratic Left. In February 1956, Lozano Díaz jailed many leaders of the 1954 strike, including Céleo González and Óscar Gale Varela.[24] Gale Varela had played a key role in the strike and in August 1954 became the first elected president of the Union of Tela Railroad Company Workers (Sitraterco, the Sindicato de Trabajadores de la Tela Railroad Company). Gale Varela was a public target, one who stood for the entire banana workers' movement. Lozano Díaz even forced Villeda Morales into exile. One curious exception to Lozano Díaz's penchant for repression was a cynical attempt to extend his illegal rule: in January 1955, the Honduran Right allowed women to register to vote for the first time in the country's history.

On August 1, 1956, the situation changed dramatically. In a coup that was welcomed, if not openly backed, by the Liberal Party, the military ousted Lozano Díaz. The military junta made two key promises: a relatively quick "return to constitutional normalcy" and a preventive attempt to deal with "the social question."[25] The junta leaders kept both promises, along with a little something for themselves. In November 1956, the military banned political demonstrations and restricted freedom of the press. The junta backed state intervention in the economy and created a number of new agencies, including the National Electric Power Company, the National Housing Institute, the National Children's Trust, the School of Social Service, and the Comptroller General of the Republic. In an attempt to integrate the mobilized workers, the military regime also passed legislation in support of railroad workers (Ley del Trabajo Ferrocarrilero) and collective bargaining (Ley de Contratación Colectiva), paving the way for the passage, in 1959, of a comprehensive labor code (Código de Trabajo). The military ruled from October 1956 until December 1957, when the junta convoked a constitutional convention in which Ramón Villeda Morales won the overwhelming support of the delegates.

The military facilitated and then permitted Ramón Villeda Morales's ascension to the presidency in 1957. The Constitution of 1957 brought two important changes: first, it contained many social democratic guarantees ("proporcionar a toda la población una existencia digna y decorosa"), and second, it granted the armed forces complete autonomy, no longer subordinating the military to the will of the president.[26] Social scientists Mario Posas and Rafael del Cid argue that this resulted in a "duality of command" that simply hid the military's true authority behind a civilian figurehead.[27] At the discretion of the military, Villeda Morales would stay in power. In other words, for the first half of the twentieth century, the United States and the United Fruit Company had a faithful ally in the National Party, but with the National Party in disarray, the United States chose to exert its influence through the Honduran military. The bilateral military agreement that was signed three weeks into the 1954 strike provided a formal institutional framework for manipulating the economic and political affairs of the country. The armed forces attempted to accelerate capitalist development, to initiate social programs that responded to the demands of the increasingly restless popular classes, and to retain their role as, in the words of historian Marvin Barahona, "the political referee."[28] That is, the civilian government of Honduras had a new overseer, the Honduran military. That overseer took its orders from a United States that had its own plan for Cold War Honduras.

Founded in August 1954, the banana workers' labor union continues to be one of the most tangible structural accomplishments of the 1954 strike. "From the very first days of the strike," construction worker Agapito

Fig. 9.5. In 1960, workers invited Rafael Platero Paz to photograph the inauguration of the new offices of their labor union, Sitraterco. The event was presided over by President Ramón Villeda Morales (standing to the right of the priest and wearing dark-rimmed glasses) and Fr. Joseph D. Wade. With the people's president, a priest, and an AFL-CIO-backed labor union, the workers were subdued by the paternalistic embrace of the state. *Courtesy of the Rafael Platero Paz Archive.*

Robleda recalls, "the leaders of our movement had the idea of creating a labor organization as a mechanism for permanent struggle."[29] By 1958, Sitraterco was nine thousand members strong.[30] The 1960 inauguration of the Sitraterco offices in La Lima was the culmination of years of work and sacrifice.

Platero Paz's images of the day are straightforward. He photographed the very Catholic priest who had ministered to the striking workers, Father Joseph Wade, now six years older, consecrating the new building as he was flanked by the union leaders and President Ramón Villeda Morales (figure 9.5). Platero Paz documented the convivial atmosphere enjoyed by the chief representatives of the government, the church, labor, and capital. In one photo, Ramón Villeda Morales is seated between Óscar Gale Varela, secretary general of Sitraterco, and Serafino Romualdi, the American Federation of Labor's longtime anticommunist labor representative in Latin America. To the right of Gale Varela is Arturo Jauregui, secretary general of the

Inter-American Regional Labor Organization (ORIT, Organización Regional Inter-Americana de Trabajadores). In the early 1950s, Romualdi and Jauregui were at the forefront of the US policy of supporting conservative labor organizations in Latin America; over the years, both men were, at various times, on the CIA's payroll.[31] The leader of the country's largest labor union, Sitraterco, and the people's president, Villeda Morales, are firmly hemmed in by their new overseers.

In another photo from the ceremony, Villeda Morales's gaze is cast warily to the side, directed either at the soldier who walks behind him or at the North American, who is wearing dark sunglasses through which he can look without people knowing exactly what he is looking at. The image is, in a sense, a chronicle of the 1963 coup foretold: in the midst of overwhelming popular support, the military will still overthrow the civilian government.

Fig. 9.6. Inside Rafael Platero Paz's studio, Foto Arte, El Progreso. *Courtesy of the Rafael Platero Paz Archive.*

Each of the photographs is suffused with the signs of official authority. They are set inside the workers' building, which is, no doubt, an achievement. But that achievement was tainted. After the United Fruit Company and the Honduran government succeeded in getting the workers' first strike committee disbanded and replaced with a much more cooperative committee, the strike began to lose its popular drive. These photographs, taken six years after the conclusion of the strike, commemorate not only the opening of the new union offices but also the integration of the workers back into the fold of the old order. In these photos, the church and the state have recaptured the labor movement. The hierarchical structure that the strike threw into question was reconstituted as the state repressed radical labor and then integrated the domesticated workers into an institutional arrangement that tilted toward the United States.

When *progreseños* crossed the threshold into Rafael Platero Paz's studio, myriad gazes immediately beckoned them to return the look (figure 9.6). As she held her flowing hair behind her left ear, a cardboard cutout of a happy young blond woman hailed consumers to "Buy Kodak Film here." Above the Kodak girl, Platero Paz hung a painted portrait of his daughter, Profesora Aída. As objects, his painted color portraits offered the nostalgia and refinement of the artisan's hand and the realism of the photographs upon which they were based. And, as Profesora Aída tells it, this particular portrait of her was a hot commodity, stolen from her father's studio by one of her admirers.[32] Following the line of young Aída's gaze, one discovers the photograph of the inauguration of Sitraterco. Upon entering the studio, the customer saw Villeda Morales and Gale Varela but also Jauregui and Romauldi, framed right above the calendar. The post-1954 order of US-backed, state-sponsored unionism had been aestheticized. It seemed right, natural, and good to have the workers represented in such august company.

In Platero Paz's studio, the intimate intersected with the public. Like the display case in the Mahchis' store, the display in Platero Paz's studio reflected images of customers back at them. Inside the case, the photographer placed examples of his mainstay: the studio portrait. His customers saw images of themselves and images of others whom they could imitate. Platero Paz's studio allowed *progreseños* to embed themselves within any number of national and transnational imagescapes: from the bonds of family in Jerusalem to the quiet intimacy of El Progreso, from the conspicuous consumption of North America to the reformist liberalism of Honduras.

A Bridge Called Democracy

The bridge and its name were products of the 1954 strike. Rafael Platero Paz was there on a Sunday in March 1963 to welcome the workers' president, Dr. Ramón Villeda Morales, to inaugurate the arch of concrete and steel over the Ulúa River (figure E.1). The bridge was named Democracia, and the banana workers across the north coast were the political base that enabled Villeda Morales to enact a number of important social reforms. His would-be successor, Modesto Rodas Alvarado, also enjoyed enthusiastic support from north coast labor and the Palestinian Honduran community, which had transformed itself from small-scale merchants into industrial capitalists. But then, just ten days before Rodas Alvarado was set to win the 1963 presidential elections, the military overthrew Ramón Villeda Morales and placed the country under martial law.

Decades later, on May 28, 2009, CNN reported that a magnitude 7.3 earthquake rattled Central America, causing six deaths, the destruction of eighty homes, and the collapse of a central section of the Democracy Bridge in El Progreso. Photographs and video of the bridge that no longer spanned the Ulúa River accompanied news of this seismological event (figure E.2).

Fig. E.1. Inauguration of a bridge called Democracy, which made the ferry obsolete. Or, as Aída López de Castillo captioned the image, "Apoteósica e inolvidable inauguración del puente 'La Democracia' el 3 de marzo de 1963 por el doctor Ramón Villena Morales y el Alcalde Salvador Delgado acompañados por miles de progreseños." *Courtesy of the Rafael Platero Paz Archive.*

Fig. E.2. The gap in Democracy. Or, as Agence France-Presse captioned the image, "One of the lanes of 'La Democracia' bridge over the Ulua River, built by the French in 1963, had its central section collapse due to an earthquake May 28, 2009, in El Progreso, 270 km north of Tegucigalpa." *Courtesy of Orlando Sierra, Agence France-Presse/ Getty Images.*

Exactly one month later, on Sunday, June 28, democracy itself collapsed in Honduras, as the Honduran military kidnapped their president, Manuel "Mel" Zelaya, and flew him to Costa Rica in his pajamas. In doing so, the military acted on behalf of the country's political and economic elites to conduct an unconstitutional transfer of power from the Left to the Right. Led by Roberto Micheletti Bain, one of the initial acts of the new government was to indefinitely suspend the laws that protected the basic civil liberties of Hondurans and to enforce a new regime of aggressive censorship of the press, including threatening the journalists in the Jesuit-run radio station in El Progreso.

"When the media lie, the walls talk," scrawled one activist in black spray paint on the side of a building. In the days following the 2009 coup, graffiti artists depicted former president Carlos Roberto Flores Facussé, a media magnate of Palestinian descent, as a man-serpent with a prodigious nose and a pointed textual message: "Carlos Flores Facusse: Media Terrorist (figure E.3)." By publicly aligning themselves with traditional creole power brokers who sent the armored personnel carriers rolling through the streets of Tegucigalpa to oust President Zelaya, Palestinian Hondurans, who had largely remained out of the public eye, suddenly became hypervisible.

Fig. E.3. Tegucigalpa, July 2009. With critical media outlets silenced, political activists took to the walls. With several visual slurs, they depicted former President Carlos Roberto Flores Facussé. *Photograph by the author.*

Fig. E.4. June 29, 2009. This photograph, taken by Esteban Felix for the Associated Press, was published in the *New York Times* and captioned, "The riot police dispersed supporters of the ousted president on Monday near the presidential palace in the capital, Tegucigalpa." *AP Photo/ Esteban Felix.*

Within hours of the coup, several hundred people gathered in El Progreso to block traffic across the Democracy Bridge's sibling, a parallel structure of more recent build that went undamaged by the earthquake. The small but outspoken group of *progreseños* responded immunologically to the violent assault on Honduran democracy. They carried ideas of participatory politics that were like antibodies, formed in the struggles for equality and recognition that had taken place in El Progreso throughout the twentieth century.[1] That the coup leaders failed to anticipate that many Hondurans would have defenses against the pathogen of authoritarian rule only demonstrates their arrogance and the depths of their historical amnesia. As the coup regime suspended the guarantees of the law, the movement to restore constitutional rule grew and nourished itself on the memory of the 1954 strike. Marking each day since the coup, the resistance movement explicitly put itself in relation to the workers who had held out for sixty-nine days. The strike thus embedded itself in the body politic as an autotherapeutic capacity that could be activated whenever the sovereignty of the country was threatened. But this time it was not a sole studio photographer and a handful of photojournalists documenting and extending the moment; now anyone with a camera phone could work to restore the civil contract. Tens of thousands of urban, middle-class folks draped themselves in the Honduran flag and orchestrated the production of images that could help to consolidate the coup regime. Meanwhile, the disenfranchised and dispossessed—an eclectic group of peasants, skilled workers, university students, and members of the local intelligentsia—took pictures of themselves at rallies as they sought to reverse the unconstitutional transfer of power. At several crucial moments, international press photographers in helmets and flack jackets let the coup regime, and its military and police forces, know that the world was watching. The struggle played out in the streets and at dinner tables, in embassies and courtrooms, on TV and in newspapers, on vulnerable bodies and on the virtual walls of Facebook pages.

Meanwhile, in an ironic twist that O. Henry would have admired, just three months after seizing power, Roberto Micheletti Bain gave something back to his native El Progreso: 17,000 square meters of land for a Railroad Museum that would be built around the now derelict locomotives of the United Fruit Company. The official legislative decree cited El Progreso as "the cradle of the Honduran workers' movement," and the museum's walls are covered in Rafael Platero Paz's blown-up photographs of dignified workers taking over the trains in 1954.[2]

ACKNOWLEDGMENTS

When I was weighing where to do my doctoral studies, I was told that if I went to Indiana University, I would find a strong cohort of Latin American-ists. It turned out to be true. I am especially grateful to two dear friends, David Díaz Arias and Sebastián Carassai. David is a generous and thought-ful reader, and I'm thankful that our bond forged in Bloomington now stretches from San José to Toronto. Meanwhile, from Buenos Aires to Toronto, Sebastián has shown me that understanding, ethical choices, and aesthetic pleasure must each be pursued with equal vigor and in the com-pany of others; Sebastián has helped me to think through several of the good ideas, as well as many of the bad ones, that you may have found in this book. What brought each of us to IU was the extraordinary faculty. Spe-cial thanks to Jeff Gould, who encouraged me to reevaluate the 1954 strike while providing me with the space to pursue my interests. Thanks also to Peter Guardino, whose rigorous historical thinking and personal integrity continue to inspire me. My greatest debt is to Danny James, a consummate scholar and one of the kindest, funniest people I know. He gave me the courage, as well as many of the conceptual tools, that I needed to undertake a project on the politics of images.

Early in my research in El Progreso, I was lucky enough to meet Profesora Aída López de Castillo, the daughter of studio photographer Rafael Platero Paz, whose thousands of pictures became the foundation for this book. Thwarting hurricanes, scorching sun, and careless relatives, Profesora Aída has singlehandedly preserved boxes containing thousands of negatives and prints. She opened her home to me and gave me the room that used to contain her father's old studio. Her family—including her husband, Don Eloy, a former timekeeper for the United Fruit Company, and her sons, Oswaldo, Pedro, and José—were enthusiastic companions in the search through pictures of El Progreso's past.

In Honduras, I was affiliated with the Equipo de Reflexión, Investigación y Comunicación (ERIC), a Jesuit research institute in El Progreso. I was glad to have the support of Fr. Ismael Moreno, a *progreseño* whose moral stature is unrivaled in contemporary Honduras. Kind and generous beyond measure was Marvin Barahona, a passionate historian of the present. I would also like to thank Guillermo Mahchi and Sammie Gabrie for sharing their family photo albums with me. A remarkable group of independent banana producers for Dole Fruit taught me about banana production—planting, cutting, detecting plant disease, processing at their packing house, and loading the harvested and selected fruit onto containers bound for Gulfport, Mississippi, in special consignments for Wal-Mart; thanks to Geovany Mejía, Daniel Díaz, Salvador García Bonilla, and Edar Hernández at the Cooperativa Agropecuaria Guanchías. María Teresa Campos de Pastor, director of the Museo de Antropologia e Historia in San Pedro Sula, generously invited me to examine her museum's collection of postcards. In Yoro, Lidia López helped me transcribe many years of municipal government and departmental immigration records. Eric Schwimmer, a Benjaminian collector who attempts to reassemble Honduran worlds that have been scattered, has proven to be the most reliable investigator one could ever hope to find. I am thankful also to Valentina Zaldivar de Farach and Wady Farach for opening their house in Tegucigalpa to my family and me for six months in 2009. During this time, I worked in the Archivo Nacional, where I benefited from the wisdom and hospitality of Mario Argueta and the assistance of Dennis Ramírez and Rolando Canizales Vijil. Yesenía Martínez was a thoughtful interlocutor, especially with respect to the incipient populism of President Juan Manuel Gálvez. For more than a decade, I have enjoyed rich and extended conversations with Darío A. Euraque, who served as the director of the Honduran Institute for Anthropology and History (IHAH) during the administration of President Manuel Zelaya Rosales. Soon after the 2009 coup d'état that deposed President Zelaya, the new and unconstitutional regime fired Darío. Through this experience, along with far less stressful conversations, I've witnessed Darío's deep intellectual and personal commitment to the past and future of Honduras.

While the United Fruit Company has notoriously appropriated public resources throughout the Caribbean Basin, it has kept most of its internal records off limits to the public. There are a couple of exceptions to what remains a sequestered archive, and I would like to thank Philippe Bourgois for sharing copies of the company's internal memoranda that he discovered in Panama. Thanks also to Melissa Murphy, in Special Collections at Harvard University's Baker Library, who was unfailingly helpful as I worked my way through the United Fruit Company Photograph Collection.

Transitioning into life as a junior professor at the University of Toronto was made easier by the support of some extraordinary colleagues. First among them is Elspeth Brown, whose warmth and originality make her the hub of so much productive activity. Another friend, Dan Bender, took the time to read an early version of the manuscript and to help me understand the significance of my argument. I am grateful to our vibrant contingent of Latin Americanists and Caribbeanists—Ken Mills, Valentina Napolitano, Eva-Lynn Jagoe, Melanie Newton, Rosa Sarabia, Susan Antebi, Kevin O'Neill, and most recently Jeffrey Pilcher and Luis van Isschot—for their support and enthusiasm. My comrades in the Department of Historical Studies ensure that neither teaching nor research is a solitary activity; thanks to Shafique Virani, Rebecca Wittmann, Kyle Smith, Mairi Cowen, Ken Derry, Christoph Emmrich, Andreas Bendlin, Joan Simalchik, Martin Revermann, Ajay Rao, Shabina Moheebulla, Sharon Marjadsingh, and, certainly not least, Duncan Hill. In the Department of History, I've found friendship and critical engagement with a great group of scholars, especially Sean Mills, Jayeeta Sharma, Steve Penfold, Bhavani Raman, Tong Lam, Ritu Birla, Nick Terpstra, Alison Smith, Nathalie Rothman, Lynne Viola. Thanks as well to Will Fysh, Erica Toffoli, Justin Douglas, Steve McClellan, and Siobhan Angus for challenging me to clarify my thinking in our Images as History graduate seminars. Dima Saad meticulously proofread the entire manuscript.

Beyond Bloomington and Toronto, I've discussed aspects of this book with friends and colleagues who have offered generous insights. I am especially grateful to Jens Andermann for reading a first draft of this manuscript and for showing me how to rethink the architecture of my argument. I've also had the pleasure of talking about this material with John Louis Lucaites, Bruno Bosteels, Esther Gabara, Barbara Weinstein, Anne Rubenstein, Gillian McGillivray, César Seveso, Natalia Milanesio, Valeria Manzano, Matt Van Hoose, Sarah Bassnet, Sarah Parsons, Matt Brower, Dot Tuer, Brian Morton, Maria Duarte, Christina Heisser, Alfio Saitta, Justin Wolfe, Sara Scalenghe, Camila Pastor de Maria y Campos, and Lila Caimari.

For material support and the time to write, I am grateful to the Andrew W. Mellon Foundation–American Council of Learned Societies; the Social Sciences and Humanities Research Council of Canada; the University of Toronto's Connaught New Researcher Award; the Fulbright-Hays Doctoral Dissertation Research Abroad Fellowship; the Bernardo Mendel Fellowship in Latin American History at Indiana University; the John H. Edwards Fellowship at Indiana University; a Samuel F. Bemis Research Grant from the Society for Historians of American Foreign Relations; and the Tinker Foundation for two separate travel grants. While studying at Indiana University, I had the good fortune to work at the *American Historical Review*; I am grateful to Michael Grossberg, Rob Schneider, Sarah Knott, Maria Bucur, Moureen Coulter, and most especially Jane Lyle. Jane, a genuinely gifted editor and a dear friend, has helped me take this project from grant proposal to published book.

If, as Walter Benjamin argued, the great tragedy of the early twentieth century was that the combined power of industrial production, mass consumption, and the myth of technological progress tended to annihilate gazes that could otherwise have been returned, then the University of Texas Press has helped me in my attempt to restore the aura of a few photographic images from El Progreso. Kerry Webb, Victoria Davis, Angélica López, and the designer have carefully imbued the imagetext in your hand with the grace that I had long dreamt it might have.

Years before I started thinking about photography as a means to create ourselves anew, I met many good people who were trying to make themselves and the world a little kinder and a bit more just. As an undergraduate philosophy major at Northern Arizona University, three remarkable teachers—George Rudebusch, Peter Kosso, and Alison Brown—attempted to cultivate in me habits of thought that were worth holding onto. When I was a Peace Corps volunteer in southern Honduras, my friends in Texiguat, San José, and Tegucigalpa taught me that in some domains of life I was the cultural equivalent of a toddler; for their friendship, I thank Jaime

Medina, Jorge Flores, Fernando Mejía, Noel Mejía, Delmy Sánchez, Juanita Padilla, Calixto Aguilar, Oscar René Cortez, Pastor López, Roberto López, Iris López, Oscar López, René Sánchez, Alejandra Padilla, Martin Rivera, and Jorge Valle-Aguiluz. Conversations with fellow volunteers helped me think through some of the ethical implications of our US–Latin American encounters; for their practical idealism, thanks to Ron Marks, Shana Yansen, Max Boycoff, Tara Pisani, and Brian Gareau. After Peace Corps, I met many good people at the University of Maryland–Baltimore County, including Jack Sinnigan and John Stolle-McAllister. While at UMBC, I was especially fortunate to find Joby Taylor, a friend whose intelligence, goodness, and openness are the standard to which I strive.

There's a photo on my desk of my mom and dad holding me as a child. They look happy and full of hope, though certainly not for a book on bananas. From the start, my parents have been loving and encouraging. My brother, Keith, and sisters, Aimee and Meghan, have been good-natured constants in my life.

In my mind's eye, I can still see Hema and Saagari in El Progreso on the morning of June 28, 2009. Just hours after the overthrow of President Manuel Zelaya, the two of them were walking across the broken bridge, La Democracia, past soldiers and the democratic activists who had wasted no time in taking up a key position. With their quirky humor and sustaining love, Hema and Saagari have accompanied me through the hardest and happiest phases of this project.

An earlier version of chapter 4 was published previously as "A Camera in the Garden of Eden," in the *Journal of Latin American Cultural Studies*, 201, no. 1 (2011): 63–96. Used here with permission from Routledge, Taylor & Francis Group, www.tandfonline.com. Part of chapter 7 was published as "Photographs of a Prayer: The (Neglected) Visual Archive and Latin American Labor History," in the *Hispanic American Historical Review*, 95, no. 3 (2015): 459–492. Used here with permission from Duke University Press Journals Division.

NOTES

PROLOGUE

1. Aída López de Castillo, oral history interview, El Progreso, August 12, 2008.

2. J. C. McDaniel, "Malaria Control Measures in 1931," in *Annual Report, 1931* (Boston: United Fruit Company [hereafter UFCo] Medical Department, 1931), 96.

3. Ibid., 97.

4. On the company's comparison with other early twentieth-century imperial enterprises, see UFCo Medical Department, "Comments on Vital Statistics and General Conditions," in *Annual Report, 1924* (Boston: UFCo, 1924), 21–55.

5. My reading of this image would not be possible without Michel Foucault's theorization of the clinical gaze; *The Birth of the Clinic: An Archaeology of Medical Perception* (New York: Pantheon Books, 1973), 22–37.

6. McDaniel, "Malaria Control Measures in 1931," 96. M. D. Rosas, "Malaria Control Measures in Chiriqui," in *Annual Report, 1931* (Boston: UFCo, 1931), 94.

7. Rosas, "Malaria Control Measures in Chiriqui," 91.

8. On the "unconscious optics" of the camera, see Walter Benjamin, "The Work of Art in the Age of Mechanical Reproduction," in *Illuminations* (New York: Schocken Books, 1969), 237.

ONE

1. Frederick Upham Adams, *Conquest of the Tropics: The Story of the Creative Enterprises Conducted by the United Fruit Company* (New York: Doubleday, 1914), 196. The literature on the United Fruit Company is extensive and includes the following: Charles Kepner and Jay Henry Soothill, *The Banana Empire: A Case Study of Economic Imperialism* (New York: Vanguard Press, 1935); Charles David Kepner, *Social Aspects of the Banana Industry* (New York: AMS Press, 1967); John Soluri, *Banana Cultures: Agriculture, Consumption, and Environmental Change in Honduras and the United States* (Austin: University of Texas Press, 2005); Lara Putnam, *The Company They Kept: Migrants and the Politics of Gender in Caribbean Costa Rica, 1870-1960* (Chapel Hill: University of North Carolina Press, 2002); Philippe Bourgois, *Ethnicity at Work: Divided Labor on a Central American Banana Plantation* (Baltimore, MD: Johns Hopkins University Press, 1989); Steve Striffler, *In the Shadows of State and Capital: The United Fruit Company, Popular Struggle, and Agrarian Restructuring in Ecuador, 1900-1995* (Durham, NC: Duke University Press, 2002); Aviva Chomsky, *West Indian Workers and the United Fruit Company in Costa Rica, 1870-1940* (Baton Rouge: Louisiana State University Press, 1996); Marcelo Bucheli, *Bananas and Business: The United Fruit Company in Colombia, 1899-2000* (New York: NYU Press, 2005); Mark Moberg, *Myths of Ethnicity and Nation: Immigration, Work, and Identity in the Belize Banana Industry* (Knoxville: University of Tennessee Press, 1997); Jason M. Colby, *The Business of Empire: United Fruit, Race, and U.S. Expansion in Central America* (Ithaca, NY: Cornell University Press, 2011).

2. The expression "landscapes and livelihoods" is John Soluri's in "Landscape and Livelihood: An Agroecological History of Export Banana Growing in Honduras, 1870-1975" (PhD diss., University of Michigan, 1998).

3. Gabriel García Márquez, *One Hundred Years of Solitude*, translation by Gregory Rabassa (New York: Avon Books, 1971), 55.

4. Esther Gabara, "Gestures, Practices, and Projects: [Latin] American Revisions of Visual Culture and Performance Studies." *E-misférica*, Spring 2010, http://hemisphericinstitute.org/hemi/en/e-misferica-71/gabara; Ricardo D. Salvatore, "Introducción: Los lugares del saber," in *Los lugares del saber: Contextos locales y redes transnacionales en la formación del conocimiento moderno* (Buenos Aires: Beatriz Viterbo Editora, 2007), 17.

5. On spatial exceptions, see Paul A. Kramer, "Power and Connection: Imperial Histories of the United States in the World," *American Historical Review* 116, no. 5 (December 2011): 1356. On contact zones, see Mary Louise Pratt, "Arts of the Contact Zone," *Profession* (1991): 33-40.

6. For this argument, see Donald Schulz and Deborah Sundloff Schulz, *The United States, Honduras, and the Crisis in Central America* (Boulder, CO: Westview Press, 1994).

7. Translations are mine unless otherwise indicated. My notes, El Progreso, Honduras, August 2008.

8. For an examination of some of the United Fruit Company photographs that do not appear in the Harvard University collection, see Kevin P. Coleman, "The Photos That We Don't Get to See: Sovereignties, Archives, and the 1928 Massacre of Banana Workers in Colombia," in *Making the Empire Work: Labor and United States Imperialism*, edited by Daniel E. Bender and Jana K. Lipman (New York: NYU Press, 2015), 104–133.

9. Nicholas Mirzoeff, "On Visuality," *Journal of Visual Culture* 5, no. 1 (2006): 66; Dipesh Chakrabarty, *Provincializing Europe: Postcolonial Thought and Historical Difference* (Princeton, NJ: Princeton University Press, 2000), 63–64.

10. Mirzoeff, "On Visuality," 66.

11. Guillermo Enrique Mahchi Carrasco, *Archivo fotográfico del ayer: El Progreso, 1900–1965* (San Pedro Sula, Honduras: Sociedad Nacional Papelera, 1992).

12. In their study of photographs in an Argentine city built around the meat-packing industry, historians Daniel James and Mirta Zaida Lobato examine how viewers must interpret visual artifacts within the social and mnemonic contexts in which they were produced; "Family Photos, Oral Narratives, and Identity Formation: The Ukrainians of Berisso," *Hispanic American Historical Review* 84, no. 1 (2004): 8.

13. I thank Sanabel Abdel Rahman for translating this postcard.

14. Karen Strassler has described the airplane as a common backdrop in the Chinese-owned studios of Indonesia and has examined the ways ethnic Chinese were considered suspect in Java; *Refracted Visions: Popular Photography and National Modernity in Java* (Durham, NC: Duke University Press, 2010), 98 and 134.

15. Robert Hariman and John Louis Lucaites, *No Caption Needed: Iconic Photographs, Public Culture, and Liberal Democracy* (Chicago: University of Chicago Press, 2007), 12–13.

16. Here I am applying to photography and collections of photographs philosopher Peter Sloterdijk's recent thinking on humans as practicing beings, *You Must Change Your Life: On Anthropotechnics*, translation by Wieland Hoban (Cambridge, England: Polity, 2013), 244.

17. Jacques Derrida puts forward a notion of the photograph as an archive of its own present, in *Copy, Archive, Signature: A Conversation on Photography*, edited by Gerhard Richter, translation by Jeff Fort (Stanford, CA: Stanford University Press, 2010), 2–3.

18. Daguerre, in Alan Trachtenberg, ed., *Classic Essays on Photography* (New Haven, CT: Leete's Island Books, 1980), 12.

19. Holmes, in Trachtenberg, *Classic Essays on Photography*, 81, emphasis in original. See also Deborah Poole's discussion of Holmes's stereoscope and his notion of a principle of equivalency between images, in *Vision, Race, and Modernity:*

262 ~ NOTES TO PAGES 23–24

A Visual Economy of the Andean World (Princeton, NJ: Princeton University Press, 1997), 114–115.

20. In invoking the idea of "forgotten futures," I have in mind Sebastián Carassai's rereading of the notion of memory in the work of Walter Benjamin, "En busca del futuro olvidado: Notas para una crítica de la memoria en Walter Benjamin," *El Ojo Mocho: Revista de Crítica Cultural y Política* 21 (Winter/Spring 2008): 81–89.

21. Alan Trachtenberg, *Reading American Photographs: Images as History, Mathew Brady to Walker Evans* (New York: Hill and Wang, 1989), 33.

22. Christopher Pinney, *"Photos of the Gods": The Printed Image and Political Struggle in India* (New Delhi: Oxford University Press, 2004); Zahid R. Chaudhary, *Afterimage of Empire: Photography in Nineteenth-Century India* (Minneapolis: University of Minnesota Press, 2012); Strassler, *Refracted Visions*; Beatriz Sarlo, *La imaginación técnica: Sueños modernos de la cultura Argentina* (Buenos Aires: Nueva Visión, 1992); Adrián Gorelik, *Miradas sobre Buenos Aires: Historia cultural y crítica urbana* (Buenos Aires: Siglo Veintiuno, 2004); Elizabeth Edwards, *The Camera as Historian: Amateur Photographers and Historical Imagination, 1885–1918* (Durham: Duke University Press, 2012); John Mraz, *Looking for Mexico: Modern Visual Culture and National Identity* (Durham, NC: Duke University Press, 2009); Esther Gabara, *Errant Modernism: The Ethos of Photography in Mexico and Brazil* (Durham, NC: Duke University Press, 2008); Andrea Noble, *Photography and Memory in Mexico: Icons of Revolution* (Manchester, England: Manchester University Press, 2010); Horacio Fernández, *The Latin American Photobook* (New York: Aperture, 2011).

23. These contributions were made by Poole, *Vision, Race, and Modernity*; Jens Andermann, *The Optic of the State: Visuality and Power in Argentina and Brazil* (Pittsburgh, PA: University of Pittsburgh Press, 2007); Gabara, *Errant Modernism*; Krista A. Thompson, *An Eye for the Tropics: Tourism, Photography, and Framing the Caribbean Picturesque* (Durham, NC: Duke University Press, 2006); Paola Cortés Rocca, *El tiempo de la máquina: Retratos, paisajes y otras imágenes de la nación* (Buenos Aires: Ediciones Colihue, 2011); Roberto Tejada, *National Camera: Photography and Mexico's Image Environment* (Minneapolis: University of Minnesota Press, 2009); Claire F. Fox, *Making Art Panamerican: Cultural Policy and the Cold War* (Minneapolis: University of Minnesota Press, 2013). Historian John Mraz's work is an exception; see his meticulous genealogy of images and imagemakers in *Photographing the Mexican Revolution: Commitments, Testimonies, Icons* (Austin: University of Texas Press, 2012).

24. Fernando Coronil, "Introduction: Can the Subaltern See? Photographs as History," *Hispanic American Historical Review* 84, no. 1 (2004): 1–4; James and Lobato, "Family Photos, Oral Narratives, and Identity Formation"; Deborah Poole, "An Image of 'Our Indian': Type Photographs and Racial Sentiments in Oaxaca, 1920–1940," *Hispanic American Historical Review* 84, no. 1 (2004): 3782; and Greg Grandin, "Can the Subaltern Be Seen? Photography and the Affects of

Nationalism," *Hispanic American Historical Review* 84, no. 1 (2004): 83–111. Robert M. Levine was the first historian to systematically treat photographs from Latin America as documents in their own right; *Images of History: Nineteenth and Early Twentieth Century Latin American Photographs as Documents* (Durham, NC: Duke University Press, 1989).

25. Rosalind C. Morris has edited a volume that includes the two versions of Spivak's essay; *Can the Subaltern Speak? Reflections on the History of an Idea* (New York: Columbia University Press, 2010).

26. Grandin, "Can the Subaltern Be Seen?," 111. The availability of photography to popular groups from the late nineteenth century onward should be tempered with an awareness that studies of early photography are "overdetermined by imperialism," as Chaudhary points out in his study of nineteenth-century India; the medium was available mostly to the upper levels of the Indian indigenous bourgeoisie. Hence if scholars want "to reopen the fracture of colonialism," he argues, they need to put remnants of subaltern communication captured in archives of colonial governance into play with elite photographic practices; *Afterimage of Empire*, 29–31.

27. Although it predates Spivak's essay, relevant here is Jacques Rancière's post-1968 challenge to his teacher Louis Althusser, whose theory of ideology Spivak rigorously applied to the "other side of the international division of labor"; Rancière, *Althusser's Lesson* (London: Continuum, 2011).

28. Here, I am adapting Alain Badiou's notion of the political subject to photography, *Theory of the Subject*, translation by Bruno Bosteels (London: Continuum, 2009), 37–39.

29. Ariella Azoulay, *The Civil Contract of Photography* (New York: Zone Books, 2008); Ariella Azoulay, *Civil Imagination: A Political Ontology of Photography*, translation by Louise Bethlehem (New York: Verso, 2012); Gareth Williams, *The Other Side of the Popular: Neoliberalism and Subalternity in Latin America* (Durham, NC: Duke University Press, 2002), 86.

30. Azoulay, *Civil Imagination*, 13.

31. Jacques Rancière, *Disagreement: Politics and Philosophy*, translation by Julie Rose (Minneapolis: University of Minnesota Press, 1999); he develops the notion of "the distribution of the sensible" in *The Politics of Aesthetics*, translation by Gabriel Rockhill (London: Continuum, 2006).

32. Azoulay, *Civil Imagination*, 27.

TWO

1. December 30, 1926, *Libros de actas de la Municipalidad de El Progreso* (hereafter *Libros de actas*), vol. 9 (1922–1929), 85, Archivo Municipal, El Progreso.

2. In their historicity, Platero Paz's photographs differ markedly from those of his more famous Argentine contemporary Horacio Coppola, who photographed Buenos Aires in the 1920s–1930s, creating atemporal themes that synthesized the city and the pampas. On Coppola, see Adrián Gorelik, *Miradas sobre Buenos Aires*, 97.

3. William "Guillermo" Bain, "Aviso: Animales robados del Ferrocarril Inter-Oceánico de Honduras," September 21, 1872, Archivo Nacional de Honduras; Guillermo Bain, "Honduras Inter-Oceanic Railroad: General Order," January 1, 1874, Archivo Nacional de Honduras.

4. January 1, 1893, *Libros de actas*, vol. 1 (1893–1898), 1.

5. Ibid., 5.

6. Ibid., January 16, 1893, 8.

7. Ibid., February 15, 1893, 16.

8. On *vecindad*, see Tamar Herzog, *Defining Nations: Immigrants and Citizens in Early Modern Spain and Spanish America* (New Haven: Yale University Press, 2003).

9. Gorelik, *Miradas sobre Buenos Aires*, 148.

10. *Libros de actas*, vol. 1, February 22, 1893, 1.

11. Ibid., May 20, 1898, and August 1, 1898.

12. Ibid., June 22, 1893.

13. Ibid., August 29, 1893.

14. Ibid., vol. 4, December 1, 1906.

15. Ibid., vol. 5, June 15, 1909.

16. Ibid.

17. On road construction, see *Libros de actas*, vol. 4, December 27, 1908, 176.

18. Nearly forty years ago, Antonio Murga Frassinetti made a similar point in more general terms in *Enclave y sociedad en Honduras* (Tegucigalpa: Universidad Nacional Autónoma de Honduras, 1978), 94. Subsequent scholars, including Darío A. Euraque and John Soluri, have since questioned the approach of historians like Murga Frassinetti who worked from within the paradigm of dependency theory; nevertheless, many of Murga Frassinetti's insights remain indispensible for understanding key macroeconomic developments in twentieth-century Honduras. See Darío A. Euraque, *Reinterpreting the Banana Republic: Region and State in Honduras, 1870–1972* (Chapel Hill: University of North Carolina Press, 1996), and Soluri, *Banana Cultures*.

19. *Libros de actas*, vol. 5, January 9, 1910. Signatures and thumbprints of the *vecinos* who ratified the proposal further reveal that even illiterate early *progreseños* participated in making some collective decisions. The exact boundaries of the agricultural and *ganaderia* land are described on page 144; see also page 168 for a full description.

20. In describing early modern seafarers as fortune-seeking and boundary-breaking project makers, Peter Sloterdijk writes that every ship "participates in

the great work of modernity: developing substance as a flow"; *In the World Interior of Capital*, translation by Wieland Hoban (Malden, MA: Polity, 2013), 83.

21. *Libros de actas*, vol. 5, January 10, 1910, Junta Popular, 135.

22. Lester D. Langley and Thomas Schoonover, *The Banana Men: American Mercenaries and Entrepreneurs in Central America, 1880–1930* (Lexington: University Press of Kentucky, 1995), 33–34.

23. For more on the Vaccaro Brothers and the Standard Fruit Company, see Antonio Canelas Díaz, *El estrangulamiento económico de La Ceiba, 1903–1965* (La Ceiba, Honduras: Editorial ProCultura, 2001), and Thomas L. Karnes, *Tropical Enterprise: The Standard Fruit and Steamship Company in Latin America* (Baton Rouge: Louisiana State University Press, 1978).

24. Kepner and Soothill, *Banana Empire*, 100; Mario Argueta, *Bananos y política: Samuel Zemurray y la Cuyamel Fruit Company en Honduras* (Tegucigalpa: Editorial Universitaria, 1989), 81; Langley and Schoonover, *Banana Men*, 37.

25. Kepner and Soothill, *Banana Empire*, 100–101; Langley and Schoonover, *Banana Men*, 38–39.

26. Langley and Schoonover, *Banana Men*, 39.

27. Kepner and Soothill, *Banana Empire*, 106; they cite Mario Ribas, *Current History*, September 1927, 921.

28. Kepner and Soothill, *Banana Empire*, 107. On Guy Molony in South Africa fighting for Her Britannic Majesty's forces against the Boers, Hermann B. Deutsch remarked, "Then he got himself into trouble by stealing his colonel's horse so that he could be photographed aboard that noble charger. He wanted to send the picture home to his mother and sister"; Hermann Deutsch, *The Incredible Yanqui: The Career of Lee Christmas* (London: Longmans Green, 1931), 83.

29. Kepner and Soothill, *Banana Empire*, 108.

30. One *manzana* of land is equivalent to 0.69 hectares.

31. *Libros de actas*, vol. 6, July 1, 1913, 9–10.

32. Kepner, *Social Aspects of the Banana Industry*, 73.

33. "Decreto número 113," *La Gaceta: Diario Oficial de la República de Honduras*, July 29, 1912, Archivo Nacional de Honduras. Kepner and Soothill discuss what appears to be a slightly different iteration of this concession; *Banana Empire*, 370n24. According to the records of *La Gaceta* that I have consulted, Decreto 113 is from July 22, 1912 (not April 8, 1912), and Article 16 provides for 6,000 hectares (not 4,000 hectares) for every twelve kilometers of railroad line.

34. Kepner, *Social Aspects of the Banana Industry*, 54–55.

35. *Libros de actas*, vol. 6, October 23, 1914.

36. The issues of law, order, and sanitation cited here were part of a special session of the municipal governement of El Progreso; "Sesión extraordinaria presidida por el señor Gobernador Político Coronel don Rafael Cobar A. y el Alcalde Juán Barahona," *Libros de actas*, vol. 7, May 30, 1916, 75–77.

37. *Libros de actas*, vol. 7, February 16, 1916.

38. "Sesión extraordinaria."

39. Ibid.

40. *Libros de actas*, vol. 7, June 30, 1917.

41. "Decreto número 113," *La Gaceta*, July 29, 1912, Archivo Nacional de Honduras.

42. *Libro registro de propiedad*, vols. 1–2 (1924), Instituto de Propiedad, Departamento de Yoro, Honduras. The denomination of the currency in these transactions was listed as "pesos oro americano," except in the case of Thornburgh, who was paid in US gold dollars.

43. "Sesión extraordinaria," September 7, 1925, *Libros de actas del consejo departamental de Yoro*, Archivo de Gobernación, Departamento de Yoro; *Libros de actas*, vol. 9, June 15, 1925; August 1, 1925; August 15, 1925.

44. Kepner and Soothill, *Banana Empire*, 76.

45. Charles Morrow Wilson, *Empire in Green and Gold: The Story of the American Banana Trade* (New York: Greenwood Press, 1968), 125–126.

46. Nicholas Mirzoeff, *The Right to Look: A Counterhistory of Visuality* (Durham, NC: Duke University Press, 2011), 50–56. On the racialized occupationanal hierarchy, we know from Charles Kepner that in 1935, "to a large extent citizens of the United States, with a scattering of Britishers and other Europeans, hold the more responsibly executive, clerical and farm positions of the United Fruit Company. In August 1930, the overseers in the Progresso and Ulua districts of Honduras consisted of six North Americans, three Britishers, two Spaniards, three Mexicans, two white Jamaicans, four Hondurans and two citizens of other Central American countries. Of the timekeepers five were North Americans and eleven were Hondurans"; Kepner, *Social Aspects of the Banana Industry*, 176.

47. Tela Railroad Company United Fruit Company, "Unit Prices for Agricultural Work as of October 1, 1933," October 1, 1933, Bocas del Toro Division, Panama, historical archives, United Fruit Company, letters (hereafter UFCo-L), Philippe Bourgois private collection.

48. Mirzoeff, *The Right to Look*, 3.

49. Carlos Enrique Ramírez, "El aparato de represión de la Tela RR.Co.," *Vanguardia Revolucionaria* (Tegucigalpa), January 10, 1950.

50. To get a sense for the vast network of Carías's secret police, see Jesús Evelio Inestroza M., *Documentos clasificados de la policía secreta de Carías (1937–1944)* (Tegucigalpa: Instituto Hondureño de Historia y Antropología, 2009). To see how the United Fruit Company used covert informants, see V. T. Mais, "Letter to G. D. Munch from V. T. Mais, Almirante," January 5, 1956, and G. D. Munch, "Letter to V. T. Mais, Chiriqui Land Company, from G. D. Munch, Almirante," January 26, 1956, UFCo-L.

51. "Overseer, Oversee," in *The Random House College Dictionary*, ed. Jess Stein (New York: Random House, 1984).

52. Maldonado González, "Mandar," *Clave: Diccionario de uso del español actual* (Madrid: Ediciones SM, 2000).

53. Giorgio Agamben, "The Archeaology of Commandment," summer seminar lecture, European Graduate School, Saas-Fee, Switzerland, 2011, http://www.you tube.com/watch?v=JVV94Fi5ChI.

54. Oswaldo Eloy Castillo, oral history interview by the author, August 14, 2008.

55. Mirzoeff describes "visualizing as the hallmark of the modern general from the late eighteenth century onward"; *The Right to Look*, 12–13.

56. United Fruit Company, Panama City, and Morgan Stone, "Letter to G. A. Myrick, Manager, Armuelles Division, from M. Stone, United Fruit Company," December 11, 1940, UFCo-L.

57. Castillo, oral history interview.

58. Wilson, *Empire in Green and Gold*, 125.

59. Arthur A. Pollan, "Circular No. B-21," memorandum, November 15, 1929, UFCo-L. Philippe Bourgois, "One Hundred Years of United Fruit Company Letters," in *Banana Wars: Power, Production, and History in the Americas*, edited by Steve Striffler and Mark Moberg (Durham, NC: Duke University Press, 2003), 103–144.

60. The case of the company's internal memo on Cálix Herrera is by no means unique. For a sampling of other such cases, see "Memorandum, Colombian Division. Labor Leaders in Ciénaga Strike," March 8, 1929, UFCo-L; United Fruit Company Headquarters, Boston, "Circular No. 32-17," September 19, 1932, UFCo-L. Bourgois, "One Hundred Years of United Fruit Company Letters"; Philippe Bourgois, *Ethnicity at Work: Divided Labor on a Central American Banana Plantation* (Baltimore, MD: Johns Hopkins University Press, 1989).

61. Ramírez, "El aparato de represión de la Tela RR.Co.," January 10, 1950.

62. The memo was accompanied by a photograph of Dougherty; United Fruit Company Headquarters, Boston, "Circular No. 32-17. Boston to Tropical Division Managers," September 19, 1932, UFCo-L.

63. Coleman, "Photos That We Don't Get to See."

64. Rina Villars, *Lealtad y rebeldía: La vida de Juan Pablo Wainwright* (Tegucigalpa: Guaymuras, 2010), 46–51.

65. Ibid., 67; Villars cites US State Department documents.

66. Ibid., 66–67; Villars cites this letter dated March 3, 1928. In addition to publishing *El Forjador*, Cálix Herrera frequently contributed to *El Martillo* and *El Trabajador Hondureño*.

67. "Acuerdo de expulsion de Manuel Cálix Herrera de la Federación Obrera Hondureña," May 11, 1928, cited in Villars, *Lealtad y rebeldía*, 67.

68. Villars, *Lealtad y rebeldía*, 97.

69. Cálix Herrera, cited in Villars, *Lealtad y rebeldía*, 103.

70. *El Cronista* (Tegucigalpa), April 29, 1931, quoted in Marvin Barahona, *Honduras en el siglo XX: Una síntesis histórica* (Tegucigalpa: Guaymuras, 2005), 90.

71. Villars, *Lealtad y rebeldía*, 53.

THREE

1. Paul Krugman, "OK, We Are a Banana Republic," *New York Times*, September 28, 2008, http://krugman.blogs.nytimes.com/2008/09/29/ok-we-are-a-banana-republic/.

2. O. Henry, *Cabbages and Kings* (New York: McClure, Phillips, 1904), 100.

3. My discussion of iconicity is indebted to Hariman and Lucaites, *No Caption Needed*.

4. Adams, *Conquest of the Tropics*, 36.

5. Criticisms of Adams's hyping of the United Fruit Company can be found in Kepner and Soothill, *Banana Empire*; Chomsky, *West Indian Workers*; Soluri, *Banana Cultures*; Thompson, *Eye for the Tropics*.

6. Adams, *Conquest of the Tropics*, 29.

7. On nineteenth-century renderings of the American West, see Martha A. Sandweiss, *Print the Legend: Photography and the American West* (New Haven, CT: Yale University Press, 2004). For an account of Oliver Wendell Holmes's reaction to Mathew Brady's Civil War pictures, see Trachtenberg, *Reading American Photographs*, 91–93.

8. Adams, *Conquest of the Tropics*, 10–11. On US stereotypes of Latin America, see Fredrick B. Pike, *The United States and Latin America: Myths and Stereotypes of Civilization and Nature* (Austin: University of Texas Press, 1992), 111.

9. Adams, *Conquest of the Tropics*, 52, 86–87, 201, 202.

10. Ibid., 25, 60, 117.

11. Ibid., 145, 208.

12. In discussing the world-historical import of mapmaking, Peter Sloterdijk demonstrates the significance of this Heideggerian insight; *In the Interior World of Capital*, 28. Martin Heidegger, "The Age of the World Picture," in *Off the Beaten Track*, edited by Julian Young, translation by Kenneth Haynes (Cambridge, England: Cambridge University Press, 2002), 71.

13. Henry Adams is quoted in Trachtenberg, *Reading American Photographs*, 146. The Frederick Upham Adams quote is from *Conquest of the Tropics*, 161–162.

14. Mary Louise Pratt, *Imperial Eyes: Travel Writing and Transculturation*, 2nd ed. (New York: Routledge, 2007), chapter 8; this quote from Pratt's translation of Bello's "La agricultura en la zona torrida" was taken from page 174.

15. On the American West as the site of America's future, see Sandweiss, *Print the Legend*, especially chapter 5. The quote from Ramón Rosa is taken from Marvin Barahona, *La hegemonía de los Estados Unidos en Honduras* (Tegucigalpa: Centro de Documentación de Honduras, 1989), 44–45.

16. Samuel Crowther, *The Romance and Rise of the American Tropics* (New York: Doubleday, Doran, 1929), v.

17. Ibid., 2.

18. On Timothy O'Sullivan's pictures, see Trachtenberg, *Reading American Photographs*, 155.

19. The images referenced in this paragraph are from Crowther, *The Romance and Rise of the American Tropics*, 15, 95, 75, 106, 131, 222.

20. Herbert C. Clark, "Venomous Snakes: Some Central American Records. Incidence of Snake-Bite Accidents," *American Journal of Tropical Medicine* s1-22, no. 1 (January 1, 1942): 37–49.

21. *Annual Report, 1927*, Medical Department, United Fruit Company. For its employees, the company produced a similarly illustrated essay, the title of which playfully conflated poisonous creatures with aboriginal peoples. See Charles T. Brues, "Poisonous Arthropods: Some Aboriginal Inhabitants of the Tropics," *Unifruitco* 4, no. 2 (September 1928): 68–72.

22. In Crowther, *The Romance and Rise of the American Tropics*, 330.

23. United Fruit Company Photograph Collection, Baker Library Historical Collections, Harvard Business School, box 9, folio 3.

24. Leticia de Oyuela, *De santos y pecadores: Un aporte para la historia de las mentalidades, 1546–1910* (Tegucigalpa: Editorial Guaymuras, 1999), 227.

25. The witticism is Rebecca Solnit's, in *As Eve Said to the Serpent: On Landscape, Gender, and Art* (Athens: University of Georgia Press, 2001), 1.

26. Oyuela, *De santos y pecadores*, 228.

27. Rachel Snow, "Tourism and American Identity: Kodak's Conspicuous Consumers Abroad," *Journal of American Culture* 31, no. 1 (2008): 7–19.

28. The reference to "Uncle Sam's New Ten Mile Strip of Empire" comes from a brochure made by the Panama Pacific Line, cited by Paul S. Sutter, "Tropical Conquest and the Rise of the Environmental Management State: The Case of US Sanitary Efforts in Panama," in *Colonial Crucible: Empire in the Making of the Modern American State*, edited by Alfred W. McCoy and Francisco A. Scarano (Madison: University of Wisconsin Press, 2009), 317.

29. Ronald Harpelle, "White Zones: American Enclave Communities of Central America," in *Blacks and Blackness in Central America: Between Race and Place*, edited by Lowell Gudmundson and Justin Wolfe (Durham, NC: Duke University Press, 2010), 308.

30. Billy Peña, oral history interview by the author, La Lima, July 25, 2007.

31. The quoted phrase is from Frances Emery-Waterhouse's 1947 *Banana Paradise*, cited in Harpelle, "White Zones," 312.

32. Henry, *Cabbages and Kings*, 328.

33. Héctor Pérez-Brignoli, "El fonógrafo en los trópicos: Sobre el concepto de banana republic en la obra de O. Henry," *Iberoamericana* 23 (2006): 127–141, 130; Henry, *Cabbages and Kings*, 323.

34. Henry, *Cabbages and Kings*, 12.

35. Alan Trachtenberg, *Reading American Photographs*, 39.

36. Henry, *Cabbages and Kings*, 12, 81, 12.

37. Ibid., 267.

38. Ibid., 271.

39. Ibid., 277–278.

40. Ibid., 279.

41. Ibid., 149.

42. Ibid., 280.

43. Ibid., 282.

44. The quote from the cruise-line brochure comes from Sutter, "Tropical Conquest," 317.

45. Henry, *Cabbages and Kings*, 339.

46. Ibid., 104.

47. Ibid., 344.

48. Ibid., 136.

49. Ibid., 344.

50. See Shari Roberts, "'The Lady in the Tutti-Frutti Hat': Carmen Miranda, a Spectacle of Ethnicity," *Cinema Journal* 32, no. 3 (1993): 3–23. The quote is from *Sintonía*, June 11, 1941, in Allen L. Woll, *The Hollywood Musical Goes to War* (Chicago: Nelson-Hall, 1983), 118.

51. Roberts, "'The Lady in the Tutti-Frutti Hat,'" 15, emphasis in the original.

52. For a full account linking the banana industry in Honduras to the consumer mass market in the United States, see Soluri, *Banana Cultures*; much of my discussion of Miss Chiquita is based on pages 161–165 of his book. The first scholar to connect Carmen Miranda and Miss Chiquita through the analytic of gender was Cynthia Enloe, *Bananas, Beaches, and Bases: Making Feminist Sense of International Politics* (Berkeley: University of California Press, 1990), 128–129.

53. "Bananas Script—Dialogue Transcript," *Drew's Script-O-Rama*, accessed July 18, 2013, http://www.script-o-rama.com/movie_scripts/b/bananas-script-transcript-woody-allen.html.

54. Henry, *Cabbages and Kings*, 9.

55. Crowther, *The Romance and Rise of the American Tropics*, 2.

FOUR

1. Henry, *Cabbages and Kings*, 38.

2. I lean here on Allan Sekula's classic reflection on photo archives, "Reading an Archive: Photography between Labour and Capital," in *Visual Culture: A Reader*, ed. Jessica Evans and Stuart Hall (London: Sage, 1999), 181–192.

3. According to his death certificate, Rafael Platero Paz died on May 6, 1983, in El Progreso; Rafael Platero Paz Archive. Other rudimentary details on Platero Paz's life are recorded in Aída López de Castillo, "Biography of Rafael Platero Paz," unpublished manuscript, 2000. For the coffee economy and the Department of La Libertad in El Salvador, see Robert G. Williams, *States and Social Evolution: Coffee and the Rise of National Governments in Central America* (Chapel Hill: University of North Carolina Press, 1994), 69–79.

4. López de Castillo, "Biography of Rafael Platero Paz"; Aída López de Castillo, oral history interview, El Progreso, August 12, 2008.

5. "Honorable Discharge from the United States Army," Rafael Platero Paz Archive, box 10.

6. The specifics of Platero Paz's migration are on his passport; Rafael Platero Paz Archive, box 10.

7. The most important study to date of Honduran masculinity is Rocío Tábora, *Masculinidad y violencia en la cultura política hondureña* (Tegucigalpa: Centro de Documentación de Honduras, 1995). For a critique of Tábora's work, see Darío A. Euraque, "En busca de Froylán Turcios: Apuntes sobre la vida y obra de Armando Méndez Fuentes," *Paraninfo: Instituto de Ciencias del Hombre, Rafael Heliodoro*, no. 23 (2003): 177–197.

8. Jean-Paul Sartre, *Being and Nothingness: An Essay on Phenomenological Ontology*, translation by Hazel E. Barnes (New York: Philosophical library, 1956), 256; for a fuller discussion of the Sartrean gaze, see my essay "A Camera in the Garden of Eden," *Journal of Latin American Cultural Studies: Travesia* 20, no. 1 (2011): 63–96.

9. Sartre, *Being and Nothingness*, 257.

10. Ibid., 256.

11. Ibid.

12. For an account of the construction of the "liberal oligarchic state," see Marvin Barahona, *Honduras en el siglo XX*. In a classic essay, Dilip Parameshwar Gaonkar critiqued ways of understanding the discourse of modernity as societal modernization and as cultural modernism. He issued an early call for site-based readings of alternative modernities, constructed through the exigencies of local histories as communities in a shrinking world negotiate the impetus to sameness and the forces that make them different; "On Alternative Modernities," *Public Culture* 11, no. 1 (1999): 1–18.

13. Charles Taylor, "Two Theories of Modernity," *Public Culture* 11, no. 1 (1999): 153–174.

14. For an ethnographic study of another in-between population, see Mark Anderson's *Black and Indigenous: Garifuna Activism and Consumer Culture in Honduras* (Minneapolis: University of Minnesota Press, 2009); for more on the official racial discourses of Honduras, see Darío A. Euraque, *Conversaciones históricas con el mestizaje y su identidad nacional en Honduras* (San Pedro Sula: Centro Editorial, 2004).

15. Roland Barthes, "The Rhetoric of the Image," in *Image, Music, Text* (New York: Hill and Wang, 1977), 51.

16. In 1934, Salvadorans made up 56 percent (1,840) of the immigrants to the Department of Yoro; *Registro especial de extranjeros residentes en Honduras: 1934*, Archivo de Gobernación, Departamento de Yoro. The quote is from my oral history interview with Aída López de Castillo, El Progreso, August 12, 2008; this account is corroborated in an interview with Ricardo Arturo Platero López, El Progreso, November 20, 2008.

17. These questions were posed to me by Joby Taylor, personal correspondence, July 1, 2010.

18. The quote is from Genesis 1:28.

19. López de Castillo, interview, August 12, 2008.

20. For the Sarlo quote and a discussion of "seeing from" Latin America, see Gabara, "Gestures, Practices, and Projects." On making the camera error, see Gabara, *Errant Modernism*.

21. For a reflection on "human salvation as a device for the self-revelation of God," see Martin Jay, *Downcast Eyes: The Denigration of Vision in Twentieth-Century French Thought* (Berkeley: University of California Press, 1993), 38. I would like to thank my friend Joby Taylor for pointing out the pre-Fall allusion of this photo, in personal correspondence, July 1, 2010.

22. Louis Althusser, "Ideology and Ideological State Apparatuses (Notes Towards and Investigation)," in *Lenin and Philosophy and Other Essays*, translation by Ben Brewster (New York: Monthly Review Press, 1972), 127–188.

23. Aída López de Castillo described how Platero Paz interacted with his clients, in her interview with me, August 12, 2008.

24. On tropicalization, see Thompson, *Eye for the Tropics*.

25. I take the quote of George Chauncey from David Bell and Ruth Holliday, "Naked as Nature Intended," *Body and Society* 6, no. 3–4 (2000): 127–140.

26. Patricia Simons, "Homosociality and Erotics in Italian Renaissance Portraiture," in *Portraiture: Facing the Subject*, edited by Joanna Woodall (Manchester, England: Manchester University Press, 1997), 29.

27. *Life* pioneered photojournalism in North America, and by 1938 it had a massive circulation of approximately eighty thousand subscribers and newsstand sales

of an additional one million copies. I take these circulation figures from "LIFE Magazine and LOOK Magazine Popularize Photojournalism in the 1930's," in *Collecting Old Magazines*, http://collectingoldmagazines.com/magazines/life-magazine/.

28. Homi K. Bhabha, *The Location of Culture*, 2nd ed. (New York: Routledge, 2004), 126.

29. Ibid., emphasis in original.

30. Putnam, *The Company They Kept*, 201.

31. Ibid., 201–202.

32. Ibid., 201.

FIVE

1. *Nuestro Criterio*, February 9, 1929, 1.

2. Ibid. In the comparative context of immigration to the United States and Mexico, Honduran policies appear far less restrictive. In 1891, for example, the US Congress passed the Disease Act, which required steamship companies to certify the health of their passengers and held the companies liable for the costs of passengers detained by US authorities, a move that effectively shifted the main port of entry for Mashreqi migrants to Veracruz, Mexico; see Theresa Alfaro-Velcamp, *So Far from Allah, So Close to Mexico: Middle Eastern Immigrants in Modern Mexico* (Austin: University of Texas Press, 2007), 31–39. For its part, Mexico banned Middle Eastern immigration in 1927, as immigrants "became scapegoats of the Mexican Revolution and post-revolutionary nation-building"; 109. For Alfaro-Velcamp's discussion of the restrictions Mexico placed on Middle Eastern immigrants during the 1930s, see 117–124. See also Camila Pastor de Maria y Campos, "The Mashreq in Mexico: Patronage, Property, and Class in the Postcolonial Global" (PhD diss., University of California, 2009), 283–289.

3. The legislation further suggested that the races most likely to cause this damage were black and Chinese. According to the 1934 registry of foreigners in the Department of Yoro, there were 157 immigrants from China and 160 immigrants from Palestine; *Registro especial de extranjeros residentes en Honduras: 1934*. Of the 145 immigrants from Palestine whose race was recorded, 79 percent were considered "white," 3 percent "black," and 18 percent *trigueño* ("dark" or "olive-skinned"). But perceptions of skin color were also influenced by perceptions of social class, as "whiteness" came to mean "economically productive." Jeffrey Lesser describes a similar process for "Arab" and "Japanese" immigrants in Brazil; *Negotiating National Identity: Immigrants, Minorities, and the Struggle for Ethnicity in Brazil* (Durham, NC: Duke University Press, 1999), 4.

4. Decreto 101, número 7860, April 2, 1929, *La Gaceta*, January–June 1929.

5. Euraque, *Reinterpreting the Banana Republic*, 34. For a detailed historical ethnography of this immigrant group often seen as "pariah entrepreneurs," see Nancie

González, *Dollar, Dove, and Eagle: One Hundred Years of Palestinian Migration to Honduras* (Ann Arbor: University of Michigan Press, 1992).

6. My application of the term "predication" is derived from Gunther Kress and Theo van Leeuwen, *Reading Images: The Grammar of Visual Design* (New York: Routledge, 2006), chapter 2.

7. On material culture as a sign system that can transform power relations, see Ian Hodder, *Reading the Past: Current Approaches to Interpretation in Archaeology*, 2nd ed. (Cambridge, England: Cambridge University Press, 1991), 8–9.

8. "Sesión extraordinaria," September 7, 1925, *Libros de actas del consejo departamental de Yoro*, 71, Archivo de Gobernación, Departamento de Yoro.

9. See Chris Otter, *The Victorian Eye: A Political History of Light and Vision in Britain, 1800–1910* (University Of Chicago Press, 2008), for a study of how technologies of lighting led to greater personal freedom in Victorian Britain.

10. *Nuestro Criterio*, December 19, 1929, 3.

11. Ibid.

12. I have not been able to identify the man standing with his hands on his hips.

13. These details were provided to me by Guillermo Enrique Mahchi Carrasco, grandson of Audelia López Moya and Salomón Mahchi, in personal correspondence, February 12, 2009. The date of Salomón Mahchi's immigration from Palestine to Honduras is listed in the *Registro especial de extranjeros residentes en Honduras: 1934*, 124.

14. Nancie González has ascertained that 92.5 percent of Palestinian marriages between 1900 and 1929 in Honduran Catholic churches were endogamous, as compared to only 27 percent (38) being endogamous between 1970 and 1979; *Dollar, Dove, and Eagle*, 116.

15. Three of Ian Hodder's claims come to mind: "all material culture is meaningfully constituted"; "context itself has to be interpreted in the data"; and "positioned subjects manipulate material culture as a resource and as a sign system in order to create and transform relations of power and domination"; *Reading the Past*, 3, 5, 9.

16. I thank Khalil Nahas for translating the note on the back of this postcard.

17. In his study of the merchants and peasants of Jabal Nablus, Beshara Doumani historicizes this language; *Rediscovering Palestine: Merchants and Peasants in Jabal Nablus, 1700–1900* (Berkeley: University of California Press, 1995), 92.

18. James and Lobato, "Family Photos, Oral Narratives, and Identity Formation," 35.

19. Edward W. Said, *Orientalism* (New York: Pantheon Books, 1978), 55.

20. Arjun Appadurai, "Disjuncture and Difference in the Global Cultural Economy," *Public Culture* 2, no. 2 (1990): 7.

21. See Doumani, *Rediscovering Palestine*, chapters 1 and 2; Ilan Pappé, *A History of Modern Palestine: One Land, Two Peoples* (Cambridge, England: Cambridge

University Press, 2004), 30; and, cited by Pappé, J. S. Szyliowicz, *Education and Modernization in the Middle East*.

22. Pappé, *History of Modern Palestine*, 61.

23. Mahchi Carrasco, *Archivo fotográfico del ayer*, front inside cover.

24. Rebecca Earle, *The Return of the Native: Indians and Myth-Making in Spanish America, 1810–1930* (Durham, NC: Duke University Press, 2007). In the contexts of late-nineteenth-century Brazil and Argentina, scholar Jens Andermann has shown how through natural science and anthropological museums, the state displayed internal otherness through the artifacts of its "primitive" peoples, facilitating a process of epistemic possession through classification that helped to produce a subject that could forge himself using a gaze of studious detachment. The national history museum played a slightly different role, as the state used it as an institution to narrate the origins of the national-self, fostering a gaze of nostalgic empathy with the creole leaders of the independence movements as the viewing subject acquired her modernity as a gift bestowed from the brave founding fathers of the past; see *The Optic of the State*, part one.

25. Mahchi Carrasco, "1905—Los Antiguos Moradores de El Progreso," in his *Archivo fotográfico del ayer*. In the caption Mahchi quotes from Enrique Peña Molina's 1952 *Monografía de la ciudad de El Progreso, D. S.* Also, Darío A. Euraque points out that the "ancient indigenous" to whom Peña refers, and whom Mahchi claims to index with this photograph, were the Tolupanes and possibly descendants of the Tolupanes exploited in the sarsaparilla trade in the 1850s and 1860s. Thus they had been suffering a civilizing modernity long before the Mahchis arrived; Euraque, personal correspondence, November 14, 2009. The earliest archaeological work on this subject was done by Samuel Zemurray's daughter, Doris Stone, "A Delimitation of the Area and Some of the Archaeology of the Sula-Jicaque Indians of Honduras," *American Antiquity* 7, no. 4 (April 1942): 376–388.

26. John Lloyd Stephens, *Incidents of Travel in Central America, Chiapas, and Yucatan* (New York: Harper and Brothers, 1841), 28.

27. The Gabrie family's immigration records can be found in the Archivo de Gobernación, Departamento de Yoro, *Registro especial de extranjeros residentes en Honduras: 1934*, 19.

28. Sammie Gabrie, oral history interview, El Progreso, September 3, 2008. In a gesture similar to donating the national seal, in 1921, members of the Syrian-Palestinian community of San Pedro Sula announced that they would build a park to be called Palestina; *La República* (Tela), August 4, 1921, 1. Darío A. Euraque analyzes the donation of a statue of Lempira in 1936 by the Syrian-Palestinian community of San Pedro Sula; "Nation Formation, Mestizaje, and Arab Palestinian Immigration to Honduras, 1880–1930s," *Critique: Critical Middle Eastern Studies* (Spring 1995): 25–37.

29. Pierre Bourdieu, *Photography: A Middle-Brow Art*, translation by Shaun Whiteside (Stanford, CA: Stanford University Press, 1990), 36–37.

30. See Annelies Moors and Steven Machlin, "Postcards of Palestine: Interpreting Images," *Critique of Anthropology* 7, no. 2 (1987): 63.

31. James and Lobato, "Family Photos, Oral Narratives, and Identity Formation," 24–25.

32. Cited in Mahchi Carrasco, *Archivo fotográfico del ayer*, on the page with photographs dated 1929.

33. Advertisement, "La Flor de Palestina," *Revista Mercurio*, November 1, 1921, 179.

34. Palestinian Honduran family photos, Guillermo Enrique Mahchi Carrasco private collection, El Progreso; Guillermo Enrique Mahchi Carrasco, oral history interview, September 16, 2008.

35. García Márquez, *One Hundred Years of Solitude*, 1. For more on the biblical plot of the novel, see Shay David, "Concepts of Time in *One Hundred Years of Solitude*: A Means for Social Criticism," *Anamesa* (Spring 2003), http://www.nyu.edu/pubs/anamesa/archive/spring_2003_democracy/03_david.htm.

36. García Márquez, *One Hundred Years of Solitude*, 1–5.

37. Ibid., 227.

38. "El incendio en La Lima," *Nuestro Criterio*, San Pedro Sula, August 18, 1928, 1.

39. John Tofik Karam maps changes in the marriage practices of the Christian Syrian-Lebanese in Brazil; *Another Arabesque: Syrian-Lebanese Ethnicity in Neoliberal Brazil* (Philadelphia: Temple University Press, 2007), 95–120. Jeffrey Lesser offers a more limited discussion of the topic but usefully juxtaposes the differing public debates around the miscegenation of Syrian-Lebanese and Japanese immigrants to Brazil; *Negotiating National Identity*, 43, 102–108. Theresa Alfaro-Velcamp examines endogamy among Middle Easterners in Mexico, *So Far from Allah, So Close to Mexico*, 140–141.

40. My regional numbers for the Department of Yoro can be compared to the overall figures for the entire country. Jorge Alberto Amaya Banegas uses various censuses to assert that in 1910 there were 200 Palestinians in Honduras, in 1926 the number jumped to 1,066, and in 1930 there were 780; *Los árabes y palestinos en Honduras, 1900–1950* (Tegucigalpa: Editorial Guaymuras, 2000), 58.

41. Euraque, *Reinterpreting the Banana Republic*, 34.

42. Reviewing secondary literature on the immigration cards of Middle Eastern immigrants to Mexico, Camila Pastor de Maria y Campos observes a similar process: "Mashreqis' race is invariably described as *blanca*, white"; "Mashreq in Mexico," 287.

43. For a genealogy of the racial classification of *trigueño*, see Euraque, *Conversaciones históricas con el mestizaje*, 146–151. Euraque argues that the term *trigueño*

emerges out of a notion of republican citizenship intended to negate the African ancestry of the segment of the Honduran population that had previously been categorized as *mulato* or *pardo*.

44. Carolina Gómez, "La panadería de los hondureños," *Revista Summa*, March 21, 2012, http://www.revistasumma.com/23918/.

45. An examination of debts paid by individuals in El Progreso in 1935 reveals that 27 percent (68 out of 251) of the people involved in disputes over small amounts of money were women. Yet, in 32 percent of the cases, a man was obligated to pay a woman money that he owed her for some good or service rendered. In 8 percent of the cases, a woman was obligated to repay another woman. In 55 percent of the cases, a man paid another man. And in 6 percent of the cases, a woman paid a man. This reveals not only the various sources of income that women in a banana-company town could generate, but also the ways that petit bourgeois women could enlist the police to get their claims repaid. "Copiador de correspondencia. Deudas pagadas por individuos," 1935, Archivo de Gobernación, Departamento de Yoro.

46. República de Honduras Secretaría de Relaciones Exteriores, "Lista de naturalizaciones y reconocimientos de nacionalidad hondureña acordados por el poder ejecutivo desde julio de 1946 hasta junio de 1956" (Tipografía Nacional, 1956), Archivo Nacional de Honduras.

SIX

1. For a fuller account of these events, see Marvin Barahona, *El silencio quedó atrás: Testimonio de la huelga bananera de 1954*, 2nd ed. (Tegucigalpa: Guaymuras, 1995), 118–119.

2. For analysis of how the regime created a network of loyal supporters, see Mario Argueta, *Tiburcio Carías: Anatomía de una época, 1923–1948* (Tegucigalpa: Editorial Guaymuras, 1989), 106–107.

3. In Barahona, *El silencio quedó atrás*, 135.

4. Tiburcio Carías Andino, "El mensaje presidencial," *Revista de Policía* 5, no. 69 (January 1939): 1–2.

5. Manuel Bonilla, "Decreto Número 7, Ley de estado de sitio," *La Gaceta*, November 18, 1898.

6. To count each instance of a declaration of martial law, I examined, with the assistance of Eric Schwimmer, each issue of *La Gaceta*, the official legislative digest of the Honduran government, between 1890 and 1956.

7. I limit myself here to discussing uses of the state of siege law under Carías. For classic theoretical statements on regimes of exception, see Carl Schmitt, *Political Theology: Four Chapters on the Concept of Sovereignty*, translation by George

Schwab (Cambridge: MIT Press, 1985); Walter Benjamin, "Critique of Violence," in *Reflections: Essays, Aphorisms, Autobiographical Writings* (New York: Harcourt Brace Jovanovich, 1978), 277–300; Giorgio Agamben, *Homo Sacer: Sovereign Power and Bare Life* (Stanford: Stanford University Press, 1998); Giorgio Agamben, *State of Exception* (Chicago: University of Chicago Press, 2005). For more contextualized work on this topic, see Ariella Azoulay, "The Loss of Critique and the Critique of Violence," *Cardozo Law Review* 26, no. 3 (2005): 1005–1039; David Dyzenhaus, *The Constitution of Law: Legality in a Time of Emergency* (Cambridge: Cambridge University Press, 2006); Paul W. Kahn, *Political Theology: Four New Chapters on the Concept of Sovereignty* (New York: Columbia University Press, 2011). Closer to home, Gareth Williams provides a trenchant theoretico-historical account of how sovereign exceptionality continues to work in cultural terms; see *The Mexican Exception: Sovereignty, Police, and Democracy* (New York: Palgrave Macmillan, 2011).

8. On the writ of habeas corpus, see Paul D. Halliday, *Habeas Corpus: From England to Empire* (Cambridge: Harvard University Press, 2010); Paul D. Halliday and G. Edward White, "The Suspension Clause: English Text, Imperial Contexts, and American Implications," *Virginia Law Review* 94, no. 3 (2008): 575–714.

9. Vicente Mejía Colindres, "Decreto No. 33, Declárase la república en estado de sitio por el término de treinta días, a contar de hoy; Decreto No. 34," *La Gaceta*, November 14, 1932, Archivo Nacional de Honduras; S. Meza Cálix, "Decreto No. 16 (Legislativo), convocar al Congreso Nacional para conocer del Decreto No. 33, Estado de sitio," *La Gaceta*, November 22, 1932, Archivo Nacional de Honduras.

10. This loan is discussed in a US State Department report dated January 10, 1933, quoted in Barahona, *La hegemonía de los Estados Unidos*, 223.

11. Abraham Williams and Honduras Congreso Nacional, "Decreto Num. 2, Aprobar el Decreto No. 33 emitido por el poder ejecutivo en consejo de ministros el 12 de noviembre de este año declarando la república en estado de sitio," *Boletín del Congreso Nacional Legislativo*, February 24, 1933, Archivo Nacional; Abraham Williams and Honduras Congreso Nacional, "Decreto Num. 3, Declarar la república en estado de sitio, sor el término de sesenta días," *Boletín del Congreso Nacional Legislativo*, February 24, 1933, Archivo Nacional.

12. Thomas J. Dodd, *Tiburcio Carías: Portrait of a Honduran Political Leader* (Baton Rouge: Louisiana State University Press, 2005), 78.

13. Ibid., 187.

14. Ibid., 79–81.

15. Tiburcio Carías Andino, "Mensaje dirigido al Congreso Nacional; Orden público, la república se mantuvo bajo el imperio del estado de sitio," *La Gaceta*, January 3, 1935.

16. R. Alcerro C., "Decreto Num. 136, Declarar subsistentes hasta el 31 de julio de este año," *Boletín del Congreso Nacional Legislativo*, June 15, 1934; Tiburcio

Carías Andino, "Mensaje dirigido al Congreso Nacional en la inauguración de sus sesiones; Estado de intranquilidad, desorganización y pobreza," *La Gaceta*, January 3, 1934.

17. In Dodd, *Tiburcio Carías*, 52.

18. I take inspiration here from a recent rereading of Schmitt's political phenomenology: Paul W. Kahn, *Political Theology: Four New Chapters on the Concept of Sovereignty* (New York: Columbia University Press, 2011).

19. In Dodd, *Tiburcio Carías*, 52.

20. Antonio C. Rivera, "Decreto No. 26, Convocar al pueblo hondureño para que elija diputados a una asamblea nacional constituyente; Constitución Política," *La Gaceta*, January 25, 1936.

21. Tiburcio Carías Andino, "Mensaje del Señor Presidente de la República, Dr. y Gral. Tiburcio Carías A., al Soberano Congreso Nacional," *La Gaceta*, December 7, 1936.

22. Dodd, *Tiburcio Carías*, 115.

23. Asamblea Nacional Constituyente, Antonio C. Rivera, and Tiburcio Carías Andino, "Se publican de nuevo la Constitución y leyes constitutivas en vigencia; Decreto No. 3, Constitución Política; Capítulo VII, De la suspensión de garantías," *La Gaceta*, April 15, 1937; Asamblea Nacional Constituyente, Antonio C. Rivera, and Tiburcio Carías Andino, "Decreto No. 9, Ley de amparo," *La Gaceta*, May 8, 1936.

24. Asamblea Nacional Constituyente, Antonio C. Rivera, and Tiburcio Carías Andino, "Se publican de nuevo la Constitución y leyes constitutivas en vigencia; Decreto No. 3, Constitución Política" and "Título XII: Del trabajo y de la familia," *La Gaceta*, April 16, 1937.

25. Plutarco Muñoz P. and Congreso Nacional, "Decreto No. 6, Declarar al Señor Presidente Constitucional de la República, Doctor y General Don Tiburcio Carías A., 'Fundador y Defensor de la Paz de Honduras y Benemérito de la Patria,'" *La Gaceta*, December 27, 1944.

26. Plutarco Muñoz P. and Congreso Nacional, "Decreto No. 3, Declarar el territorio de la república en estado de sitio; con motivo de la agresión del impero de Japón a los Estados Unidos de Norte América," *La Gaceta*, December 20, 1941; Plutarco Muñoz P. and Honduras Congreso Nacional, "Decreto No. 25, Derogar el decreto legislativo No. 3, emitido el 9 de diciembre de 1941, por el que se declara la república en estado de sitio," *La Gaceta*, February 1, 1946.

27. T. Cerrato Callejas, "Circular; Censura del correo; Habiendo sido declarado el estado de guerra y estando suspensas las garantías individuales," *La Gaceta*, December 12, 1941.

28. Tiburcio Carías Andino, "Decreto No. 62, Establécese la censura de la emisión del pensamiento por la prensa o por cualquier otro medio," *La Gaceta*, June 10, 1943.

29. Héctor M. Leyva, *Imaginarios (sub)terráneos: Estudios literarios y culturales de Honduras* (Tegucigalpa: Plural, 2009), 124–155.

30. Ibid., 128.

31. Alejandro Bados Murillo, "Ética policial," *Revista de Policía* 97, no. 7 (April 1941): 14–15.

32. *Revista de Policía*, January 1939, cited in Leyva, *Imaginarios (sub)terráneos*, 130.

33. Jens Andermann, "State Formation, Visual Technology and Spectatorship: Visions of Modernity in Brazil and Argentina," *Theory, Culture, and Society* 27, no. 7–8 (2010): 164; Andermann, *Optic of the State*.

34. Ambrocio Bueso, "Ha causado indignación la criminal actitud de los enemigos del gobierno. Su fracaso en San Pedro Sula," *La Época*, July 5, 1944.

35. Dodd, *Tiburcio Carías*, 212.

36. Leslie Bethell and Ian Roxborough, *Latin America between the Second World War and the Cold War, 1944–1948* (New York: Cambridge University Press, 1992).

37. Plutarco Muñoz P. and Honduras Congreso Nacional, "Decreto No. 95, Los extranjeros culpables de actividades totalitarias y disociadoras serán castigados," *La Gaceta*, March 13, 1946.

38. Dodd, *Tiburcio Carías*, 222.

39. US Embassy Tegucigalpa, "President Galvez to Retire at End of Present Term" (University Publications of America, February 19, 1952), US State Department Confidential Central Files. Honduras, 1950–1954. Internal Affairs Decimal Numbers 715, 815, 915, and Foreign Affairs Decimal Numbers 615 and 611.15.

40. Camilo Gómez and Congreso Nacional, "Decreto No. 44, Ley de trabajo de menores y mujeres," *La Gaceta*, February 18, 1952.

41. "Impidamos la aprobación de la contrata de la Tela RR. Co.," *Vanguardia Revolucionaria*, August 31, 1949.

42. I am indebted here to Jens Andermann's reading of Juan Gutiérrez's photograph of the statue of General Osorio; "State Formation, Visual Technology, and Spectatorship."

43. Marianne Hirsch, *Family Frames: Photography, Narrative, and Postmemory* (Cambridge: Harvard University Press, 1997), 272.

44. "Detalles de la manifestación del domingo," *Prensa Libre*, August 31, 1949.

45. See, for example, "Patriótica manifestación estudiantil contra la Tela Railroad Company recorrió el día de ayer las calles de Tegucigalpa," *El Día*, August 29, 1949; "Defensa nacional," *Prensa Libre*, September 2, 1949; "Impidamos la aprobación de la contrata de la Tela RR. Co.," *Vanguardia Revolucionaria*, August 31, 1949.

46. "Jefe ferroviario impone jornadas de 50 y 60 horas," *Vanguardia Revolucionaria*, August 31, 1949.

47. Darío Montes, "Defensa nacional," *Prensa Libre*, August 29, 1949.

48. Agamben, *Homo Sacer*. In his subsequent book, *State of Exception*, Agamben attempts to historicize this notion of the sovereign decision. Political theorist Bruno Bosteels harnesses the thought of the Argentine Freudo-Marxist philosopher León Rozitchner to critique Agamben's notion of the "Vitae necisque potestas"; *Marx and Freud in Latin America: Politics, Psychoanalysis, and Religion in Times of Terror* (London: Verso, 2012), 140.

49. Agamben, *Homo Sacer*, 88–90.

50. On ekphrasis, or "textual pictures," see W. J. T. Mitchell, *Picture Theory: Essays on Verbal and Visual Representation* (Chicago: University of Chicago Press, 1995), chapter 5.

SEVEN

1. On the notion of ascetic self-making that I assume here, see Sloterdijk, *You Must Change Your Life*, 220.

2. Joseph D. Wade, "The Light of the Dawn Becomes the Light of Day: The History of the Catholic Church in Honduras from 1854 through 1965" (unpublished manuscript, 1982), 2:289.

3. Ibid.

4. Ibid., 2:290.

5. Ibid., 2:288.

6. In Barahona, *El silencio quedó atrás*, 137.

7. "Centro América convulsa," *El Día*, May 15, 1954.

8. Wade, "Light of the Dawn," 2:292.

9. Ibid., 2:293.

10. Agapito Robleda Castro, *La verdad de la huelga de 1954 y de la formación del SITRATERCO: 54 años después*, 2nd ed. (San Pedro Sula, Honduras: Litográfica San Felipe de Jesús, 2008), 80; Wade, "Light of the Dawn," 2:291.

11. Robleda Castro, *La verdad de la huelga*, 81.

12. "Pronunciamiento del PDRH en favor de 'la Soberania' y 'las Libertades,'" *El Día* (Tegucigalpa), April 29, 1954.

13. Whiting Willauer, "Guatemalan Plane Landed Puerto Cortes," May 10, 1954, US State Department Confidential Central Files, Honduras: Internal Affairs and Foreign Affairs, 1950–1954; Mario Argueta, *La gran huelga bananera: 69 días que conmovieron a Honduras* (Tegucigalpa: Editorial Universitaria, 1995), 66–67.

14. Trachtenberg, *Reading American Photographs*, 54–55.

15. Thanks to Will Fysh for alerting me to the workers' engagement with the issue of reproducibility in this photograph.

16. In Barahona, *El silencio quedó atrás*, 179.

17. On dehabituation, see Jon Beasley-Murray, *Posthegemony: Political Theory and Latin America* (Minneapolis: University of Minnesota Press, 2010), 211.

18. "Los huelgistas están aumentando su número en la División de Tela," *La Época* (Tegucigalpa), May 7, 1954, cited in Argueta, *La gran huelga bananera*, 67.

19. Robleda Castro, *La verdad de la huelga*, 82.

20. Testimony of Rivera, in Barahona, *El silencio quedó atrás*, 164.

21. Laclau, *On Populist Reason* (New York: Verso, 2007), 71.

22. Wade, "Light of the Dawn," 2:293.

23. Ibid.

24. Ibid., 2:294.

25. Murphy, in ibid. 2:294.

26. Ibid., 2:296–297.

27. Barahona, *El silencio quedó atrás*, 167.

28. Argueta, *La gran huelga bananera*, 83.

29. "Honduran Public Opinion Favors Strikers," Central Intelligence Agency, May 22, 1954, quoted in Nick Cullather, *Secret History: The CIA's Classified Account of Its Operations in Guatemala, 1952–1954*, 2nd ed. (Stanford, CA: Stanford University Press, 2006), 79.

30. For the logic of how "the part that has no part" comes to stand for the whole, see Slavoj Žižek, "Afterword: The Lesson of Rancière," in *The Politics of Aesthetics*, by Jacques Rancière, translation by Gabriel Rockhill (London: Continuum, 2006), 70.

31. "Que la Virgen de Suyapa está en la huelga," *Prensa Libre* (Tegucigalpa), June 2, 1954, quoted in Barahona, *El silencio quedó atrás*, 36.

32. Willauer to Department of State, June 5, 1954, telegram no. 419, quoted in Argueta, *La gran huelga bananera*, 96.

33. "Que la Virgen de Suyapa está en la huelga," quoted in Barahona, *El silencio quedó atrás*, 37.

34. Ibid.

35. I am playing here with an idea about how religion organizes submission to authority that I found in Bruno Bosteels's discussion of León Rozitchner's *La cosa y la cruz*; see Bosteels, *Marx and Freud*, chapter 5.

36. For a meditation on dehabituation through freely accepted discipline, see Peter Sloterdijk, *You Must Change Your Life*.

EIGHT

1. Cullather, *Secret History*, 80.

2. Whiting Willauer and US Embassy Tegucigalpa, "Honduran Chief of Staff Velasquez Long Object Suspicions Guatemalan Affiliations" (University Publications of America, May 26, 1954), US State Department Confidential Central Files, Honduras, 1950–1954. Internal Affairs Decimal Numbers 715, 815, 915

and Foreign Affairs Decimal Numbers 615 and 611.15 (hereafter cited as US State Department files, Honduras, 1950–1954).

3. Whiting Willauer and US Embassy Tegucigalpa, "Prompt Implementation of Organization and Training of Honduran Combat Battalion under Military Assistance Agreement of 1954" (University Publications of America, June 12, 1954), US State Department files, Honduras, 1950–1954. Four days after workers struck at various fruit company sites throughout the north coast, the Honduran press began publicly discussing the US-Honduran military agreement; "Un convenio bilateral celebrará el Gobierno Hondureño con los EEUU," *El Día* (Tegucicalpa), May 2, 1954.

4. Willauer, "Prompt Implementation."

5. Philip L. Shepard, quoted in Walter LaFeber, *Inevitable Revolutions: The United States in Central America* (New York: Norton, 1983), 310.

6. *Life*, June 14, 1954.

7. Captions from "The End of a 12-Day Civil War," *Life*, July 12, 1954, 20–22; "Reds' Priority: Pin War on Us," *Life*, July 5, 1954, 8–10.

8. I have only reproduced here a few key pages from the *Bohemia* article. To see the full photoessay and other supplementary visual source material, visit http://kevincoleman.org/archives-2/.

9. In W. J. T. Mitchell's account of the means by which consciousness stitches the seeable to the sayable, it is precisely between images and perspectives that the operation of Lacanian suture, "the junction between the imaginary and the symbolic" indexed by the "I," takes place; Mitchell, *Picture Theory*, 92.

10. Henry Wallace, "La huelga de los trabajadores hondureños: Un grito que ha resonado en todo el mundo," *Bohemia*, June 1954, translation by Alberto Rubiera, Archivo Nacional de Honduras.

11. Rancière, *Disagreement*, 18.

12. In Alain Badiou's analysis of March 18, 1871, the first day of the Paris Commune, we find tools for thinking the subject who opens up an event and in the process gives birth to itself as a new kind of political being; "Logic of the Site," *Diacritics* 33, no. 3 (2003): 141–150.

13. Wallace, "La huelga de los trabajadores hondureños." For an etymology of *chatas*, see Eric Schwimmer, *Dictionary of Honduran Colloquialisms, Idioms, and Slang*, 2nd ed. (Tegucigalpa: Litografía López, 2004).

14. Jens Andermann describes the relation between showing and seeing in modern formations of political power through a close reading of Juan Gutiérrez's photographs of Brazilian state rituals in the 1890s; "State Formation, Visual Technology, and Spectatorship," 161–183.

15. Hariman and Lucaites, *No Caption Needed*, 18.

16. Henry F. Holland and US Embassy Tegucigalpa, "Proposed Memorandum for the President on Conditions in Honduras" (University Publications of America, May 7, 1954), US State Department files, Honduras, 1950–1954.

17. Raymond G. Leddy and US State Department, Washington, DC, "Honduran Situation—Conversation with Ambassador Willauer" (University Publications of America, May 9, 1954), US State Department files, Honduras, 1950–1954.

18. This official statement from the Tela Railroad Company's Office of Public Relations was given in "Unos 22 mil trabajadores participan del movimiento huelguistico norteño," *El Día*, May 12, 1954.

19. Whiting Willauer and US Embassy Tegucigalpa, "Situation North Coast Honduras" (University Publications of America, May 10, 1954), US State Department files, Honduras, 1950–1954.

20. Raymond G. Leddy and US State Department, Washington, DC, "Department has Conflicting Reports Re Government Control North Coast" (University Publications of America, May 10, 1954), US State Department files, Honduras, 1950–1954.

21. Ibid.

22. Argueta, *La gran huelga bananera*, 74–75.

23. Ibid., 60.

24. As of June 1953, the United Fruit Company kept the following farm labor rates in effect: overseers earned $165 to $190 per month, day laborers $0.21 to $0.60 per hour, and road clearers $0.01 per length yard; Tela Railroad Company United Fruit Company, "Reconstruction Finance Corporation—Honduras Abaca Project," June 8, 1953, UFCo-L.

25. "Testimonio de Gabriel David Galeano," in Barahona, *El silencio quedó atrás*, 252.

26. United Fruit Company Headquarters, Boston and Franklin Moore, "Letter to G. D. Munch from Franklin Moore, UFCo Boston," March 2, 1954, UFCo-L.

27. The United Fruit Company imported English-speaking West Indians to Costa Rica and Panama, creating, in some cases deliberately, dissension within the ranks of black, mestizo, and indigenous workers; Bourgois, *Ethnicity at Work*; Putnam, *The Company They Kept*.

28. United Fruit Company Headquarters, Boston and G. A. Myrick, "Letter to G. A. Myrick, Puerto Armuelles, to A. A. Pollan, Executive Vice President, United Fruit Company, and W. W. Turnbull, Division Managaer, La Lima," October 18, 1945, UFCo-L; United Fruit Company and G. A. Myrick, "Repatriating Honduran agitators—Letter to J. F. Aycock, La Lima, Honduras, from G. A. Myrick, Almirante," December 7, 1946, UFCo-L.

29. United Fruit Company, Bocas Division, "Letter to Franklin Moore, UFCo Boston, from Chiriqui Land Company, Bocas Division," February 25, 1952, UFCo-L.

30. United Fruit Company Headquarters, Boston and Walter Turnbull, "Letter to V. E. Scott, Tegucigalpa, from W. W. Turnbull, Division Manager, La Lima," April 21, 1951, UFCo-L.

31. United Fruit Company Headquarters, Boston and Franklin Moore, "Letter

to C. W. Diebold from Franklin Moore, UFCo Boston," February 6, 1952, UFCo-L.

32. United Fruit Company, Bocas Division, "Letter to Franklin Moore, UFCo Boston, from Chiriqui Land Company, Bocas Division," July 28, 1953, UFCo-L.

33. Tela Railroad Company United Fruit Company and V. E. Scott, "Letter to J.F. Aycock, Manager, La Lima, from V.E. Scott, Manager, Tela Railroad Company," July 22, 1953, UFCo-L.

34. Fernando A. Vargas, "Lista de los miembros del Sindicato de Trabajadores de la Chiriqui Land Company," March 13, 1954, UFCo-L.

35. Mario Posas, *Luchas del movimiento obrero hondureño* (Ciudad Universitaria Rodrigo Facio, Honduras: Editorial Universitaria Centroamericana, 1981), 140.

36. Ezequiel Escoto, *El Pueblo*, May 24, 1954, quoted in Argueta, *La gran huelga bananera*, 56.

37. Karl Marx, "Letters from the Deutsch-Französische Jahrbücher," cited in Bosteels, *Marx and Freud in Latin America*, 174.

NINE

1. "El ferrocarril pasa al gobierno," *Orientación*, May 20, 1954.

2. Mario Posas and Rafael del Cid, *La construcción del sector público y del Estado nacional en Honduras, 1876–1979* (San José, Costa Rica: Editorial Universitaria Centroamericana, 1983), 173.

3. Arturo Taracena Arriola, "Liberalismo y poder político en Centroamérica (1870–1929)," in *Historia general de Centroamárica*, vol. 4, edited by Víctor Acuña Ortega (Madrid: Sociedad Estatal Quinto Centenario, 1993), 168.

4. Víctor Acuña Ortega, conclusion, *Historia general de Centroamérica*, vol. 4, edited by Víctor Acuña Ortega (Madrid: Sociedad Estatal Quinto Centenario, 1993), 399–401.

5. Marvin Barahona periodizes the collapse of the liberal oligarchic state from 1954 to 1956, that is, from the 1954 strike through the unconstitutional seizure of power by Julio Lozano Díaz in November 1954 to the popular-military assault on the army barracks in Tegucigalpa in 1956. I am not disagreeing with Barahona; on the contrary, I am merely identifying a key moment in the changing character and function of the Honduran state; *Honduras en el siglo XX*, 178–187.

6. "Being-unto-the-goal" is the way Peter Sloterdijk characterizes "the temporal mode of the practicing life"; *You Must Change Your Life*, 482.

7. The notions of "visual subcultures" and "scopic regimes" were put forward by Martin Jay in "Scopic Regimes of Modernity," in *Vision and Visuality*, edited by Hal Foster (Seattle: Bay Press, 1988), 33–38.

8. See, for example, the photographs accompanying the internal company memo that marked labor leaders in Colombia for elimination, exile, or imprisonment; Unsigned, "Memorandum, Colombian Division. Labor Leaders in Ciénaga

Strike" (United Fruit Company, March 8, 1929), UFCo-L, which I examine in "The Photos That We Don't Get to See."

9. Elspeth H. Brown, *The Corporate Eye: Photography and the Rationalization of American Commercial Culture, 1884–1929* (Baltimore, MD: Johns Hopkins University Press, 2005).

10. Michel-Rolph Trouillot, *Silencing the Past: Power and the Production of History* (Boston: Beacon Press, 1995), 48.

11. Chakrabarty, *Provincializing Europe*, 64.

12. Quote, ibid., 66.

13. This idea of photography as "translation" is put forward by Vilém Flusser in "The Gesture of Photography," translation by Nancy Ann Roth, *Journal of Visual Culture* 10, no. 3 (2011): 279–293.

14. Roland Barthes, *Camera Lucida: Reflections on Photography*, 2nd ed. (New York: Hill and Wang, 1982), 76–77.

15. Barthes, "Rhetoric of the Image," 34–36.

16. Jacques Derrida, *The Politics of Friendship*, translation by George Collins (London: Verso, 2006), 306.

17. Jacques Derrida, *Specters of Marx: The State of the Debt, the Work of Mourning, and the New International*, translation by Peggy Kamuf (New York: Routledge, 1994), 99.

18. Mirzoeff, *The Right to Look*, 4.

19. Ibid., 3.

20. D. R. Coerr Wymberley and US Embassy Tegucigalpa, "Liberals Flogged by Orders of Reformist Commandant" (University Publications of America, October 20, 1954), US State Department Confidential Central Files. Honduras, 1950–1954. Internal Affairs Decimal Numbers 715, 815, 915 and Foreign Affairs Decimal Numbers 615 and 611.15.

21. Ibid.

22. The Liberal Party won 121,000 votes and twenty-six legislative seats as compared to the National Party's 78,000 votes and nineteen seats and the National Reformist Movement's 53,000 votes and eleven seats; see Mario Argueta, *Ramón Villeda Morales: Luces y sombras de una primavera política* (Tegucigalpa: Editorial Guaymuras, 2009), 46.

23. Julio Lozano Díaz, "Decreto No. 1: Durante el actual estado de emergencia, el Jefe de Estado gobernará el país," *La Gaceta*, December 6, 1954.

24. Euraque, *Reinterpreting the Banana Republic*, 99.

25. Quoted in Posas and Cid, *La construcción del sector público*, 157.

26. Ibid., 163.

27. Ibid., 171.

28. Barahona, *Honduras en el siglo XX*, 186.

29. Robleda Castro, *La verdad de la huelga*, 167.

30. Argueta, *Ramón Villeda Morales*, 122.

31. For a discussion of the relationship between Sitraterco, ORIT, the CIA, and funds from the Alliance for Progress, see Euraque, *Reinterpreting the Banana Republic*, 98–102. In the wake of the US overthrow of Árbenz in Guatemala, CIA leadership instructed its chief of plans: "The AFL, either acting through the ORIT or independently, should be urged to send immediately a highly qualified team of labor instructors to assist anti-Communist Guatemalan labor leaders in the purging and re-organization of both urban and rural unions. These instructors should be men willing and able to cooperate with the Catholic Church in Guatemala"; from "Document 9," quoted in Cullather, *Secret History*, 159.

32. López de Castillo, oral history interview, August 18, 2008.

EPILOGUE

1. On the practicing subject as *homo imunologicus*, see Sloterdijk, *You Must Change Your Life*, 10.

2. Congreso Nacional, "Decreto No. 183-2009," *La Gaceta*, December 22, 2009, Archivo Nacional de Honduras.

BIBLIOGRAPHY

ARCHIVES

El Progreso
    Archivo Municipal
        Libros de actas de la Municipalidad de El Progreso, vols. 1–37 (1893–1969).
        Gabrie, Sammie, photo collection. Private collection of Sammy Gabrie.
        Mahchi, Guillermo, photo archive. Private collection of Guillermo Enrique Mahchi Carrasco.
        Platero Paz, Rafael, archive. Private collection of Aída López de Castillo.
        Society of Jesus archive. Equipo de Reflexión, Investigación y Comunicación.

La Ceiba
    Archivo de Gobernación del Departamento de Atlántida
        Libro copiador de cartas, 1920s.
        Libro de matrícula de agricultores y ganaderos, 1928–1935.
        Registro de propiedad, vol. 1, 1926.
        Libros de actas de la Municipalidad de La Ceiba

San Pedro Sula
   Museo de Antropología e Historia de San Pedro Sula, collection of postcards
   and photographs.

Tegucigalpa
   Archivo Nacional de Honduras
   Colección Guilbert, Instituto Hondureño de Antropología e Historia.
   Inestrosa M., Jesús Evelio, private collection of military and police
   photographs.
   Schwimmer, Eric, private collection of Honduran photographs and postcards.

Tela
   Libros de actas de la Municipalidad de Tela

United Fruit Company (UFCo)
   Bocas del Toro Division, Panama. Historical archives, letters (UFCo-L), private
   collection of Philippe Bourgois.
   Medical Department, Boston, *Annual Report.*
   Unifruitco
   United Fruit Company Photograph Collection, Baker Library Historical Collec-
   tions, Harvard Business School.

US Department of State
   Confidential Central Files. Honduras, 1893–1956.

Yoro
   Archivo de de Gobernación, Departamento de Yoro
      Libro copiador de la correspondencia. Deudas pagadas por individuos, 1935.
      Libro en el que la gobernación política del Dep. de Yoro llevará el conocimiento de
      la solicitudes de inscripción de extranjeros, 1946.
      Libro registro de propiedad, vols. 1–2, 1924.
      Libro rehabilitado en donde el secretario de la gobernación política consignara
      las remisiones de documentos de extranjería, 1968–1969.
      Libros de actas del consejo departamental de Yoro
      residentes en la República de Honduras, 1939–1943, 1946–1948.
      Registro especial de extranjeros residentes en Honduras
   Instituto de la Propiedad
   Juzgado de Letras, archivo muerto
      Juzgado de Paz de lo Criminal, El Progreso
      Juzgado de Letras de lo Civil, El Progreso

ORAL HISTORY INTERVIEWS

Castillo, Oswaldo Eloy. El Progreso, August 2008.
Gabrie, Sammie. El Progreso, August–September 2008.
    López de Castillo, Aída. El Progreso, August 2008.
Mahchi Carrasco, Guillermo Enrique. El Progreso, August–September 2008.
Peña, Billy. La Lima, July 2007.
Platero López, Ricardo Arturo. El Progreso, November 20, 2008.
Robleda, Sylvia. El Progreso, September 2008.

PERIODICALS

Bohemia (Havana)
El Ciudadano (Tegucigalpa)
El Cronista (Tegucigalpa)
El Día (Tegucigalpa)
Diario Comercial (San Pedro Sula)
La Época (Tegucigalpa)
El Gráfico (Tegucigalpa)
La Gaceta (Tegucigalpa)
Life
Mercurio (Tegucigalpa)
New York Times
Nuestro Criterio (San Pedro Sula)
Orientación (San Pedro Sula)
El Pueblo (Tegucigalpa)
Revista de Policía (Tegucigalpa)
Revista Todo (Mexico City)
Tiempo (San Pedro Sula)
Time
Vanguardia (Tegucigalpa)
Vanguardia Revolucionaria (Tegucigalpa)

SECONDARY SOURCES

Acuña Ortega, Víctor. Conclusion. *Historia general de Centroamérica*. Vol. 4, edited by Victor Acuña Ortega, 167–253. Madrid: Sociedad Estatal Quinto Centenario, 1993.
Adams, Frederick Upham. *Conquest of the Tropics: The Story of the Creative Enterprises Conducted by the United Fruit Company*. New York: Doubleday, 1914.

Agamben, Giorgio. "The Archaeology of Commandment." Summer seminar lecture, European Graduate School, Saas-Fee, Switzerland, 2011. http://www.youtube.com/watch?v=JVV94Fi5ChI.

———. *Homo Sacer: Sovereign Power and Bare Life*. Stanford, CA: Stanford University Press, 1998.

———. *State of Exception*. Chicago: University of Chicago Press, 2005.

Alfaro-Velcamp, Theresa. *So Far from Allah, So Close to Mexico: Middle Eastern Immigrants in Modern Mexico*. Austin: University of Texas Press, 2007.

Althusser, Louis. "Ideology and Ideological State Apparatuses (Notes Towards an Investigation)." In *Lenin and Philosophy and Other Essays*, translation by Ben Brewster, 127–188. New York: Monthly Review Press, 1972.

Amaya Banegas, Jorge Alberto. *Los árabes y palestinos en Honduras, 1900–1950*. Tegucigalpa: Editorial Guaymuras, 1997.

Andermann, Jens. "State Formation, Visual Technology, and Spectatorship: Visions of Modernity in Brazil and Argentina." *Theory, Culture, and Society* 27, nos. 7–8 (2010): 161–183.

———. *The Optic of the State: Visuality and Power in Argentina and Brazil*. Pittsburgh, PA: University of Pittsburgh Press, 2007.

Anderson, Mark. *Black and Indigenous: Garifuna Activism and Consumer Culture in Honduras*. Minneapolis: University of Minnesota Press, 2009.

Appadurai, Arjun. "Disjuncture and Difference in the Global Cultural Economy." *Public Culture* 2, no. 2 (1990): 1–24.

Argueta, Mario. *Bananos y política: Samuel Zemurray y la Cuyamel Fruit Company en Honduras*. Tegucigalpa: Editorial Universitaria, 1989.

———. *La gran huelga bananera: 69 días que conmovieron a Honduras*. Tegucigalpa: Editorial Universitaria, 1995.

———. *Ramón Villeda Morales: Luces y sombras de una primavera política*. Tegucigalpa: Editorial Guaymuras, 2009.

———. *Tiburcio Carías: Anatomía de una época, 1923–1948*. Tegucigalpa: Editorial Guaymuras, 1989.

Azoulay, Ariella. *The Civil Contract of Photography*. New York: Zone Books, 2008.

———. *Civil Imagination: A Political Ontology of Photography*. Translation by Louise Bethlehem. New York: Verso, 2012.

———. "The Loss of Critique and the Critique of Violence." *Cardozo Law Review* 26, no. 3 (2005): 1005–1039.

Badiou, Alain. "Logic of the Site." *Diacritics* 33, no. 3 (2003): 141–150.

———. *Theory of the Subject*. Translation by Bruno Bosteels. London: Continuum, 2009.

"Bananas Script—Dialogue Transcript." *Drew's Script-O-Rama*. Accessed July 18, 2013. http://www.script-o-rama.com/movie_scripts/b/bananas-script-transcript-woody-allen.html.

Barahona, Marvin. *La hegemonía de los Estados Unidos en Honduras, 1907–1932*. Tegucigalpa: Centro de Documentación de Honduras, 1989.

———. *Honduras en el siglo XX: Una síntesis histórica*. Tegucigalpa: Guaymuras, 2005.

———. *El silencio quedó atrás: Testimonio de la huelga bananera de 1954*. 2nd ed. Tegucigalpa: Guaymuras, 1995.

Barthes, Roland. *Camera Lucida: Reflections on Photography*. 2nd ed. New York: Hill and Wang, 1982.

———. "The Rhetoric of the Image." In *Image, Music, Text*, 32–51. New York: Hill and Wang, 1977.

———. "Striptease." In *Mythologies*, 84–88. New York: Hill and Wang, 1972.

Beasley-Murray, Jon. *Posthegemony: Political Theory and Latin America*. Minneapolis: University of Minnesota Press, 2010.

Bell, David, and Ruth Holliday. "Naked as Nature Intended." *Body and Society* 6, no. 3–4 (November 1, 2000): 127–140.

Benjamin, Walter. *Illuminations*. Translation by Harry Zohn, edited by Hannah Arendt. New York: Schocken Books, 1969.

———. *Reflections: Essays, Aphorisms, Autobiographical Writings*. Edited by Peter Demetz. New York: Harcourt Brace Jovanovich, 1978.

Bethell, Leslie, and Ian Roxborough. *Latin America between the Second World War and the Cold War, 1944–1948*. New York: Cambridge University Press, 1992.

Bhabha, Homi K. *The Location of Culture*. 2nd ed. New York: Routledge, 2004.

Bosteels, Bruno. *Marx and Freud in Latin America: Politics, Psychoanalysis, and Religion in Times of Terror*. London: Verso, 2012.

Bourdieu, Pierre. *Photography: A Middle-Brow Art*. Translation by Shaun Whiteside. Stanford, CA: Stanford University Press, 2003.

Bourgois, Philippe. *Ethnicity at Work: Divided Labor on a Central American Banana Plantation*. Baltimore, MD: Johns Hopkins University Press, 1989.

———. "One Hundred Years of United Fruit Company Letters." In *Banana Wars: Power, Production, and History in the Americas*, edited by Steve Striffler and Mark Moberg, 103–144. Durham, NC: Duke University Press, 2003.

Brown, Elspeth H. *The Corporate Eye: Photography and the Rationalization of American Commercial Culture, 1884–1929*. Baltimore, MD: Johns Hopkins University Press, 2005.

Brues, Charles T. "Poisonous Arthropods: Some Aboriginal Inhabitants of the Tropics," *Unifruitco* 4, no. 2 (September 1928): 68–72.

Bucheli, Marcelo. *Bananas and Business: The United Fruit Company in Colombia, 1899–2000*. New York: NYU Press, 2005.

Canelas Díaz, Antonio. *El estrangulamiento económico de La Ceiba, 1903–1965*. La Ceiba, Honduras: Editorial ProCultura, 2001.

Carassai, Sebastián. "En busca del futuro olvidado: Notas para una crítica de la memoria en Walter Benjamin." *El Ojo Mocho: Revista de Crítica Cultural y Política* 21 (Winter/Spring 2008): 81–89.

Carroll, Lewis. *The Complete Works of Lewis Carroll*. New York: Barnes and Noble, 1994.

Chakrabarty, Dipesh. *Provincializing Europe: Postcolonial Thought and Historical Difference*. Princeton, NJ: Princeton University Press, 2000.

Chaudhary, Zahid R. *Afterimage of Empire: Photography in Nineteenth-Century India*. Minneapolis: University of Minnesota Press, 2012.

Chomsky, Aviva. *West Indian Workers and the United Fruit Company in Costa Rica, 1870–1940*. Baton Rouge: Louisiana State University Press, 1996.

Clark, Herbert C. "Venomous Snakes. Some Central American Records. Incidence of Snake-Bite Accidents." *American Journal of Tropical Medicine* s1–22, no. 1 (January 1, 1942): 37–49.

Colby, Jason M. *The Business of Empire: United Fruit, Race, and U.S. Expansion in Central America*. Ithaca, NY: Cornell University Press, 2011.

Coleman, Kevin P. "A Camera in the Garden of Eden." *Journal of Latin American Cultural Studies: Travesia* 20, no. 1 (2011): 63–96.

———. "The Photos That We Don't Get to See: Sovereignties, Archives, and the 1928 Massacre of Banana Workers in Colombia." In *Making the Empire Work: Labor and United States Imperialism*, edited by Daniel E. Bender and Jana K. Lipman, 104–133. New York: NYU Press, 2015.

Coronil, Fernando. "Introduction: Can the Subaltern See? Photographs as History." *Hispanic American Historical Review* 84, no. 1 (2004): 1–4.

Cortés Rocca, Paola. *El tiempo de la máquina: Retratos, paisajes y otras imágenes de la nación*. Buenos Aires: Ediciones Colihue, 2011.

Crowther, Samuel. *The Romance and Rise of the American Tropics*. New York: Doubleday, Doran, 1929.

Cullather, Nick. *Secret History: The CIA's Classified Account of Its Operations in Guatemala, 1952–1954*. 2nd ed. Stanford, CA: Stanford University Press, 2006.

Daguerre, Louis Jacques Mande. "Daguerreotype." In *Classic Essays on Photography*, edited by Alan Trachtenberg, 11–13. New Haven, CT: Leete's Island Books, 1980.

David, Shay. "Concepts of Time in *One Hundred Years of Solitude*: A Means for Social Criticism." *Anamesa* (Spring 2003). http://www.nyu.edu/pubs/anamesa/archive/spring_2003_democracy/03_david.htm.

Derrida, Jacques. *Copy, Archive, Signature: A Conversation on Photography*. Edited by Gerhard Richter. Translation by Jeff Fort. Stanford, CA: Stanford University Press, 2010.

———. *The Politics of Friendship*. Translation by George Collins. London: Verso, 2006.

———. *Specters of Marx: The State of the Debt, the Work of Mourning, and the New International*. Translation by Peggy Kamuf. New York: Routledge, 1994.

Deutsch, Hermann. *The Incredible Yanqui: The Career of Lee Christmas*. London: Longmans Green, 1931.

Dodd, Thomas J. *Tiburcio Carías: Portrait of a Honduran Political Leader*. Baton Rouge: Louisiana State University Press, 2005.

Doumani, Beshara. *Rediscovering Palestine Merchants and Peasants in Jabal Nablus, 1700–1900*. Berkeley: University of California Press, 1995.

Dyzenhaus, David. *The Constitution of Law: Legality in a Time of Emergency*. Cambridge, England: Cambridge University Press, 2006.

Earle, Rebecca. *The Return of the Native: Indians and Myth-Making in Spanish America, 1810–1930*. Durham, NC: Duke University Press, 2007.

Edwards, Elizabeth. *The Camera as Historian: Amateur Photographers and Historical Imagination, 1885–1918*. Durham, NC: Duke University Press, 2012.

Emery-Waterhouse, Frances. *Banana Paradise*. New York: Stephen-Paul, 1947.

Enloe, Cynthia. *Bananas, Beaches, and Bases: Making Feminist Sense of International Politics*. Berkeley: University of California Press, 1990.

Euraque, Darío A. *Conversaciones históricas con el mestizaje y su identidad nacional en Honduras*. San Pedro Sula, Honduras: Centro Editorial, 2004.

———. "En busca de Froylán Turcios: Apuntes aobre la vida y obra de Armando Méndez Fuentes." *Paraninfo: Instituto de Ciencias del Hombre, Rafael Heliodoro Valle*, no. 23 (2003): 177–197.

———. "Nation Formation, Mestizaje, and Arab Palestinian Immigration to Honduras, 1880–1930s." *Critique: Critical Middle Eastern Studies* 4, no. 6 (1995): 25–37.

———. *Reinterpreting the Banana Republic: Region and State in Honduras, 1870–1972*. Chapel Hill: University of North Carolina Press, 1996.

Fernández, Horacio. *The Latin American Photobook*. New York: Aperture, 2011.

Flusser, Vilém. "The Gesture of Photography." Translation by Nancy Ann Roth. *Journal of Visual Culture* 10, no. 3 (2011): 279–293.

Foucault, Michel. *The Birth of the Clinic: An Archaeology of Medical Perception*. New York: Pantheon Books, 1973.

———. "Security, Territory, Population." In *Ethics: Subjectivity and Truth*, edited by Paul Rabinow, translation by Robert Hurley, 67–71. New York: New Press, 1997.

Fox, Claire F. *Making Art Panamerican: Cultural Policy and the Cold War*. Minneapolis: University of Minnesota Press, 2013.

Gabara, Esther. *Errant Modernism: The Ethos of Photography in Mexico and Brazil*. Durham, NC: Duke University Press, 2008.

———. "Gestures, Practices, and Projects: [Latin] American Re-visions of Visual Culture and Performance Studies." *E-misférica*, Spring 2010. http://hemi sphericinstitute.org/hemi/en/e-misferica-71/gabara.

García Márquez, Gabriel. *One Hundred Years of Solitude*. Translation by Gregory Rabassa. New York: Avon Books, 1971.

Gómez, Carolina. "La panadería de los hondureños." *Revista Summa*, March 21, 2012. http://www.revistasumma.com/23918.

González, Maldonado. "Mandar." *Clave: Diccionario de uso del español actual*. Madrid: Ediciones SM, 2000.

González, Nancie. *Dollar, Dove, and Eagle: One Hundred Years of Palestinian Migration to Honduras*. Ann Arbor: University of Michigan Press, 1992.

Gorelik, Adrián. *Miradas sobre Buenos Aires: Historia cultural y crítica urbana*. Buenos Aires: Siglo Veintiuno, 2004.

Grandin, Greg. "Can the Subaltern Be Seen? Photography and the Affects of Nationalism." *Hispanic American Historical Review* 84, no. 1 (2004): 83–111.

Gusfield, Joseph. "Benevolent Repression: Popular Culture, Social Structure, and the Control of Drinking." In *Drinking: Behavior and Belief in Modern History*, edited by Susanna Barrows and Robin Room. Berkeley: University of California Press, 1991.

Halliday, Paul D. *Habeas Corpus: From England to Empire*. Cambridge: Harvard University Press, 2010.

Halliday, Paul D., and G. Edward White. "The Suspension Clause: English Text, Imperial Contexts, and American Implications." *Virginia Law Review* 94, no. 3 (2008): 575–714.

Hariman, Robert, and John Louis Lucaites. *No Caption Needed: Iconic Photographs, Public Culture, and Liberal Democracy*. Chicago: University of Chicago Press, 2007.

Harpelle, Ronald. "White Zones: American Enclave Communities of Central America." In *Blacks and Blackness in Central America: Between Race and Place*, edited by Lowell Gudmundson and Justin Wolfe, 307–333. Durham, NC: Duke University Press, 2010.

Heidegger, Martin. "The Age of the World Picture (1938)." In *Off the Beaten Track*, edited by Julian Young, translation by Kenneth Haynes, 57–85. Cambridge, England: Cambridge University Press, 2002.

Henry, O. *Cabbages and Kings*. New York: McClure, Phillips, 1904.

Herzog, Tamar. *Defining Nations: Immigrants and Citizens in Early Modern Spain and Spanish America*. New Haven, CT: Yale University Press, 2003.

Hirsch, Marianne. *Family Frames: Photography, Narrative, and Postmemory*. Cambridge: Harvard University Press, 1997.

Hodder, Ian. *Reading the Past: Current Approaches to Interpretation in Archaeology*. Cambridge, England: Cambridge University Press, 1986.

Holmes, Oliver Wendell. "The Stereoscope and the Stereograph." In *Classic Essays on Photography*, edited by Alan Trachtenberg, 71–82. New Haven, CT: Leete's Island Books, 1980.

Horkheimer, Max, and Theodor W. Adorno. *Dialectic of Enlightenment: Philosophical Fragments*. Edited by Gunzelin Schmid Noerr. Translation by Edmund Jephcott. Stanford, CA: Stanford University Press, 2002.

Inestroza M., Jesús Evelio. *Documentos clasificados de la policía secreta de Carías (1937–1944)*. Tegucigalpa: Instituto Hondureño de Historia y Antropología, 2009.

James, Daniel, and Mirta Zaida Lobato. "Family Photos, Oral Narratives, and Identity Formation: The Ukrainians of Berisso." *Hispanic American Historical Review* 84, no. 1 (2004): 5–36.

Jay, Martin. *Downcast Eyes: The Denigration of Vision in Twentieth-Century French Thought*. Berkeley: University of California Press, 1993.

———. "Scopic Regimes of Modernity." In *Vision and Visuality*, edited by Hal Foster, 3–38. Seattle: Bay Press, 1988.

Kahn, Paul W. *Political Theology: Four New Chapters on the Concept of Sovereignty*. New York: Columbia University Press, 2011.

Karam, John Tofik. *Another Arabesque: Syrian-Lebanese Ethnicity in Neoliberal Brazil*. Philadelphia: Temple University Press, 2007.

Karnes, Thomas L. *Tropical Enterprise: The Standard Fruit and Steamship Company in Latin America*. Baton Rouge: Louisiana State University Press, 1978.

Kepner, Charles David. *Social Aspects of the Banana Industry*. New York: AMS Press, 1967.

Kepner, Charles, and Jay Henry Soothill. *The Banana Empire: A Case Study of Economic Imperialism*. New York: Vanguard Press, 1935.

Kim, Yeon-Soo. *Family Album: Histories, Subjectivities, and Immigration in Contemporary Spanish Culture* (Lewisburg, PA: Bucknell University Press, 2005).

Kramer, Paul A. "Power and Connection: Imperial Histories of the United States in the World." *American Historical Review* 116, no. 5 (December 2011): 1348–1435.

Kress, Gunther R., and Theo Van Leeuwen. *Reading Images: The Grammar of Visual Design*. New York: Routledge, 1996.

Laclau, Ernesto. *On Populist Reason*. New York: Verso, 2007.

LaFeber, Walter. *Inevitable Revolutions: The United States in Central America*. New York: Norton, 1983.

Langley, Lester D., and Thomas Schoonover. *The Banana Men: American Mercenaries and Entrepreneurs in Central America, 1880–1930*. Lexington: University Press of Kentucky, 1995.

Lesser, Jeffrey. *Negotiating National Identity: Immigrants, Minorities, and the Struggle for Ethnicity in Brazil*. Durham, NC: Duke University Press, 1999.

Levine, Robert M. *Images of History: Nineteenth and Early Twentieth Century Latin American Photographs as Documents*. Durham, NC: Duke University Press, 1989.

Leyva, Héctor M. *Imaginarios (sub)terráneos: Estudios literarios y culturales de Honduras*. Tegucigalpa: Plural, 2009.

López de Castillo, Aída. "Biography of Rafael Platero Paz." Unpublished manuscript, 2000.

Mahchi Carrasco, Guillermo Enrique. *Archivo fotográfico del ayer: El Progreso, 1900–1965*. San Pedro Sula, Honduras: Sociedad Nacional Papelera, 1992.

Marx, Karl. "Letters from the Deutsch-Französische Jahrbücher." March 1843. Reproduced at marxist.org, https://www.marxists.org/archive/marx/works/1843/letters/43_03.htm.

McDaniel, J. C. "Malaria Control Measures in 1931." In *Annual Report, 1931*, 96–98. Boston: UFCo Medical Department, 1931.

Mercer, Kobena. "Reading Racial Fetishism: The Photographs of Robert Mapplethorpe." In *Visual Culture: The Reader*, edited by Jessica Evans and Stuart Hall, 435–447. London: Sage, 1999.

Mirzoeff, Nicholas. "On Visuality." *Journal of Visual Culture* 5, no. 1 (2006): 53–79.

———. *The Right to Look: A Counterhistory of Visuality*. Durham, NC: Duke University Press, 2011.

Mitchell, W. J. T. *Picture Theory: Essays on Verbal and Visual Representation*. Chicago: University of Chicago Press, 1995.

Moberg, Mark. *Myths of Ethnicity and Nation: Immigration, Work, and Identity in the Belize Banana Industry*. Knoxville: University of Tennessee Press, 1997.

Moors, Annelies, and Steven Machlin. "Postcards of Palestine: Photographic Essay." *Critique of Anthropology* 7, no. 2 (1987): 61–77.

Morris, Rosalind C., ed. *Can the Subaltern Speak? Reflections on the History of an Idea*. New York: Columbia University Press, 2010.

Mraz, John. *Looking for Mexico: Modern Visual Culture and National Identity*. Durham, NC: Duke University Press, 2009.

———. *Photographing the Mexican Revolution: Commitments, Testimonies, Icons*. Austin: University of Texas Press, 2012.

Noble, Andrea. *Photography and Memory in Mexico: Icons of Revolution*. Manchester, England: Manchester University Press, 2010.

Nora, Pierre. "Between Memory and History: Les Lieux de Memoire." *Representations* 26, no. 1 (1989): 7–24.

Murga Frassinetti, Antonio. *Enclave y sociedad en Honduras*. Tegucigalpa: Universidad Nacional Autónoma de Honduras, 1978.

Otter, Chris. *The Victorian Eye: A Political History of Light and Vision in Britain, 1800–1910*. Chicago: University of Chicago Press, 2008.

Oyuela, Leticia de. *Constructores artísticos entre siglos*. San Pedro Sula, Honduras: Grupo OPSA, 2010.

———. *De santos y pecadores: Un aporte para la historia de las mentalidades, 1546–1910*. Tegucigalpa: Editorial Guaymuras, 1999.

Pappé, Ilan. *A History of Modern Palestine: One Land, Two Peoples*. Cambridge, England: Cambridge University Press, 2004.

Parameshwar Gaonkar, Dilip. "On Alternative Modernities." *Public Culture* 11, no. 1 (1999): 1–18.

Pastor de Maria y Campos, Camila. "The Mashreq in Mexico: Patronage, Property, and Class in the Postcolonial Global." PhD diss., University of California, 2009.

Peña Molina, Enrique. *Monografía de la ciudad de El Progreso*. Tegucigalpa: Imprenta Calderón, 1952.

Pérez-Brignoli, Héctor. "El fonógrafo en los trópicos: Sobre el concepto de banana republic en la obra de O. Henry." *Iberoamericana* 23, no. 6 (2006): 127–141.

———. *La reforma liberal en Honduras*. Tegucigalpa: Editorial Nuevo Continente, 1973.

Pike, Fredrick B. *The United States and Latin America: Myths and Stereotypes of Civilization and Nature*. Austin: University of Texas Press, 1992.

Pinney, Christopher. *"Photos of the Gods": The Printed Image and Political Struggle in India*. New Delhi: Oxford University Press, 2004.

Poole, Deborah. "An Image of 'Our Indian': Type Photographs and Racial Sentiments in Oaxaca, 1920–1940." *Hispanic American Historical Review* 84, no. 1 (2004): 37–82.

———. *Vision, Race, and Modernity: A Visual Economy of the Andean World*. Princeton, NJ: Princeton University Press, 1997.

Posas, Mario. *Luchas del movemiento obrero hondureño*. Ciudad Universitaria Rodrigo Facio, Honduras: Editorial Universitaria Centroamericana, 1981.

Posas, Mario, and Rafael del Cid. *La construcción del sector público y del Estado nacional en Honduras, 1876–1979*. San José, Costa Rica: Editorial Universitaria Centroamericana, 1983.

Pratt, Mary Louise. "Arts of the Contact Zone." *Profession* (1991): 33–40.

———. *Imperial Eyes: Travel Writing and Transculturation*. 2nd ed. New York: Routledge, 2007.

Putnam, Lara. *The Company They Kept: Migrants and the Politics of Gender in Caribbean Costa Rica, 1870–1960*. Chapel Hill: University of North Carolina Press, 2002.

Rancière, Jacques. *Althusser's Lesson*. Translation by Emiliano Battista. London: Continuum, 2011.

———. *Disagreement: Politics and Philosophy*. Translation by Julie Rose. Minneapolis: University of Minnesota Press, 1999.

———. *The Politics of Aesthetics.* Translation by Gabriel Rockhill. London: Continuum, 2006.

Roberts, Shari. "'The Lady in the Tutti-Frutti Hat': Carmen Miranda, a Spectacle of Ethnicity." *Cinema Journal* 32, no. 3 (1993): 3–23.

Robleda Castro, Agapito. *La verdad de la huelga de 1954 y de la formación del SITRATERCO: 54 años después.* 2nd ed. San Pedro Sula, Honduras: Litográfica San Felipe de Jesús, 2008.

Rosas, M. D. "Malaria Control Measures in Chiriqui." In *Annual Report, 1931,* 91–95. Boston: UFCo, 1931.

Rozitchner, León. *La cosa y la cruz: Cristianismo y capitalismo (en torno a las Confesiones de San Agustín).* Buenos Aires: Losada, 1997.

Rudé, George. *The Crowd in History: A Study of Popular Disturbances in France and England, 1730–1848.* New York: Wiley, 1964.

Said, Edward W. *Orientalism.* New York: Pantheon Books, 1978.

Salvatore, Ricardo D. *Los lugares del saber: Contextos locales y redes transnacionales en la formación del conocimiento moderno.* Buenos Aires: Beatriz Viterbo Editora, 2007.

Sandweiss, Martha A. *Print the Legend: Photography and the American West.* New Haven, CT: Yale University Press, 2004.

Sarlo, Beatriz. *La imaginación técnica: Sueños modernos de la cultura argentina.* Buenos Aires: Nueva Visión, 1992.

Sartre, Jean-Paul. *Being and Nothingness: An Essay on Phenomenological Ontology.* Translation by Hazel E. Barnes. New York: Philosophical library, 1956.

Schmitt, Carl. *The Concept of the Political.* Expanded ed. Chicago: University of Chicago Press, 2007.

———. *Political Theology: Four Chapters on the Concept of Sovereignty.* Translation by George Schwab. Cambridge: MIT Press, 1985.

Schulz, Donald, and Deborah Sundloff Schulz. *The United States, Honduras, and the Crisis in Central America.* Boulder, CO: Westview Press, 1994.

Schwimmer, Eric. *Dictionary of Honduran Colloquialisms, Idioms, and Slang.* 2nd ed. Tegucigalpa: Litografía López, 2004.

Sekula, Allan. "Reading an Archive: Photography between Labour and Capital." In *Visual Culture: A Reader,* edited by Jessica Evans and Stuart Hall, 181–192. London: Sage, 1999.

Simons, Patricia. "Homosociality and Erotics in Italian Renaissance Portraiture." In *Portraiture: Facing the Subject,* edited by Joanna Woodall. Manchester, England: Manchester University Press, 1997.

Sloterdijk, Peter. *In the World Interior of Capital.* Translation by Wieland Hoban. Malden, MA: Polity, 2013.

———. *You Must Change Your Life: On Anthropotechnics*. Translation by Wieland Hoban. Cambridge, England: Polity, 2013.

Snow, Rachel. "Tourism and American Identity: Kodak's Conspicuous Consumers Abroad." *Journal of American Culture* 31, no. 1 (2008): 7–19.

Solnit, Rebecca. *As Eve Said to the Serpent: On Landscape, Gender, and Art*. Athens: University of Georgia Press, 2001.

Soluri, John. *Banana Cultures: Agriculture, Consumption, and Environmental Change in Honduras and the United States*. Austin: University of Texas Press, 2005.

———. "Landscape and Livelihood: An Agroecological History of Export Banana Growing in Honduras, 1870–1975." PhD diss., University of Michigan, 1998.

Stein, Jess, ed. "Overseer, Oversee." *The Random House College Dictionary*. New York: Random House, 1984.

Stephens, John Lloyd. *Incidents of Travel in Central America, Chiapas, and Yucatan*. New York: Harper and Brothers, 1841.

Stone, Doris. "A Delimitation of the Area and Some of the Archaeology of the Sula-Jicaque Indians of Honduras." *American Antiquity* 7, no. 4 (1942): 376–388.

Strassler, Karen. *Refracted Visions: Popular Photography and National Modernity in Java*. Durham, NC: Duke University Press, 2010.

Striffler, Steve. *In the Shadows of State and Capital: The United Fruit Company, Popular Struggle, and Agrarian Restructuring in Ecuador, 1900–1995*. Durham, NC: Duke University Press, 2002.

Sutter, Paul S. "Tropical Conquest and the Rise of the Environmental Management State: The Case of U.S. Sanitary Efforts in Panama." In *Colonial Crucible: Empire in the Making of the Modern American State*, edited by Alfred W. McCoy and Francisco A. Scarano, 317–326. Madison: University of Wisconsin Press, 2009.

Szyliowicz, Joseph S. *Education and Modernization in the Middle East*. Ithaca, NY: Cornell University Press, 1973.

Tábora, Rocío. *Masculinidad y violencia en la cultura política hondureña*. Tegucigalpa: Centro de Documentación de Honduras, 1995.

Tagg, John. *The Disciplinary Frame: Photographic Truths and the Capture of Meaning*. Minneapolis: University of Minnesota Press, 2009.

Taracena Arriola, Arturo. "Liberalismo y poder político en centroamérica (1870–1929)." In *Historia general de centroamérica*. Vol. 4, edited by Víctor Acuña Ortega, 167–253. Madrid: Sociedad Estatal Quinto Centenario, 1993.

Taylor, Charles. "Two Theories of Modernity." *Public Culture* 11, no. 1 (1999): 153–174.

Tejada, Roberto. *National Camera: Photography and Mexico's Image Environment*. Minneapolis: University of Minnesota Press, 2009.

Thompson, Krista A. *An Eye for the Tropics: Tourism, Photography, and Framing the Caribbean Picturesque*. Durham, NC: Duke University Press, 2006.

Trachtenberg, Alan, ed. *Classic Essays on Photography*. New Haven, CT: Leete's Island Books, 1980.

———. *Reading American Photographs: Images as History, Mathew Brady to Walker Evans*. New York: Hill and Wang, 1989.

Trouillot, Michel-Rolph. *Silencing the Past: Power and the Production of History*. Boston: Beacon Press, 1995.

Turner, Frederick Jackson. *The Frontier in American History*. Henry Holt, 1920.

United Fruit Company (UFCo) Medical Department. "Comments on Vital Statistics and General Conditions." In *Annual Report, 1924*, 21–55. Boston: UFCo, 1924.

Umaña, Helen. *Panorama crítico del cuento hondureño, 1881–1999*. Tegucigalpa: Editorial Iberoamericana, 1999.

Villars, Rina. *Lealtad y rebeldía: La vida de Juan Pablo Wainwright*. Tegucigalpa: Guaymuras, 2010.

———. *Porque quiero seguir viviendo . . . Habla Graciela García*. Tegucigalpa: Guaymuras, 1991.

Wade, Joseph D. "The Light of the Dawn Becomes the Light of Day: The History of the Catholic Church in Honduras from 1854 through 1965." 2 vols. Unpublished manuscript, 1982.

Wallace, Henry. "La huelga de los trabajadores hondureños: Un grito que ha resonado en todo el mundo." Translation by Alberto Rubiera. *Bohemia*, June 1954.

Williams, Gareth. *The Mexican Exception: Sovereignty, Police, and Democracy*. New York: Palgrave Macmillan, 2011.

———. *The Other Side of the Popular: Neoliberalism and Subalternity in Latin America*. Durham, NC: Duke University Press, 2002.

Williams, Robert G. *States and Social Evolution: Coffee and the Rise of National Governments in Central America*. Chapel Hill: University of North Carolina Press, 1994.

Wilson, Charles Morrow. *Empire in Green and Gold: The Story of the American Banana Trade*. New York: Greenwood Press, 1968.

Woll, Allen L. *The Hollywood Musical Goes to War*. Chicago: Nelson-Hall, 1983.

Žižek, Slavoj. "Afterword: The Lesson of Rancière." In *The Politics of Aesthetics*, by Jacques Rancière, translation by Gabriel Rockhill. London: Continuum, 2006.

INDEX

landscapes and livelihoods, 10. *See also* countervisuality

Wade, Joseph D., 177–182, 194–196, 200, 240, *246, 246*
Wainwright, Juan Pablo, 240
Wallace, Henry, 210, *210*, 243
Waller Lumber Company, 37
Weekend in Havana (film), 91
White Zones, 79. *See also* American Zones
Willauer, Whiting, 198, 202–203, 220
Williams Calderón, Abraham, 198
Williams, Gareth, 26, 277–278n7
Wilson, Charles Morrow, 47–49, 53

yet-to-come, the, 179, 239

Zelaya, José Santos, 34
Zelaya Rosales, Manuel "Mel," 240, 251
Zemurray, Sam "The Banana Man," 29, 40–42, 46–47, 87, 275n25
Zúñiga Huete, José Ángel, 160